THE FIRST
CONSPIRACY

Also by Brad Meltzer

THE FIRST
CONSPIRACY

The Secret Plot to Kill George Washington

Brad Meltzer
and Josh Mensch

FLATIRON
BOOKS
NEW YORK

Portrait on page 35 courtesy of the North Carolina Museum of History. Recruitment poster image on page 44 © Everett Historical / Shutterstock. Forty-shilling image on page 89 is from the National Numismatic Collection at the Smithsonian Institution. Banner image on page 93 is from *The Pictorial Field Book of the Revolution*. 2 vols. New York: Harper, 1851–52. Rifle image on page 153 courtesy of Cowan's Auctions Inc., Cincinnati, Ohio. Musket image on page 153 © Ken Backer / Dreamstime .com. Bayonet image on page 153 courtesy of Skinner, Inc. www .skinnerinc.com. John Jay portrait on page 204 © New-York Historical Society.

www.flatironbooks.com

Design by Donna Sinisgalli Noetzel

The Library of Congress Cataloging-in-Publication Data is available upon request.

ISBN 978-1-250-13033-4 (hardcover)
ISBN 978-1-250-23122-2 (signed edition)
ISBN 978-1-250-13034-1 (ebook)

Our books may be purchased in bulk for promotional, educational, or business use. Please contact your local bookseller or the Macmillan Corporate and Premium Sales Department at 1-800-221-7945, extension 5442, or by email at MacmillanSpecialMarkets@macmillan.com.

First Edition: January 2019

10 9 8 7 6 5 4 3 2 1

For Dale Flam,
my mother-in-law,
the quiet leader,
who does all the heavy lifting,
but never takes the credit.
—B.M.

For Mary and Malcolm, with all my love.
—J.M.

Contents

Author's Note

This book started as a detective story. Nearly a decade ago, I found my first clues where all the best clues are found—in the footnotes. I forget the name of the book, but there it was: a supposed plot to kill George Washington.

Naturally, I started with skepticism. Was this true, or just some overhyped myth? Weeks went by and I couldn't shake it. A bit of digging found small mentions in many scholarly works. Some called it a plot to kill George Washington; others said the goal was to seize or kidnap him, but I couldn't find an entire book written on the subject.

Searching for information, and wondering if this should be my new project, I eventually reached out to Pulitzer Prize–winning historian Joseph J. Ellis. As the author of *His Excellency: George Washington*, I thought he'd know a thing or two about the subject. Naturally, he'd heard the story. He was fascinated by it too, and when I told him I was thinking about writing a book about it, he warned me how hard the project would be. This was a story about espionage—a secret plot—and the clandestine investigation to stop that plot. For everyone involved, including George Washington's inner circle, their entire purpose was to ensure there was no record of their actions. As Ellis told me that day, "You can find the number of slaves at Mount Vernon; you'll never find all his spies. By its nature, this is something that will always be elusive."

He was right. Thankfully, with the help of Josh Mensch, as well as historian and Washington expert Barnet Schecter, there was still plenty to find. You'll see the evidence in these pages—from private letters, to pension requests, to the transcripts of secret trials—each detail an additional puzzle piece.

Along the way, one key question remained: Were they trying to kill George Washington, kidnap him, or something else? The evidence, along with our analysis and conclusions, are in these pages, though whether it was killing or kidnapping, the result would most likely have been the same. During the Revolution, if those at the top level of American leadership were captured, they expected to be hanged as traitors. Only at lower levels were officers like Major General Charles Lee, Washington's second-in-command, exchanged for their British counterparts. Does that tell us definitively what was in the heart of each and every conspirator back then? Of course not. Like Ellis said during out first conversation, some details are forever elusive.

In the end, you'll see how the plot against George Washington was planned. You'll see how it was foiled. And most important, when it came to Washington himself, you'll see how easily history could've turned out differently.

—*Brad Meltzer*

Notes on the Text

When quoting directly from eighteenth-century written sources, we've standardized the original spelling, capitalization, and punctuation to make the language more accessible to modern readers. The wording itself is not changed, unless otherwise indicated in the text or endnotes.

Also, many chapters begin with a heading that indicates the location, using the familiar "City, State" construction. The states were still colonies during most of the time period we cover, but because the colony and state names are the same in every case, we've opted to use the modern format.

We must, indeed, all hang together, or
most assuredly we shall all hang separately.

—ATTRIBUTED TO BENJAMIN FRANKLIN,

JULY 4, 1776

THE FIRST
CONSPIRACY

Prologue

———·———

April 1776

The trap is set.

It's quiet on this night. Moonlight shines over a clearing in a dense wood.

The silence is broken by the drumbeat of hooves in the distance, growing steadily louder. Soon several uniformed men on horseback emerge from the blackness. The party halts not far from a large wooden manor house that sits at the clearing's edge. A few of the riders dismount and prime their muskets, standing guard. They scan the clearing, apparently thinking all is safe.

They're wrong.

A moment later, another rider steps down from his horse. He's taller than the rest and wears a long officer's coat.

His name is George Washington, the Commander-in-Chief of the Continental army.

There is a traitorous plan against him. He has no idea it's coming.

For the last ten months, since the day he was appointed to his command, Washington has had a nearly impossible task: to organize a scattered mess of backwoods militias and untrained volunteers into a functioning national army. And not just any army. This small, inexperienced, poorly equipped group of soldiers needs to stand up to what is probably the biggest and most powerful military force in the world. By any normal measure, they don't stand a chance—and Washington knows this, just as he knows that with every decision he makes, thousands of young soldiers' lives could be lost.

Tonight, even more is at risk.

Washington has just arrived in the western woods of Manhattan, about two miles north of New York City's bustling commercial district, which covers the island's southern tip. He's just finished a weeklong journey from Boston, and he's here now to fortify the city against the first major British offensive of the war. What he's facing is terrifying: Sometime in the next few weeks or months, a massive fleet of the vaunted British navy will swarm into New York Harbor—hundreds of ships and tens of thousands of soldiers prepared to invade the city.

They're coming. It's just a question of when.

The colonies have placed all their hope and trust in him. It is up to this one man, George Washington, to lead the small Continental army and withstand the massive attack.

Tonight, among the soldiers accompanying Washington, a few are dressed differently from the rest, in short blue-and-white coats with brass buttons. They're known as the "Life Guards," an elite group of specially trained soldiers handpicked to serve as Washington's bodyguards. He takes particular pride in these men, whom he trusts above all others.

In the faint moonlight, Washington walks slowly toward the nearby manor house that will serve as his lodging for the next few critical weeks before the British attack.

Yet what George Washington doesn't know is that here in Manhattan, the coming battle isn't the only thing he should fear.

There are other enemies waiting for him—enemies more dangerous than even the British army.

At this exact moment, three miles away due southeast in New York Harbor, a ship is anchored in the darkness. On board is one of the most powerful men of the colonies—the exiled Governor of New York—and he is masterminding a clandestine plan to sabotage the colonies' rebellion. In the dead of night, small boats carrying spies shuttle back and forth to him, delivering intelligence from shore.

At the same time, two miles away from where Washington now stands, the Mayor of New York City, working in concert with the Governor, carries a secret cache of money. His plan is to tempt Washington's soldiers to betray their army and their countrymen in a breathtaking act of treason.

And several blocks from the Mayor's office, in one of the city's underground jails, three prisoners whisper to each other in a dank cell, out of earshot of the guards. They have no idea that their quiet murmurs could change the future of the continent.

They are all players in an extraordinary plot:

A deadly plot against George Washington.

Most extraordinary of all, some of the key members of this plot are in George Washington's own inner circle—the very men in whom he has placed his greatest trust.

You could call it America's first great conspiracy—but at this moment, America doesn't yet exist.

Some of the details of this scheme are still shrouded in mystery, but history provides enough clues for an astonishing story. This is a story of soldiers, spies, traitors, Redcoats, turncoats, criminals, prostitutes, politicians, great men, terrible men, and before it's over, the largest public execution at the time ever to take place on North American shores. It all happens, amazingly, within days of the signing of the Declaration of Independence.

That's not all. The discovery of this plot, and the effort to investigate it, will lead colonial authorities to devise new systems of intelligence gathering and counterespionage. In many ways, this plot against George Washington would lead to the creation of a whole new field of American spycraft—now known as counterintelligence.

At its center is a deadly conspiracy against the one man on whose life the very future of America depends.

PART I

The Commander

Prelude

———•———

It's a hot summer day in Virginia, and this young man is full of sorrow.

He's barely twenty years old, with no college education. He's a terrible speller, though better at math. He grew up mostly in a rural farming region in King George County, across the Rappahannock River from Fredericksburg.

His name is George Washington, and today his world has been shattered. He just found out that his older half brother, Lawrence, has died. For several years Lawrence had been suffering from tuberculosis, which has been sweeping through the southern colonies. Doctors had warned that the illness could be fatal, and lately Lawrence has been bedridden by coughs and fever. Still, Lawrence had always been strong. Handsome. Thirty-four years old and in his prime. The family couldn't believe that Lawrence would succumb to the disease; certainly George couldn't.

Nine years earlier, when George was eleven, their father, Augustine, died unexpectedly, leaving his family in grief and financial turmoil. George's mother was left to raise five young children on her own, and to run their estate without an income. After this tragedy, it was Lawrence, then a dashing man in his midtwenties, who swept in and took George under his wing.

Born to a different mother, Lawrence had grown up in relative privilege; he had traveled to London for his college education, and soon served as an officer within the provincial forces under the British navy. After his return to Virginia, he had married into a wealthy and powerful family and become a leader in local affairs. Fortune had smiled on Lawrence: He was worldly, ambitious, and sophisticated.

Young George, a country boy, was none of these things. But Lawrence took a great interest in this younger brother whom their father had left behind. Lawrence mentored George, taught him social graces, and invited him to stay at the grand estate of his wife's family. Thanks to Lawrence, George's world expanded. The two were often inseparable. Lawrence was many things to George: a role model, a hero, and a surrogate father. When Lawrence was hit by tuberculosis, it was George who often sat by his bed.

Now Lawrence is gone too. For the second time in his life George has been left alone.

When the final estate papers are read, it's revealed that Lawrence has set aside two small parcels of land for George. There is also the possibility that he might one day inherit Lawrence's own beloved estate, Mount Vernon. According to his brother's will, these gifts are "in consideration of the natural love and affection which he hath and doth bear unto his loving brother George Washington."

But for George, now twenty years old, gaining a few parcels of land doesn't begin to fill the void left by the loss of his brother. Lawrence's death devastates George, taking away arguably the most important man in his life—the person he has looked up to more than anyone else.

Reflecting on his older brother's varied accomplishments, perhaps what George most admires is Lawrence's past glory as a military officer. Fulfillment of a greater duty, dedication to a larger cause—these ideals had transformed his brother's life and provided him a grand purpose.

Now, with Lawrence gone, George is searching for a purpose of his own.

For the past few years, during his late teens, George has worked as a land surveyor. In the rapidly growing colonies, land speculation is a great way to make money; George's surveying skills are in high demand. He serves prominent clients and has started to invest in land deals of his own, putting him on a path to gain wealth and property.

Yet the death of his brother stirs within George a deeper craving. A month earlier, in June 1752, while Lawrence lay on his deathbed, George wrote a letter to the Lieutenant Governor of the colony of Virginia. His goal? To apply for a position in the local militia, run by the colony's royal government. It is, in fact, a position formerly held by Lawrence—a position that would now be vacant.

George has no military experience or skills to speak of, so all his letter offers is an earnest promise to do his best and honor his brother's work: "[I] should take the greatest pleasure in punctually obeying . . . your Honor's commands; and by a strict observance of my Duty, render myself worthy of the trust reposed in me."

Perhaps because of the letter's sincerity, or because of Lawrence's reputation, or perhaps just due to good timing, George receives the position. Within weeks after the death of his boyhood hero, he puts aside his surveyor's tools and prepares to wear a uniform for the first time.

Up to this point, George Washington's youth has been characterized by death and loss. But now he is ready to embark on a new path.

Maybe, as a soldier, he will find his deeper purpose.

This young man from Virginia, George Washington, is now on the road to fulfill a destiny greater than he could ever imagine.

And nothing—not even the fear of death itself—will stop him.

1

---·---

TWENTY-THREE YEARS LATER . . .

Philadelphia, Pennsylvania

May 10, 1775

Philadelphia feels alive.

For the past few days, the most prominent leaders in the colonies have been arriving in the city. Coaches and carriages are pulling in, almost by the hour, often met by cheering crowds and marching bands. Onlookers fill the streets and watch from porches and windows. The inns are full to capacity; the taverns are bustling.

The mood is mostly festive. But the air is also charged with something else: that unique mix of anticipation and fear that comes with the feeling that the world is about to change, though no one knows quite how.

The occasion is momentous: a meeting of the Second Continental Congress. Delegates chosen from every colony are meeting here for one purpose—to debate the possibility of war with England.

Just a year earlier such a notion was unthinkable except to the most radical. But in recent months, longstanding disputes have grown and multiplied between the Crown and its colonial subjects across the ocean. Arguments over trade, taxes, and tariffs have turned into deep, irreconcilable grievances. On the colonists' side, rallies and protests against the Crown's repressive policies have grown louder, larger, and angrier. England has responded by sending soldiers to clamp down on protests and reassert the mother country's absolute power. In the New England colonies, local rebel militias have been preparing to stand up to the royal authorities. Earlier in the year, King George III declared the colony of Massachusetts to be in a state of "rebellion" against England.

And recently, outside Boston, blood has been spilled.

On the night of April 19, a regiment of British soldiers stationed in the city marched from Boston toward the neighboring towns of Lexington and Concord, to arrest two rebel leaders and seize a cache of munitions that the colonial militias were stockpiling. The colonists learned of the plan in advance, and as the British arrived in Lexington a band of armed locals was there to meet them. In the melee that followed, the British forces killed eight townspeople and lost only a horse. When the British troops advanced towards Concord, however, they encountered a much larger colonial militia. No one knows which side began shooting first, but whoever pulled the first trigger fired the "shot heard 'round the world." Both the British and the colonists suffered heavy casualties in sustained fighting.

Within forty-eight hours, the British soldiers were driven back into Boston and royal authorities put the city under lockdown. An uneasy truce was reached, but tensions in the city were now at an all-time high.

The bloodshed sent shockwaves throughout the colonies, especially in New England. Dr. Matthew Thornton, the president of the New Hampshire Provincial Congress, captured the prevailing mood in a public address:

> Painful beyond expression have been those scenes of blood and devastation which the barbarous cruelty of British troops have placed before our eyes. Duty to God, to ourselves, to posterity, enforced by the cries of slaughtered innocents, have urged us to take up arms in our defense. Such a day as this was never before known, either to us or to our fathers.

The future is uncertain. Was this violence a local Boston skirmish or the start of a larger war? Is peaceful reconciliation still possible—or is it time for the colonies to mobilize and raise arms?

These are the urgent questions the Second Continental Congress is now convened to face.

But from England's perspective, the very meeting of this so-called Congress is itself an act of rebellion. England doesn't recognize the Congress as legitimate. England never authorized any such gathering of delegates from around the colonies, and in fact forbade it. From the point of view of the British Parliament and the Crown, this Congress has no authority, wields no power, and represents nothing.

And yet, here they are.

They have come from Rhode Island, New Jersey, Connecticut, and the far-off northern lands of New Hampshire. They've come from Delaware, Maryland, even from the southern swamps of South Carolina. There are sixty-five delegates in all, representing twelve of the thirteen colonies. Only one colony, Georgia, has declined to participate; though soon, it too will send a representative.

Just the logistical effort of organizing all these delegates to meet at one time and place is a major accomplishment. With the transportation technology of the day—namely, horses—the trip for some delegates from their home cities may take as long as two weeks, not including delays for weather or getting lost. This means eight hours of travel per day, on coach seats or saddles over bumpy roads, with bathroom breaks often taking place in the swamps or brush by the side of the road.

The invitations themselves were all handwritten letters, also delivered on horseback with long delays. The delegates had to commit to leaving behind businesses, families, and local affairs for what they knew might be a period of many months.

Adding high drama to the proceedings, two of the delegates from Massachusetts—Samuel Adams and John Hancock—had to hide out in fields and farmhouses during the first part of their journey, for fear of British soldiers who had been sent to detain them for their roles in organizing the Boston revolt. They secretly met up en route with the other Massachusetts delegates—including Samuel Adams's cousin John Adams—then escaped across the colony line to merge with the Connecticut delegation for the trip to Pennsylvania. Word quickly spread of this dramatic journey, and by the time the group arrived in

Philadelphia, they were greeted as heroes—escorted by a band of militiamen and cheered on by crowds as they pass.

"All ranks and degrees of men are in Arms," observes Joseph Hewes, the delegate from North Carolina, upon arriving in the city. Even here in normally peace-loving Philadelphia, known for its university and its large population of Quakers, the drums of war are beating.

Yet some of the delegates sense a consequence even larger than the immediate fate of the colonies. A new idea has slowly been forming, borrowed from philosophers in Europe and filtered through the specific experience of the American colonists. At the heart of it lies a fundamental question: Is it natural and just for people to be ruled by the absolute power of a monarch who claims divine authority? Or, in fact, do people have a right—an *inherent* right—to choose their own government and therefore rule themselves?

Such a simple idea today. But back then, this was a radical concept—and a *dangerous* one. In pamphlets, a new word is being thrown around—"liberty"—and this word represents an incredible threat. It's not just a challenge to the powerful royal family in England; it's a challenge to centuries of vested power and authority everywhere, a threat to royal families all over Europe and indeed the world.

As Thomas Paine will soon write: "We have it in our power to begin the World over again."

It's an exhilarating time, but also terrifying—because in order to exercise that power, the fragile colonies must raise arms against one of the greatest military powers that history has ever known.

The air is alive in Philadelphia, and the world is about to change.

2

———·———

They call it the Pennsylvania State House—the designated meeting place for the Continental Congress. It's on Chestnut Street between Fifth and Sixth Streets in Philadelphia, five or so blocks west of the Delaware River. The State House sits at one end of a broad grassy common that has recently become a regular gathering place for rallies and speeches. The structure, a grand red-brick Georgian with a handsome white steeple and bell tower, is an appropriately august setting for what's about to happen. The official meeting room, known as the Main Assembly Hall, is just past the foyer through the large white front doors; it's a two-story space, modest but functional, and just big enough for the assembled delegates.

This is the room.

This is where, in daily meetings in the coming weeks and months, the future of America will be decided. As in most meeting rooms of the era, there are a few spittoons placed around the room for those who chew tobacco or pinch a bit of snuff.

The delegates convened here are, as a group, some of the most educated and respected men in the colonies. Most of them wear the standard breeches, frocks, and waistcoats fashionable at the time, typical for their positions as lawyers, businessmen, or politicians in their home colonies.

Yet one man stands out from the rest.

He arrives wearing a full military officer's uniform, with a long blue coat and brass buttons. At a time when the average height is five feet seven, his over-six-foot stature and perfect posture towers over the group. He has impeccable manners and a quiet but commanding presence.

This is Col. George Washington, delegate from Virginia. At forty-three years old, he's a veteran of the French and Indian War two decades earlier, and the former leader of the Virginia militia. Now he's a wealthy landowner and planter. He hasn't served the military in almost fifteen years, but for this extraordinary occasion, he wears his uniform as a former officer.

Clearly, this man means business.

The other delegates take notice. "[Colonel] Washington appears at Congress in his uniform and, by his great experience and abilities in military matters, is of much service to us," John Adams writes. "He has so much martial dignity in his deportment that you would distinguish him to be a general and a soldier from among ten thousand people," the Pennsylvania delegate Benjamin Rush gushes in a letter to a friend.

It's not just Washington's appearance that makes him stand out, though. The Congress is full of highly educated talkers who use ornate, flowery language. Washington never went to college. He speaks simply or, more often, he listens. As the other delegates compete to talk as much as possible, Washington exerts a gravity and power by withholding opinions. He has, as John Adams later puts it, the "gift of silence." But when he does speak, the words have conviction.

That Washington would make such a strong impression is in some ways a surprise, given that he is not really a new face to the other delegates, or at least that he shouldn't be. He also attended the First Continental Congress, held in this same room less than a year earlier and comprised of many of the same delegates. At that earlier session, however, Washington was barely noticed—he wore civilian clothes, didn't give a single speech, and generally made little impression.

But so much has changed in a year. Last time, the idea of independence from England had been just that—a vague notion. It was abstract, an article of political theory to debate in coffeehouses and taverns.

This time, the stakes are higher. Lives have been lost. Now all the fancy oratory in the world means less than the real-world experience of someone who understands the actuality of war. Washington is selected to be on multiple committees at the Congress related to military affairs, and the other delegates soon consider his opinion vital to every decision.

Simply put, people want someone who knows how to fight.

Still, the Congress's position on war is complicated. On the one hand, most delegates agree that they need to pursue some sort of peaceful solution before plunging headlong into an armed conflict against England's massively superior armed forces. Maybe they can negotiate more favorable policies and more autonomy without resorting to bloodshed—or, for starters, at least persuade England to recognize the authority of their Congress. Maybe then a compromise can be reached. Either way, these debates will take time, and any potential negotiation with the British Parliament could take months if not years to resolve.

But in the meantime, there's the situation in Boston. Every day the delegates receive new reports: British troops have occupied the major forts in the city, imposing strict martial law. They've confiscated some two thousand firearms from the citizens, who now live in fear if they haven't already fled. Trade has mostly ceased, cutting off the food supply. Any day now, the British soldiers could march to surrounding towns.

In response, loose-knit rebel militias have gathered outside Boston, having marched there from all over Massachusetts, Connecticut, Rhode Island, and New Hampshire. These militiamen are ready to raise arms against British soldiers if necessary and, if nothing else, prevent their movement to other cities.

So even as the delegates in Philadelphia begin to debate the larger political questions, they still need an immediate plan to coordinate the scattered militias on the ground in New England into a coherent fighting force, in the event they need to confront the British troops. In other words, the colonies need to form a national army, a *Continental* army.

These realizations come swiftly in the first few weeks of the Congress, and sorting through the details of how to create such an army quickly becomes the first critical task.

Once you have an army, you need someone to lead it. Choosing who among them should command this new army will be the *next* critical task.

There are several candidates. But one clearly stands out: How about the guy from Virginia who showed up in the uniform? On June 14, 1775, John Adams calls a session to formalize the creation of a Continental army, and to debate which of the candidates should lead it. On the first point everyone agrees: A national army will be created. On the second, Adams reads several names aloud as contenders. Naturally, Washington is one of them.

There's only one problem: George Washington has disappeared.

3

Honor, honor, honor.

So much in George Washington's life has been centered around the pursuit of this ideal. It's perhaps the greatest lesson from his youth, learned when his older brother Lawrence first introduced him to Virginia society: A reputation for integrity and honor is something you can take anywhere, and it will never let you down.

George may not have come from wealth, he may not have come from a noble family, but he would always have *character*—an unimpeachable code of personal honor that could not be taken from him.

It's a subject that will come up again and again in his letters—a reflection upon the values of integrity, duty, and trust. "I hope I shall possess firmness and virtue enough to maintain what I consider the most enviable of all titles, the character of an honest man," he once wrote to Alexander Hamilton; and, in a moment of reflection to his aide Joseph Reed: "I have but one capital object in view, I could wish to make my conduct coincide with the wishes of mankind, as far as I can consistently."

He could sometimes judge others harshly for failing to live up to his high standards of virtue, but he often reserved the toughest judgment for himself.

It started when he was young. One of the few remaining documents from George Washington's boyhood is a list of 110 "rules of civility" he carefully transcribed by hand, probably in his early teens. They're from a well-known book of the time, *Rules of Civility & Decent Behavior in Company and Conversation*. Originally written by French Jesuits in 1595, it was later translated into English and became popular both in Britain and the colonies.

Some of the rules provide an amusing take on basic manners, like Rule 5: "If you cough, sneeze, sigh, or yawn, do it not loud but privately; and speak not in your yawning, but put your handkerchief or hand before your face and turn aside," or another, Rule 7, which still provides good advice today: "Put not off your clothes in the presence of others, nor go out [of] your chamber half dressed."

However, some of the rules that Washington carefully copied speak to a deeper sense of graciousness toward others, like the very first: "Every action done in company, ought to be with some sign of respect, to those that are present," or Rule 43: "Do not express joy before one sick or in pain for that contrary passion will aggravate his misery."

We still don't know if the task of writing out these rules was a mandatory schoolhouse exercise assigned by a teacher or whether young George chose to do so for his own use, but the emphasis on decorum and courtesy seems to have made an impact. George Washington may not have been born into nobility, but he could *learn* to be a gentleman; he could work hard to improve himself; he could, through his character alone, earn the respect of anyone he might meet.

But for Washington, this personal code of honor and integrity was not something to brag about or put on display. Later in life, after he had become one of the most famous people in the world, those who met him were often surprised by his quiet modesty. As the French nobleman Prince de Broglie wrote after first meeting him, "He is a foe to ostentation and to vainglory. . . . Modest even to humility, he does not seem to estimate himself at his true worth. He receives with perfect grace all the homages which are paid him, but he evades them rather than seeks them." No matter the circumstance, he was almost always deferential, always gracious. After all, bragging and boasting aren't honorable; what's honorable is doing one's duty and sacrificing oneself for a noble cause.

It's as if, after losing his father and his brother, Washington learned to cling fiercely to these personal ideals of honor and integrity. This way, he had something he could rely on within himself.

Certainly, Washington's carefully cultivated reputation will serve him well as a young adult. It's what led Virginia's Governor, Robert Dinwiddie, to entrust twenty-one-year-old George Washington to lead one of the first crucial expeditions of the French and Indian War—a highly unusual assignment for someone so young. It's what later led to his appointment as a personal aide to Gen. Edward Braddock, one of the most prominent British generals in the war; and, when Braddock was mortally wounded in battle, it was Washington's sense of duty that led him to brave a hail of bullets to secure the dying officer's body and provide his superior officer a proper burial.

Washington's reputation also served him well after the war, when he pursued the hand of the young widow Martha Custis, a woman of far greater wealth than himself. And, once he was married and established as a prosperous landowner, his reputation got him elected to a seat in Virginia's House of Burgesses, a body that then appointed him as one of the delegates to represent the colony at the Continental Congress.

Now, here in Philadelphia, it is George Washington's sense of honor that makes him literally flee the room when John Adams stands before the Congress and announces Washington's name as a candidate for the command of the Continental army.

Why does he flee? Washington doesn't want it to look in any way as if he is *hoping* to win the position out of vanity or arrogance, or that he is somehow suggesting his own superiority over the others. Even the *appearance* that he might be coveting the role for personal reasons—rather than for the greater good—would be immodest, and not worthy of the sacred duty of the command.

So, while the other contenders try to lobby and jockey to obtain the position, Washington simply disappears.

After the Congress considers the candidates and puts the matter before the floor, the delegates vote unanimously that George Washington should receive the command. Washington doesn't learn of his appointment until later that night, when he runs into a few congressmen on the street and they stop to give him a salute.

"General," they call him.

Honor, honor, honor.

4

———•———

Just like that, everything has changed.

The colonies officially have an army—or at least they have a plan to create one—and George Washington from Virginia will lead it.

"This Congress doth now declare that they will maintain and assist and adhere to him, the said George Washington, with their lives and fortunes," John Hancock announces to the delegates the next day, in a session to formalize the decision and allow the new Commander to speak.

Washington is seemingly overwhelmed by the weight of the responsibility he now bears. When he advances to the podium to accept the command, his speech is brief and almost painfully modest. He expresses gratitude for the "high honor" of the position, declines the offered payment, and concludes on the humblest possible note: "Lest some unlucky event should happen unfavorable to my reputation . . . I beg it may be remembered by every Gentleman in this room, that I this day declare with the utmost sincerity, I do not think myself equal to the command I am honored with."

The other delegates are moved by Washington's words, although a few, like Eliphalet Dyer from Connecticut, are almost taken aback by his humility: "He is clever, and if any thing too modest. . . . He seems discreet and virtuous, no harum-scarum ranting swearing fellow, but sober, steady, & calm."

Washington's modesty is not just a display for the Congress. In the next few days, he echoes the same humble tone in personal correspondence to family members. In a private letter to his wife he calls the new position "a trust too great for my capacity," and in a letter to his brother-in-law, Burwell Bassett, he writes this:

I am now embarked on a tempestuous ocean from whence, perhaps, no friendly harbor is to be found. . . . I can answer but for three things: a firm belief of the justice of our cause—close attention to the prosecution of it—and the strictest integrity. If these cannot supply the places of ability & experience, the cause will suffer.

Even more telling, fellow Virginian Patrick Henry encounters Washington outside by himself the night following the appointment, and sees that the new Commander has tears in his eyes. As Henry recalls it, Washington confides to him: "Remember, Mr. Henry, what I now tell you: From the day I enter upon the command of the American armies, I date my fall, and the ruin of my reputation."

For Washington, it seems, the responsibility and trust given him are so awesome, that the very possibility of failing in his duty—of letting down his countrymen who have placed their faith in him—is almost impossible to bear.

A few days later, John Adams writes of Washington: "I hope the people of our Province, will treat the General with all that confidence and affection, that politeness and respect, which is due to one of the most important characters in the world. The liberties of America depend upon him, in a great degree."

No pressure.

5

---·---

New York, New York

June 1776

The sky above Manhattan is overcast.

Almost exactly one year into George Washington's command, at eleven o'clock in the morning, thousands of troops gather in a large field due north of New York City, divided into four standing brigades. Most of the Continental army is here, officers and soldiers alike.

General Washington, the Commander-in-Chief of the Continental forces, had ordered that the troops march here from their encampments, in uniform, and stand at attention.

Separate from the army, a huge crowd of ordinary citizens is also gathered in the field, comprised of onlookers and residents from all over the region. In total some twenty thousand people are here, soldiers and civilians, all watching and waiting.

Although the troops are in full uniform and carry their weapons, today there will be no battle, or parade, or military exercise. The crowd is silent, and the mood is somber.

A chaplain stands there, waiting.

After a few quiet minutes, several soldiers escort a prisoner before the crowd, his hands bound by rope. He's of medium height, well built, with pale skin and dark hair. The soldiers flanking the prisoner march him slowly forward.

On this very day, the colonies are at war with Great Britain; yet this prisoner is not an enemy soldier. He wears the colors of the Continental army, not those of the British.

Who is this man? And what awful crime could warrant this somber public spectacle?

Among the onlookers is a young army surgeon, barely twenty-three years old, by the name of William Eustis. He stands at attention with the rest of his unit, watching.

Several hours later, the surgeon is back at his quarters in New York City. There, sitting alone, he brings out a quill, dips it in his inkstand, puts it to paper, and begins to compose a letter.

"You will doubtless have heard of the discovery of the greatest and vilest attempt ever made against our country," he writes. "I mean the *plot*, the *infernal plot*, which has been contrived by our worst enemies."

For Eustis, writing the letter, the very idea of this plot is so terrible that he can't even conjure an ordinary word to describe it. Instead, he invents a new one: *Sacricide.*

From the Latin roots, it means "slaughter of the sacred," or "slaughter of the good."

And the target of this plot?

The young man continues:

Their design was upon the first engagement which took place, to have murdered (with trembling I say it) the best man on earth: General Washington was to have been the subject of their unheard of SACRICIDE . . . and in short the most accursed scheme was laid to give us into the hands of the enemy, and to ruin us.

Centuries later, it is a moment mostly lost to the history books. A plot to kill George Washington.

In 1776, in the first full year of the Revolutionary War, George Washington is the leader of the Continental army, and the man on whom the colonies have placed all of their hopes. For any person of the colonies, conspiring to assassinate George Washington is treasonous almost beyond measure—an act that single-handedly threatens the existence of America itself.

Who would undertake such a dangerous act?

How was the plot uncovered?

And what happened to those responsible?

This is the story of the first conspiracy.

6

---•---

Philadelphia, Pennsylvania

June 1775

In the days immediately following his appointment as the new leader of the Continental army, George Washington races to do three things in Philadelphia before he leaves for Boston to assume his command:

1. He orders a new uniform based almost entirely on his old one from the Virginia militia. Blue coat. Epaulettes on his shoulders. Yellow buttons. There is no time for anyone to come up with a new design.
2. He sends instructions to a lawyer friend to draw up his will, just in case. He and Martha have no children together, but Martha has children from her previous marriage, and Washington has several siblings, nieces, and nephews. Should he not return from battle, he needs to provide for those he leaves behind.
3. He orders several books on military strategy. These include Roger Stevenson's *Military Instructions for Officers*, recently published in Philadelphia; also, a new edition of one of Washington's favorites, Humphrey Bland's *A Treatise of Military Discipline*, originally published in 1727 and considered the "bible of the British army." It has been fifteen years since

Washington has seen any real military combat, and he wants
to be ready.

In fact, Washington's request for these books highlights something else: his lack of experience for the position he has just assumed.
Washington may be one of the more seasoned military veterans in
the colonies, but that isn't saying much. Colonial officers like Washington were given inferior positions compared to their British
counterparts. As a colonel, Washington was a midlevel officer who
had never led more than a hundred men in actual battle. He has
no experience remotely like commanding a national force in a large-
scale war.

Now, as Commander-in-Chief of the Continental army, he'll be
responsible for organizing a national army and leading thousands of
troops against the world-renowned generals of the mighty British military forces.

He better read those books.

On June 22, 1775, barely a week after Washington's appointment,
the delegates gather outside the Pennsylvania State House to see their
new Commander off. A handful of newly appointed officers, also selected from among the delegates, will join him for the trip.

As Washington strides toward one of the five white horses that have
been readied for the journey, his new aide-de-camp, a young congressman named Thomas Mifflin, runs out in front of the General, kneels,
and cups his hands by the horse's stirrup to help the new Commander
mount. It's a ceremonial gesture, a demonstration of respect, and the
crowd breaks into spontaneous applause.

George Washington, once a rural boy from Virginia, is now one
of the most important men in the colonies.

Before their departure, Washington had instilled in the other generals his conviction that anytime they appear in public, their presentation must be exemplary. In order to persuade young men to become
soldiers—and to win the faith and confidence of the public—it is essential always to *appear* confident, to *appear* organized, and to *appear*
disciplined, even under the worst circumstances.

No matter how hastily they have planned this endeavor, and no matter how under-resourced and inexperienced they are, Washington tries to make sure he and his generals *look* like officers prepared to conquer the world.

So, on the road from Philadelphia to Boston, his new entourage appears every bit the embodiment of military leaders. Washington himself rides in a small carriage known as a phaeton followed by teams of aides and servants on horseback. Before they pass through each town, Washington jumps out of his carriage and onto a single white horse to lead the procession in dramatic fashion. By this time word has spread through the colonies that a Continental army has been formed, and townspeople line the streets to get a glimpse of the new Commander.

After they travel north from Pennsylvania and up through New Jersey, the most important stop is on the third day of their trip: New York City.

At midday on June 25, now ten days after he had accepted the command, Washington and his generals arrive in Newark, New Jersey, and then travel northeast to the Hudson River, where they board a ferry across the water to Manhattan Island.

At the time, the entirety of New York City comprised only the southernmost tip of Manhattan Island. The northern city limit was the equivalent of today's Chambers Street; most of the island above that was unpopulated woods, grasslands, rivers, and rolling hills, dotted by the occasional farm or wealthy estate. Today's boroughs of Brooklyn and Queens were part of Long Island—not considered New York City at all—and usually referred to by their county names: Kings County and Queens County, respectively.

Although geographically relatively small, New York City was nonetheless a vibrant, bustling place, and its busy port district along the southeast corner of the island—today's South Street Seaport—was a commercial hub of the northeastern and mid-Atlantic colonies. With a population of about 25,000, New York City was the second largest city in the colonies after Philadelphia.

Once Washington and his generals cross the Hudson and arrive on the western shore of Manhattan, a small troop of militia greets them. Then the entire entourage advances to the city and parades through the busy streets. New Yorkers had learned in advance of Washington's arrival, and crowds line the sidewalks to cheer the man whose name has become almost instantly famous.

As Washington's procession rides down Broadway close to Wall Street, it passes near the small campus of King's College (later to be moved uptown, as Columbia University), and the cheers grow especially loud.

Among the onlookers is a fresh-faced nineteen-year-old named Alexander Hamilton, then an undergraduate student and budding revolutionary, dazzled to catch a glimpse of the new Commander. Hamilton is likely accompanied by his classmate Hercules Mulligan—and these two friends, perhaps inspired by seeing Washington, will soon enlist in the Continental army and play their own roles in the sweeping events to come.

But cheering revolutionaries-to-be like Hamilton and his classmates aren't the only ones closely watching George Washington that day.

Although many New York City residents cheer on Washington and the new Continental army, there are also many who don't support them. New York is, in fact, a major power center for Loyalists—the name given to those who live in the colonies but still support the Crown, and who oppose the colonies' rebellion.* Indeed, the New York City region has almost as many Loyalists as Patriots, with allegiances often changing. Right now, in the summer of 1775, these two opposing factions are locked in a volatile battle for the soul of the city.

There are many reasons why New York City is a base for Loyalist sentiment. Prominent families with deep royal ties live in and around the city, giving support and resources to the pro-British cause. Most of the city's countless merchants are also loyal to England and the trade it provides. The Anglican Church—literally, the "Church of

---

* "Tory" is another common term used to describe British sympathizers within the colonies during this period. Although "Tory" refers specifically to the pro-Crown political party, and "Loyalist" is a more general term, the two words are often interchangeable.

England"—is dominant in New York, and most of its flock won't betray their faith and turn against the mother country. Then as now, New York was full of immigrants, and workers from various European countries had any number of reasons to support one side or the other. Unlike George Washington's genteel Virginia, New York City is a teeming, unpredictable place full of shifting loyalties and competing agendas.

In fact, on that very same afternoon that Washington's procession rides along Broadway, a very different procession is also under way in the city, in honor of a very different man.

By sheer coincidence William Tryon, the Governor of the colony of New York and a staunch Loyalist, has that same day returned to New York City from an almost yearlong trip to England. Therefore a procession is also due in *his* honor, only a few blocks from where Washington and his generals pass. That morning, the city's planning committee, run by the New York Provincial Congress, was caught in the awkward position of having to provide a public reception to two politically opposed leaders on the same afternoon. The committeemen, doing their best, first instructed the greeting militias to be "ready to receive either the Generals or Governor Tryon, which ever shall first arrive, and to wait on both as well as circumstances will allow."

Soon realizing they should avoid two simultaneous competing processions, however, the city officials then change their strategy and intentionally delay Tryon's arrival until early evening, shortly after Washington's parade has passed. As a reflection of the city's confused politics, some of the same crowds move right from one procession to the other.

In his leadership of the colony, Governor Tryon has remained a strong supporter of British rule. He believes the "revolutionary" movement is illegitimate and has been fighting against it.

Having been at sea during the past several weeks, the Governor probably didn't learn until arriving in the port that the Continental Congress had just announced the formation of an army, and that its leader would be riding through New York City on the same day as his own ceremonial return from England.

So when Governor Tryon finally disembarks on the ferry landing's stairs in the evening to be escorted through the city, he is not pleased at having had to wait several hours for the Continental army's parade to end. As one city official who witnessed Tryon's arrival puts it, "He appeared grave this evening and said little."

The Governor's mood surely isn't improved by the sound of "much shouting in the procession," probably coming from the city's more radical contingent, which came out to see Washington and is now heckling the newly returned Governor.

Tryon, accustomed to calling the shots in his own colony, must in fact be appalled that this enemy, this so-called Commander, would parade through Manhattan right under his nose. After all, New York is Tryon's city, and the public should be cheering *him*—not some usurper representing an illegal subversion of proper royal authority.

George Washington.

It's a name William Tryon won't soon forget.

Indeed, Governor Tryon is the last person to be intimidated by so-called rebels, radicals, or revolutionaries—something he demonstrated just a few years earlier, in a most controversial fashion.

7

———•———

William Tryon was born in Surrey, England, in 1729. Raised in an aristocratic family, as a young man he was inclined toward military service, enlisting as an officer to serve the British army against France during the Seven Years' War in Europe.

By the late 1750s, Tryon had achieved the rank of Lieutenant Colonel when a bullet wound to his leg ended his service in the war.

Like many ambitious Englishmen at the time, Tryon turned his attention to the American colonies as a place to find success, wealth, and opportunity.

In 1764, Tryon received an appointment to serve the Crown in the colony of North Carolina, first as Lieutenant Governor, then as Governor in 1765. It was there that William Tryon had his first memorable run-in with colonial subversives or "rebels" who dared to challenge the authority of the royal government.

In the late 1760s a group of poor backwoods farmers in North Carolina—a group that became known as the Regulators—had begun organizing to protest oppressive taxes and fines that British officials routinely levied against them. These farmers could barely feed their families, yet had to pay increasingly large fees every month. If they couldn't pay, additional fines were levied against them. Stuck

Before serving as Governor of New York, William Tryon served as Governor of North Carolina from 1765 to 1771. This painting from 1767, originally attributed to the artist John Wollaston, has long been thought to be the only surviving portrait of Tryon. However, researchers now suspect that the portrait may not really be the work of Wollaston, and the subject may not be Tryon.*

in a cycle of debt, many had their humble farms confiscated and were sometimes forced into indentured servitude.

One of these farmers' most hated taxes was in fact one imposed directly by Governor Tryon to pay for a vast, lavish mansion he was

---

* The original provenance of the portrait was based on an inked inscription that appears on the back: "Govr Wm Tryon of No Carolina J. Wollaston, pint. Anno D. 1767." The inscription refers to John Wollaston, a popular portrait artist of the day. However, according to researchers at the State Library of North Carolina, where the painting is housed, there is no evidence that in 1767 either Wollaston or Tryon visited New York City, where the painting was purportedly executed. In other words, the inscription could be an error or a fraud. If so, the subject is someone else and there may be no surviving portrait of Tryon.

building for himself at public expense. This luxurious Governor's residence, known around the colony as "Tryon's Palace," became a symbol of royal luxury and greed at a time when many rural residents lived in near poverty.

As the Regulator movement in North Carolina gained greater numbers, Governor Tryon chose to act decisively and set an example. Rather than negotiate with the protesting farmers or respond to their demands, Tryon hired a band of well-armed mercenary soldiers, and personally rode with them to a riverside grove where several hundred of the Regulators had gathered. After a tense standoff with the encamped group, Tryon sent a written demand that the Regulators lay down any weapons and surrender their leaders for arrest within an hour's time. The message ended with these words: "By accepting these terms within one hour from the delivery of this dispatch, you will prevent an effusion of blood, as you are in this time in a state of REBELLION against your King, your country, and your laws. [Signed]William Tryon."

When the group's leaders failed to come forward and offer themselves up for arrest, Tryon's militia charged the encampment.

In this so-called Battle of Alamance, Tryon's forces overwhelmed the poorly armed farmers, killed or wounded several dozen, and shackled the group's leaders. Under Tryon's direction, the leaders were quickly tried and sentenced to death for treason. On June 19, 1771, the chief justice of Hillsborough pronounced their gruesome sentence:

The prisoner should . . . be drawn from thence to the place of execution and hanged by the neck; that he should be cut down while yet alive; that his bowels should be taken out and burned before his face; that his head should be cut off, and that his body should be divided into four quarters, which [are] to be placed at the King's disposal, and may the Lord have mercy on your soul.

We don't know if this horrific punishment, called drawing and quartering, was carried out, but in total six of the Regulator leaders were hanged, others were jailed, and the movement never recovered.

Tryon's swift, brutal response to the uprising set an example for anyone who dared question royal authority.

Tryon's North Carolina governorship lasted six years until 1771, when he was transferred to serve as Governor of a larger and even more tumultuous colony: New York.

Now, in 1775, Tryon is a nine-year veteran of the colonies with long experience in government. In New York City, he is a powerful man and a cunning politician. He understands the levers of power in the city, and curries the support of the most influential families and wealthy merchants. On his return from his trip to England, he's determined to strike back at the revolutionaries and reassert his own power.

As for Washington and his officers, after a post-parade ceremonial dinner, they settle down in their Manhattan lodgings. They need rest for the next day's journey toward Boston. But that night, Washington is uneasy. He has learned about Governor Tryon's arrival coinciding with his own, and is uncomfortable about the proximity. He knows of Tryon's past in North Carolina, and his violent repression of the Regulator movement.

Now he has a feeling that New York City could pose some future danger to his army—and in particular he distrusts the Governor.

As tired as Washington must have been that night, he takes the time to write a letter to his general Philip Schuyler, whom he has just put in charge of the New York region. Washington relates his uneasy feeling, and gives Schuyler specific instructions:

> Keep a watchful eye upon Governor Tryon; and if you find him attempting directly or indirectly any measures inimical to the common cause use every means in your power to frustrate his designs . . . if forceable measures are adjudged necessary respecting the person of the Governor, I should have no difficulty in ordering of it.

When Schuyler receives the instructions, he writes back only that Governor Tryon's conduct has thus far been "unexceptional," and doesn't seem to share Washington's concerns about Tryon. Schuyler declines to take any concrete actions against the Governor, let alone "forceable" ones.

But Washington is right to be worried. The coincidence of these two opposing men arriving in the city the same day—the Continental Commander-in-Chief, George Washington, and New York's royal Governor, William Tryon—is a foreshadowing of a dark confrontation that lies ahead, when these two men cross paths once again.

PART II

Spies in Boston

8

---•---

Cambridge, Massachusetts

July 1775

On Sunday, July 2, 1775, George Washington and his aides arrive in Cambridge, Massachusetts, on the outskirts of Boston, after an eight-day journey from New York City. The trip was made both longer and more exhausting by obligatory ceremonial stops in every town and city along the way, so local leaders and public crowds could see and meet the now-famous George Washington in person for the first time.

But for the Commander and his generals, there is no joy in making this trip.

During his journey up to Massachusetts, Washington had received news of yet more bloodshed in Boston. On June 17, a group of colonial militias occupied Breed's Hill and nearby Bunker Hill, north of the city, as a defensive posture against the British troops stationed in Boston. British officers in Boston learned in advance of the militias' plans, and led fifteen hundred soldiers from their downtown garrisons against the colonists. In a dramatic battle, the better-armed British troops charged Breed's Hill with successive waves of infantry. The British soldiers eventually prevailed and took the hill from the colonists, but only after paying a price: 226 soldiers killed and 828 wounded. The Patriots, after a bloody retreat, counted 140 deaths and 310 wounded.

Word of the battle—soon known as the Battle of Bunker Hill, although the actual fighting occurred on Breed's Hill—quickly spreads around New England and throughout the colonies. The heavy casualties, as well as reports that British soldiers had slaughtered with bayonets the injured colonists who lay on the hill in the wake of the fighting, underscore the gravity of the circumstances and heighten patriotic resolve.

Once again the violence is followed by a tense cease-fire, as both England and the colonies determine a response.

In the aftermath of this battle, Washington's arrival in Massachusetts takes on even more urgent dimensions. Although the Continental Congress continues on its course of reconciliation, colonists feel more than ever the possibility of a full-scale war.

Upon their arrival outside Cambridge, Washington and his generals are met by a greeting committee consisting of two of the most prominent Patriots in Massachusetts: Moses Gill, a politician who had overseen supplying arms for the rebels at Bunker Hill, and Dr. Benjamin Church, a member of the legendary Sons of Liberty who also served in the Massachusetts Provincial Congress. In keeping with his name, Church is someone people trust: a Harvard-educated physician and Patriot who once served as John Adams's personal doctor. In a few weeks the Continental Congress will appoint him Chief Physician & Director General of the Army's Medical Service, effectively making Dr. Church the army's first Surgeon General.

These two local Patriots, Gill and Church, escort Washington to a formal officers' dinner, where Washington learns more from local leaders about the Massachusetts militias and additional volunteers from nearby colonies that have gathered and await his command. These militiamen and new recruits, currently encamped in fields fanning out west of Boston and numbering somewhere around fourteen thousand, are the beginning of his new army.

That night, Washington sleeps in the Harvard Square home of the college president, who had offered it for the Commander-in-Chief's use. Early the next morning, July 3, 1775, Washington and his generals ride to the encampments, where the sound of fifes and drums greets them.

It's time to meet the troops.

Nothing in Washington's experience, as an officer for the British during the French and Indian War or as a leader of the Virginia militia, could have prepared him for what he is about to see.

The troops are, as one observer says, "the most wretchedly clothed, and as dirty a set of mortals as ever disgraced the name of a soldier." In fact, many of them aren't really soldiers at all. They are farmers, common laborers, ex-criminals, and beggars—some suspiciously old, some suspiciously young.

Many wield pitchforks and shovels as weapons, while others carry no weapon at all. Some of them wear the uniforms of the local colonial militias from Massachusetts, Rhode Island, Connecticut, and New Jersey, but a majority wear dirty work shirts and tattered pants.

The men had arrived and are still arriving from all directions, from different colonies, with no system in place for how to organize or feed them. They are spread out in disorganized encampments over a stretch of several miles, with no running water or sanitation system. The stench of brimming open latrines is overwhelming, and, as one orderly describes it, when the latrines are full the men spread "excrement about the fields perniciously."

The soldiers are housed in makeshift tents, cobbled together using whatever materials they can find: "Some are made of boards, some of sailcloth. . . . Others are made of stone and turf and others again of birch and other brush . . . curiously wrought with wreaths . . . in the manner of a basket."

This is the army, and these are the men, with whom Washington is supposed to fight against the biggest, most powerful, most feared military in the world.

And these are just first impressions. Beyond the initial sights, sounds, and smells of the camps, Washington has more to learn about the state of his new army. Not just their lack of supplies and accommodations, but the lack of training of most men. "[I] found a numerous army of provincials under very little command, discipline, or order," he writes.

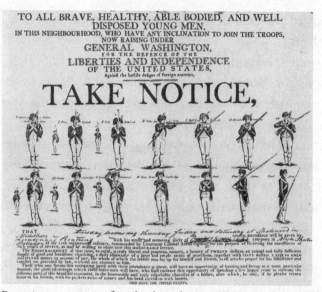

Recruitment poster for the brand-new Continental army, under the leadership of Gen. George Washington. Although the poster appeals to the Patriotic spirit, the finer print also highlights the payment offered. Most of the new recruits come from poor backgrounds, with no military experience.

Aside from their poor personal hygiene, the men's profane language and lack of soldierly manners goes against everything Washington has learned as a proper soldier and officer. In a letter to John Hancock, the president of the Continental Congress, Washington complains that "licentiousness and every kind of disorder triumphantly reign" among the militias and volunteers, and he worries if this motley crew of men and boys can ever be trained.

Washington's grim assessment also applies to many of the militias' officers, who had supposedly been providing guidance to the fledgling army. Although a few of the men who had led troops in the earlier Boston battles have provided heroic leadership—and these men will soon become Washington's top officers—overall Washington is dismayed to find that many officers are simply in it to make money, and some are even scamming to earn a little extra.

Of the Massachusetts militia he writes: "Their officers are generally speaking the most indifferent kind of people I ever saw. I have already broke [punished] one Colonel and five Captains for . . . draw-ing more pay and provisions than they had men in their companies." In general, Washington encounters a great "dearth of public spirit and want of virtue . . . such a dirty, mercenary spirit pervades the whole that I should not be at all surprised at any disaster that may happen."

Of all the setbacks and disappointments that Washington encoun-ters in his army-to-be, one perhaps alarms him most: the lack of gun-powder. Back at the Congress and during his journey to Boston he had repeatedly made requests for proper quantities of powder, without which even the finest troops in the world would be defenseless. At first, on arrival in Cambridge, he is told the troops have 308 barrels of powder, a modest but serviceable amount. But soon, a brigadier general named John Sullivan sheepishly informs him that the num-ber is a mistake, and doesn't account for the powder already used during the Bunker Hill battle. The real number is thirty-eight barrels.

As Sullivan describes it, after he informed the general of this laugh-ably small amount, Washington "did not utter a word for half an hour." The army has barely enough ammunition for training drills, let alone to fight a battle.

The enemy forces are just across the Back Bay in Boston, barely a mile away, and fully armed. Should the British choose to attack to-morrow, Washington's soldiers would be slaughtered, unable even to defend themselves.

One thing is clear: Nothing in this war will be easy.

9

New York, New York

August 1775

New York City is slipping. The Governor can sense it.

Ever since the so-called Commander, George Washington, and his procession of generals marched through New York City earlier in the summer, Governor William Tryon of New York has watched as upstart radicals and revolutionaries threaten the authority and governing principles that he believes are the foundation of the city.

As far as Governor Tryon is concerned, revolutionary fervor has ripped New York City apart at the seams. Former friends have become bitter enemies. Neighbors attack neighbors. Mobs of rebel demonstrators, with no respect for the law, bring chaos and fear to the streets. What used to be a war of pamphlets—New York City is home to many printing presses, and writers and activists on both sides are waging a propaganda war—has become a war of intimidation, mob violence, and destruction.

But Tryon remains optimistic. He still believes that at its core, New York is a city of Loyalists—that is, colonists who maintain their allegiance to the Crown. The city's powerful merchant classes, dependent on secure trade with the mother country, support England and oppose the upheaval of rebellion. Many of the wealthiest and most powerful families in the region—and Governor Tryon knows all of them—retain close ties to England. The farming communities of Long Island, Staten Island, and the Hudson Valley are also full of Loyalists.

Furthermore, Tryon believes that in the end, most people will follow strength, and it's just a matter of time before England's clear superiority, military and otherwise, will lead the public to abandon the foolish idea of rebellion and return to good sense: the good sense of strong British rule.

When Tryon returned to New York City from England that day in late June 1775, he had to endure not just the insult of George Washington parading through his city, but also the jeers from an unruly crowd of rebels shouting at their Governor. He had returned from a yearlong visit to England, lobbying there *on behalf* of the colony, only to be received with insults from the rabble.

Nevertheless, a few days later, on July 5, when Tryon addresses a gathering of the top officials in the colony, he makes sure to adopt an elevated and conciliatory tone:

> I receive with satisfaction your congratulations on my return to this Country . . . and of your continued confidence in me at this melancholy crisis of public affairs, already carried to an extreme much to be lamented by every good man and well-wisher of his King and Country.

He wants to make clear that he, Tryon, is on the side of the just and the good—which is to say, on the side of the Crown's clear authority.

> I confess my disappointment at the change of circumstances in this Government, and feel the weightiest distress at the present unfriendly aspect of the times. . . . At the same time, my breast glowing with an ardent zeal for the honour of my Sovereign. . . . [I] cherish the wish of the Nation for a speedy and happy reconciliation between Great Britain and her Colonies.

Tryon ends his speech with a message of reconciliation on behalf of the King himself: "I am authorized to say, that nothing can give greater satisfaction to the royal breast, than to see us again a happy and united people."

Tryon had hoped that his return as Governor after many months' absence, together with his generous remarks, would serve to bring good sense back to the city, and dampen revolutionary fervor.

Instead, the opposite is true.

The city has slipped even further into chaos. Throughout the late summer Tryon has borne witness to all manner of unspeakable acts. The city's businesses have been subjected to boycott and abuse by radicals. Some of the established city leaders, those who proclaim steadfast loyalty to the King, have been tarred and feathered, or jailed.

Earlier in the summer, a mob of revolutionaries had stormed King's College, forcing the Loyalist college president, Myles Cooper, to flee the city by boat in the middle of the night.

In some counties just outside the city, local prisons are overflowing, mostly with men sent there for refusing to swear an oath of allegiance to the American colonies rather than to England.

Now, as summer turns to fall in 1775, a particularly gruesome practice known as "riding the rail" has become common. Angry mobs, when wishing to inflict pain and humiliation on someone deemed an enemy, seat their victim astride a long sharp beam of wood, apply weights to his feet to enhance the pain, and parade him through the streets while onlookers spit or throw stones.

All the while, radicals circulate leaflets containing vile language against His Majesty the King, a constant affront to the Crown's authority.

Governor Tryon knows that the Loyalists in the city had been eagerly awaiting his return from England, hoping that he could apply a firm hand and restore proper authority to their city. Unfortunately, Tryon now finds that many tools of his governorship have been stripped away.

The governing bodies of the city, once consolidated under Tryon's leadership, have during his absence fallen into weakness or have been entirely disbanded; instead new governments set up by colonists are wielding power in the city and the colony.

In the last year and a half alone, the Patriots have created a confusing succession of ad hoc governing bodies in New York: First there was the Committee of Correspondence, then the Committee of Fifty, then the Committee of Fifty-One, then the Committee of One Hundred, then the Continental Association, now the New York Provincial Congress.

Clearly, these people have no idea what they're doing.

The colony's former royal legislative body, the New York Assembly, was left to die in Tryon's absence and superseded by the rebel-controlled New York Provincial Congress, which elected and sent delegates to the Second Continental Congress, a body that England considers illegitimate. The last bastion of royal authority in the colony is Governor Tryon himself, along with his appointed Governor's Council.

In New York as in many of the colonies, the revolutionaries are emboldened like never before. Now they brag about their army up in Boston, raising arms against British soldiers.

It's not just their army they brag about, but also their *Commander*.

George Washington. His name is on every rebel's lips, in every pamphlet, a new hero to the political movement that Tryon must fight against.

As Tryon and other Loyalists in the colonies must concede, the very existence of this army and its new leader has unleashed a new fervor among the radicals, based on their unrealistic hope that a brand-new collection of raw soldiers can stand up to the vast might of the British army.

The rebels' hope may be false, but their new confidence is real—and in New York, the resulting fervor has unmoored the city. It will take a leader of strength and cunning to restore it.

Governor Tryon wants to win his city back. It's as simple as that. If political solutions fail, then other means are necessary. After all, before he was a politician, Tryon was a soldier—with a bullet wound in his leg to prove it—and he is not one to back down from a fight.

If Tryon learned anything from his time governing North Carolina, it's that showing clear strength is the best way to win over a population. In North Carolina, it was pretty straightforward: When there was a rebellion of poor farmers—the so-called Regulators—he crushed it by force and hanged the leaders. Everyone fell quickly into line after that.

But here in New York, it won't be so easy. Here many of the rebels are from prominent families and have important connections. Unlike the dirt-poor farmers of North Carolina, Tryon can't just slaughter them. As the Governor himself put it to the English Parliament, "It would not do to treat the New Yorkers as I did the Regulators; they are a very different kind of men."

Even if he wanted to, Governor Tryon knows that the Crown would never let him hire his own militia, much less run it through the city streets to assault his enemies. The politics of the day are too fragile.

He will have to come up with another plan. Something secretive, something clandestine.

In a city like New York, knowledge is power, so Tryon's first move is to establish an intelligence operation to keep tabs on revolutionary activity in the region and to share it with his Loyalist allies throughout the colonies. Using his many connections in the city, he'll infiltrate rebel circles, both among the politicians and the lower classes. With his spies, he'll find their weak spots and figure out how to strike.

William Tryon doesn't need an assembly, or a congress, or anyone else. The Governor is ready to take matters into his own hands.

He has money.

He knows the city as well as anyone.

He has friends in high places—and low places.

Tryon is sure that one way or another, his side will win and the rebels will fall. And so will their Commander.

10

Cambridge, Massachusetts

August 1775

Order from chaos.

At every step, that's been George Washington's answer. When his father died, and then when his brother died, he learned to overcome the loss by exercising control, by being more disciplined, by working harder.

This army in Boston is a mess; but now it's *his* army, and it's his job, in fact his *duty,* to control it.

Every day, Washington rides with his generals through the encampments, inspecting, problem solving, imposing rules, and making plans.

Because Washington's face isn't yet known to these men, and because his hastily made uniform doesn't distinguish him as their leader, Washington places an unusual order with a local seamstress: a single light-blue sash. He wears it diagonally down his chest as a kind of totem, so his men will always recognize him. It's a "ribband to distinguish myself," he writes in his journal, and, along with his trademark gray horse, this simple ribbon will soon become a visual icon of the early years of the war.

No matter the chaos around him, while he's in front of the men, Washington always exhibits perfect poise, perfect manners, perfect horsemanship, perfect appearance. It's a small thing, but it sets the tone.

"His excellency was on horseback, in company with several other military gentlemen," writes a field doctor named James Thacher. "It was not difficult to distinguish him from the others; his personal appearance is truly noble and majestic."

But however impressive his bearing, the problems and difficulties Washington faces are staggering. Every day he has endless meetings and writes letter after letter to the Continental Congress, to other officers, to local committees, and to colonial leaders, trying to coordinate the Herculean task of organizing, feeding, supplying, transporting, paying, and training the thousands of men who have arrived from every direction with only the clothes on their backs.

With approval from Congress, he quickly appoints dozens of officers, most of them inexperienced, and then he must devise complicated chains of command from scratch, with no existing structure. Most national armies have decades if not centuries of established routines and protocol; Washington is trying to create these systems in a matter of weeks, with poor supplies, untrained soldiers, and inexperienced officers. The logistics are overwhelming, and new problems arise every day.

He begins a ritual of writing and sending daily general orders for officers to read aloud to all troops at their breakfast, an attempt to establish rules, priorities, and structure. These orders cover every facet of the army's day-to-day operations, from the most critical issues to the most mundane.

In his first few general orders, Washington introduces with great formality the names of his top generals. But he also takes tallies of blankets and kettles, responds to complaints that the daily bread is "sour and unwholesome," and singles out a soldier accused of stealing two horses from a farm: "It is ordered that he be discharged, and after receiving a severe reprimand, be turned out of camp."

Desperately, Washington tries to impose discipline on the mass of unruly young men who are living in squalor and prone to cursing, drinking, and fistfights.

He starts with a regimen of basic cleanliness, for hygiene and appearance. This isn't so easy, because every time it rains, the fields turn into mud and the open latrine ditches overflow into the muck. When some troops try to stay clean by bathing in a nearby river, Washington must respond to a different problem:

> Where it has been observed and complained of, that many men, lost to all sense of decency and common modesty, are running about naked upon the bridge, whilst passengers, and even ladies of the first fashion in the neighborhood, are passing over it, as if they meant to glory in their shame.

Clearly, these soldiers are not familiar with *The Rules of Civility & Decent Behavior*.

Washington also cracks down on the rampant drunkenness among the soldiers, castigating the officers for allowing liquor in the camps that leads to "the troops being continually debauched, which causes them to neglect their duty, and to be guilty of all those crimes which a vicious, ill habit naturally produces."

In addition to liquor, Washington has an aversion to gambling—something he considers unfit for the dignity of a soldier—and in one of his general orders announces a new policy that no "games of chance" will be allowed at the camp:

> Any officer, non-commissioned officer, or soldier, who shall here-after be detected playing at Toss-up, Pitch & Hustle, or any other games of chance, in, or near the camp or villages bordering on the encampments; shall without delay be confined and punished for disobedience of orders.

Washington usually appeals first and foremost to the soldiers' sense of honor and duty as their prime motivation to obey the various rules, sometimes using lofty language to do so. When it comes to soldiers stealing food or clothing from one another, he writes:

> [The General] hopes, and indeed flatters himself, that every private soldier will detest, and abhor such practices, when he considers,

that it is for the preservation of his own rights, liberty and property, and those of his fellow countrymen, that he is now called into service: that it is unmanly and sullies the dignity of the great cause, in which we are all engaged.

Nevertheless, if his appeals to the nobler sentiments of the men prove ineffective, Washington and his generals also impose strict punishments for every infraction, enforceable by court-martial. Punishments range from lashes on the back to expulsion and even imprisonment for serious crimes.

More than anything, Washington tries to instill in the troops from so many colonies that they are now fighting as one army, joined in a new American cause. Coming from so many regions, and without a common uniform or even a common flag to bind them, the new army will have to unite behind the *idea* of a shared purpose. In his general orders of July 4, 1775, Washington appeals to this lofty aspiration of national unity:

> The Continental Congress having now taken all the troops of the several Colonies. . . . They are now the troops of the United Provinces of North America; and it is hoped that all distinctions of Colonies will be laid aside; so that one and the same spirit may animate the whole, and the only contest be, who shall render, on this great and trying occasion, the most essential service to the great and common cause in which we are all engaged.

Unfortunately, Washington's high-minded plea is, at least at first, a total failure. In the coming weeks the various regional groups and militias quickly devolve into bitter rivalries and jealousies against one another, sometimes expressed with insults, fists, or knives. These petty fights are a constant source of frustration for Washington. Already carrying the massive burden of trying to organize and lead this vast operation, he can't seem to grasp why his soldiers don't share his exalted sense of common duty and mission.

The general's aggravation reaches something of a boiling point one day in early winter, a few months after he has assumed command. A regiment of backwoods Virginia riflemen had just arrived to join the Continental force, and after their long journey are to be housed in some vacant buildings on Harvard Yard before being sent to the camps. A group of Massachusetts troops, the so-called Marblehead regiment, happen to be recessing in the Yard when the Virginians arrive, and, rather than greet them, the Marblehead soldiers begin to shout mocking insults about the newcomers' uniforms, which, in the rural Virginia mode, are made of "white linen frocks, ruffled and fringed."

A ten-year-old boy named Israel Trask, the son of a Massachusetts officer, is in Harvard Yard at the time and describes what follows. The insults between the Marbleheaders and the Virginians get more heated, and then:

> Both parties closed, and a fierce struggle commenced with biting and gouging on the one part, and knockdown on the other part with as much apparent fury as the most deadly enmity could create. Reinforced by their friends, in less than five minutes more than a thousand combatants were on the field, struggling for the mastery.

Instead of fighting the British, the soldiers are fighting one another. The unholy brawl continues for several minutes, spilling into every corner of Harvard Yard. Just as the chaos threatens to spiral out of control, the sound of beating hooves fills the Yard, and George Washington himself gallops from around a corner and plunges into the fray:

> With the spring of a deer, he leaped from his saddle, threw the reins of his bridle into the hands of his servant, and rushed into the thickest of the melee, with an iron grip seized two tall, brawny, athletic, savage-looking riflemen by the throat, keeping them at arm's length, alternately shaking and talking to them.

At the sight of Washington, the hundreds of brawlers "[take] flight at the top of their speed in all directions from the scene of the conflict," and "less than fifteen minutes' time had elapsed from the commencement of the row before the general and his two criminals were the only occupants of the field of action."

After incidents like these, at times it seems to Washington that no matter how hard he works, the obstacles and difficulties are insurmountable.

In a moment of darkness, Washington writes a candid letter to his friend, fellow Virginia delegate Richard Henry Lee, expressing his frustration at the never-ending parade of problems: "There [have] been so many great, and capital errors, & abuses to rectify . . . that my life has been nothing else (since I came here) but one continued round of annoyance and fatigue."

The Commander-in-Chief's growing despair doesn't go unnoticed by those around him; as one aide writes: "I pity our good general, who has a greater burden on his shoulders and more difficulties to struggle with than I think should fall to the share of so good a man." And, in a moment of near hopelessness Washington confides to his aide Joseph Reed: "Could I have foreseen what I have and am like to experience, no consideration upon earth should have induced me to accept this command."

Yet at the end of the day, Washington knows that the command *is* his, and he can't escape it. To give up now, to abandon his charge, would be an act of dishonor that's simply unthinkable.

The fact is the army *needs* George Washington.

He's all they've got.

11

New York, New York

June 1776

It's a rainy Thursday in New York City. The city is filthy, full of mud.

The Continental army is everywhere, living in homes, walking the streets. These soldiers are here to defend the city. Many civilians have fled for fear of what is to come.

At this very moment, the first wave of the massive British fleet—hundreds of ships carrying tens of thousands of soldiers—is sailing toward the city. They're only a few days away.

It will be the first large-scale battle of the Revolutionary War.

And yet, in this tense moment, word has slowly spread about another danger—not coming from across the ocean but from right here, within the city. Maybe even from within the army.

On this rainy day, inside one home in the city, a quill touches parchment. A man's hand scrawls these words in dark ink: "You have no doubt heard of a most horrid conspiracy lately discovered in this place."

A conspiracy. In New York City.

The conspirators will "stop at nothing, however villainous and horrible, to accomplish their designs."

Their designs are against the Continental army, and not just against the army, but against its leader. The letter continues: "All our important men were to be seized or murdered. . . . General Washington was among the first that were to be sacrificed, and the rest in succession, according to their importance."

George Washington, murdered.

Such an act would devastate the army, especially when timed as the British arrive.

Interestingly, according to the letter, this plan does not originate from British forces. The plot is treasonous—it emerges from within.

The letter continues: "From the weight of the persons who have appeared to prosecute the inquiry, and the circumstances that have been mentioned, I have no doubt of the truth of the general charge."

In fact, at that moment, military and civilian officials are racing to uncover the details of this plot to try to stop it.

If what's in the letter is true, the implications are almost unfathomable: George Washington, murdered in 1776, in the first year of the Revolutionary War—murdered before the Declaration of Independence is even signed—before the United States of America even exists.

The quill comes to a stop. The letter, now finished, is sealed. The writer will send it by mail to Hartford, Connecticut.

12

NINE MONTHS EARLIER . . .

Cambridge, Massachusetts

It's late September 1775.

Washington's slowly growing army remains in a tense stalemate with the British troops occupying Boston. The Continental forces doesn't have the troops, weapons, or ammunition to try and win back the city—and even if it did, such action would likely precipitate an all-out war, which the Continental Congress is still hoping to avoid through negotiation.

The British, meanwhile, don't have sufficient troops in Boston or nearby Bunker Hill to expand and march to other cities. Washington's army is spread out in positions fanning out north, west, and south of the city, preventing any real British movement without a major confrontation. England's position seems to be to avoid more bloodshed, at least for now, while the two sides negotiate.

Still, both armies know that this stalemate could break in an instant, turning into a battle. In this tense environment both armies are eager for any information about the other—trying to gather intelligence about troop numbers, supplies, plans, and intentions.

That's when a stranger appears at Washington's doorstep.

One of Washington's top generals, Nathanael Greene, is the one who brings him. They arrive together at Washington's headquarters.

The stranger carries with him a mysterious letter.

His name, he says, is Godfrey Wenwood. He is a baker from Newport, Rhode Island, whose only claim to fame is a recipe for biscuits—known as "Wenwood's butter biscuits"—popular among the sailors and seamen who frequent his shop on Bannister's Wharf in Newport.

Why has General Greene brought a Rhode Island biscuit maker before the Commander-in-Chief of the Continental army?

The answer lies in the letter. It's a document written in code, and the baker says he was given the letter and asked to deliver it to British military officials stationed in Rhode Island.

Washington inspects the document, and indeed it contains a series of jumbled letters, apparently some kind of encrypted message.

Washington asks the obvious question: Who gave Wenwood the letter and asked him to deliver it to the British?

The answer: a woman.

She's the baker's former girlfriend, a love interest from the past, who is now a "woman of ill repute"—a prostitute—living here in Cambridge, Massachusetts. This former girlfriend unexpectedly came to visit the baker in Newport, and asked if he would deliver the letter, sealed at the time, to one of three British officials currently docked at a ship in Newport. She said she didn't know what was in the letter, only that she was just delivering it for an unnamed friend.

The baker explains to Washington that he felt very nervous about the woman's request. Although British seamen and officers stationed in Newport often visit his shop, he has no allegiance to them—in fact, he sides with the Patriots—and in any case he's just a humble man who makes biscuits for a living and isn't looking for trouble. He says that once the woman left, he held on to the letter rather than deliver it. Together with a friend, he opened the seal on the letter to see its contents, and was surprised to see that the enclosed document was in some sort of code.

The baker chose not to deliver the document, instead simply hiding it in the storeroom of his shop.

The letter might just have stayed in that storeroom forever, but then the baker's former-lover-turned-prostitute wrote him a follow-up note, wondering why the intended recipient hadn't yet received it: "I much wonder you never sent what you promised to send," she wrote. "If you did [he] never received it, so pray let me know by the first opportunity."

Now the baker is even more uneasy. How did she know the letter hadn't been sent? Why was she so concerned about it? And what business did she have delivering a coded letter to the British, anyway?

What's more, with tensions high in Rhode Island between Loyalists and Patriots, and with members of both groups frequenting his bakery and buying his famous biscuits, the last thing the baker needs is to get caught in the middle of some secret military scheme.

This time, the baker takes preemptive action. He carries the letter to a local Patriot leader, Rhode Island Secretary of State Henry Ward, and tells his story. Ward, immediately alarmed that someone in Cambridge is trying to deliver a coded letter to British officers in Rhode Island, sends the baker to meet with Gen. Nathanael Greene—also stationed in Rhode Island—who becomes similarly concerned. Greene beckons the baker to travel with him to Cambridge, to present the letter and his story to George Washington.

And so here they are now, in the Commander's headquarters.

The baker recounts his story once again to Washington. Satisfied that the man is telling the truth, Washington quizzes him for everything he knows about the woman and commends him for taking the letter to the proper authorities.

Clearly, to get to the bottom of this episode, Washington must speak to the woman herself.

For this, Washington enlists the help of another general, Israel Putnam, a Connecticut native sometimes known as "Old Put," who had become a hero here in Massachusetts for his leadership at Bunker Hill. Washington gives Putnam the order to track down the woman in Cambridge, arrest her, and bring her to headquarters.

A few days later, Washington looks out the window of his Cambridge headquarters to see a rather extraordinary sight: Old Put, famously rotund, is galloping on horseback up Brattle Street toward the headquarters, with a young woman—the baker's former paramour and current lady of the night—riding pillion, sitting on the horse just behind the large general and trying her best to wrap her arms around his waist.

Minutes later, the young woman is sitting quietly before both General Putnam and the tall Commander-in-Chief. Washington, who had once been an examining magistrate in Virginia, puts to use his skills as an interrogator and questions her.

It doesn't take long for her to break. She admits she traveled to Newport with the letter, intending to deliver it to designated British officials stationed on a ship at the wharf. She couldn't get to them herself, so she left the letter with her former boyfriend, the baker, who happened to operate a shop in Newport. She says she has no idea what's in the letter—she never opened the seal or saw the contents. She was just delivering the letter for a friend.

So who was this friend? Who in Cambridge was trying to deliver a secret encrypted document to the British military, and sending a prostitute to do so?

The woman won't say. She refuses to reveal his name.

With matters of war at stake, the generals continue to press her, and Washington threatens her with punishment for crimes of treason against the colonies if she doesn't buckle. "For a long time, she was proof against every threat and persuasion, to discover the author," as Washington later described the situation to John Hancock. But then, after several hours of interrogation, "at length she was brought to a Confession."

Finally, the woman agrees to reveal the identity of the man who gave her the encrypted letter and asked her to deliver it to the enemy.

When she whispers the name, George Washington can scarcely believe it.

13

———.———

At last, the young woman whispers a name.

To this day, we have no idea how Washington reacted at that moment—but his face must have been frozen in shock.

Dr. Benjamin Church.

The trusted one. The first surgeon general of the Continental army—and one of the two men who greeted and escorted Washington into Cambridge when he first arrived. Dr. Church, the Harvard-educated surgeon, personal physician of John Adams, former member of both the Sons of Liberty and the Massachusetts Provincial Congress.

It simply doesn't make sense that one of the most respected Patriots in Massachusetts would secretly be sending coded messages to British officers.

Washington turns to the woman again. How does she know Dr. Church? And how was it that he gave her a message to deliver to the British?

The woman explains that she is Church's secret mistress. Church, a married man, is her "benefactor," as they called it then. The woman says that Church asked her to deliver the mysterious letter to the British officers in Newport, said that it was urgently important—and told her that she absolutely mustn't tell anyone else about it.

The embarrassing personal details about Church are mortifying enough. But the idea that such an esteemed man could be secretly consorting with the enemy seems unthinkable.

For Washington, there's only one way to learn the truth.

Within hours, officers detain Dr. Church at his home and bring him to Washington's headquarters for questioning. Washington later describes Church's explanation:

> Upon his first examination he readily acknowledged the letter, said it was designed for his brother Fleming, and when deciphered would be found to be nothing criminal. . . . [He] made many protestations of the purity of his intentions.

Church proclaims his devotion to the Patriot cause and explains that because his brother-in-law Fleming lives within Boston, behind enemy lines, he sometimes sends letters through British channels to reach him. That's all.

It's a dubious story, but a man of Church's reputation deserves the benefit of the doubt. Washington decides that the only way to determine the truth is to discern the text of the letter itself.

Unfortunately neither Washington nor any of his inexperienced officers have any idea how to decipher the coded letter. The Continental army barely has any gunpowder, let alone a cryptography service. So with Dr. Church still detained, Washington inquires around Cambridge and eventually finds a few civilians who can do the one thing he needs: break codes. He quickly hires all of them.

To double-check their work, Washington divides these cryptographers into two teams and instructs them to independently try to crack the cipher in the letter. After several hours, both teams separately break the code, and their resulting translations match almost perfectly.

Church's "innocent" letter is in fact a report on the status of the Continental army, including some details about troop numbers, weapons, supplies, and plans. It's critical and confidential information.

Even worse, although ostensibly written to Church's brother-in-law, the letter is in fact intended for a British officer—and not just any British officer, but Gen. Thomas Gage, the Commander of all British forces in America and the most senior British military official in the colonies.

Dr. Benjamin Church, long one of the most respected Patriots in Boston, is a full-fledged traitor and a spy, secretly delivering intelligence to the enemy.

14

——— · ———

The Church affair stuns every Patriot in Massachusetts. It stuns the members of the Continental Congress. Most of all, it stuns George Washington.

For a man whose entire life has been based on the pursuit of honor and integrity, the reality that a supposedly trustworthy Patriot could so terribly betray his countrymen is surely beyond unsettling. Church's actions are, as a committee of the Massachusetts Provincial Congress will soon put it, "wicked and detestable practices" for which the punishment should be severe. To set an example, the colonial authorities must "testify to the world their utmost abhorrence of such deceitful conduct, horrible ingratitude, and breach of trust."

While Church is held in custody to determine his fate and punishment, the disgraced surgeon writes a letter to George Washington himself, in which he again changes his story. Church claims that the encrypted letter was in fact a clever ruse to confuse the British with misinformation. He writes that "I can honestly appeal to Heaven for the purity of my intentions" and begs "the magnanimous, the compassionate George Washington to shield me from undeserved infamy."

Unconvinced, Washington convenes a council of war with his top officers to discuss the evidence of the case, and the council unanimously agree that Church is guilty. Because the army's rules of conduct lack the scope to determine adequate punishment for this treasonous act, Washington sends Church's case directly to the Continental Congress to review. Meanwhile, Church himself is sent to a Connecticut prison to contemplate his wrongdoings from behind bars.

In fact, Church's crimes were even worse than Washington and the Congress realized at the time. Dr. Church had been secretly consorting with the enemy for a period of almost two years, providing intelligence on the early Patriot movement in Boston, and later sending dispatches to the British with details from his visits to the Continental Congress.

His motives? Apparently nothing more than money. British officers were paying him handsomely for each report. His spying supported a lavish lifestyle. He wore fine clothes, built a grand home in Cambridge, and kept a paid mistress, the very mistress who tried to deliver the letter to British officers in Rhode Island.

For the Commander-in-Chief of the Continental army, the entire episode raises a profound question: If you can't trust a man like Dr. Benjamin Church, who *can* you trust?

In the revolutionary era, the answer is: No one, really.

George Washington's previous military experience had not prepared him for this sort of subterfuge. In the French and Indian War, British soldiers were fighting French soldiers in wilderness battlefields. The two sides wore different uniforms and spoke different languages. You always knew who the enemy was.

In the revolutionary era, the two sides are porous and always changing. Unlike in a conventional war, where one nationality or one religion is facing another, here the lines are constantly blurred. In this war, the ability to discern loyalties—in soldiers and citizens alike— is just as important as military planning. Allegiance in the conflict is not determined by language, birthplace, or race, but simply by whatever a person declares his or her loyalty to be at any given moment.

Washington should know this from his own army. Two of his top generals, Horatio Gates and Charles Lee, were in fact born in England, and came of age in the British military before recently switching sides to join the colonists' cause. Many other rebel soldiers or leaders were also born in Great Britain. Even Thomas Paine, the great writer of the revolutionary movement whose hugely influential treatise *Common Sense* would soon be published, was an Englishman who had moved to the colonies only two years earlier.

Similarly, many people born and raised in the colonies choose to support the British side; these are the Loyalists. Many of these British sympathizers will choose to bear arms for Great Britain or otherwise provide aid to the Crown for reasons of family, business interests, or political conviction.

Apart from the Patriots and Loyalists, yet more colonists have allegiances that are up for grabs. They'll switch to whichever side will benefit them at any given moment, or whichever side will pay them more, or whichever side they think is most likely to win.

Throughout the colonies, these divided and shifting loyalties create an environment of distrust and confusion within cities, within neighborhoods, even within families. Dramatic examples abound, even among the most prominent players on both sides of the struggle.

For example, Thomas Gage, the top British commander in America, had lived and worked in the colonies for decades; during this time he married a young New York woman named Margaret Kemble. Once the hostilities began, Margaret's brother and other family members became prominent Patriots, while her husband oversaw the British occupation of Boston. To this day, many suspect that Margaret shared top-secret British military intelligence with her Patriot brothers.

Divided loyalties also rip apart the family of one of the most beloved Patriot heroes. Benjamin Franklin's own son, New Jersey Governor William Franklin, becomes a Loyalist in the years leading up to the war, and as hostilities begin he uses his position to fight the revolutionary movement and give aid to the British. The father and son stop speaking, and when colonial authorities later arrest William, his father does nothing to intervene or prevent his imprisonment.

Then there's the case of Robert Rogers, a decorated veteran of the French and Indian War. During the revolutionary era, he has a bizarre series of adventures in which he is arrested by the British for committing treason, then arrested by the Americans on suspicion of being a traitor, and for a while travels the countryside disguised in Native American garb to avoid capture by either side.

One thing is clear: With so many divided loyalties and shifting allegiances, the landscape is ripe for treachery, spying, and double-crossing. Espionage and intelligence gathering are a critical part of warfare—in many cases more so than pure military might.

George Washington is not entirely new to the world of spies. As a young officer, he had some experience with intelligence gathering during the French and Indian War. Continental army ledgers also show that one of Washington's first big expenditures upon his arrival in Cambridge was payment for a spy posing as a Loyalist he sent to cross into Boston and gather information about the British army.

Not much is known about this spy, but obviously Washington was at least pursuing some avenues of espionage. Later in the war, Washington will become a much more sophisticated spymaster, overseeing teams of secret agents—including the legendary Culper Ring—who are versed in the use of ciphers, codes, and invisible ink.

However, what the Church episode plainly reveals is that sending out spies to gather intelligence is only part of the equation.

The more vexing question is: How to prevent the *enemy*'s agents and spies from plotting, scheming, and infiltrating one's own side? When it comes to espionage in time of war, how do you play defense as well as offense?

Clearly, Washington caught Dr. Church later than he should have—and only because a biscuit maker in Rhode Island voluntarily came forward to report his story. Otherwise, Dr. Church may have continued to sell intelligence to the British indefinitely. No one was on Church's trail, despite the doctor's often reckless methods of spying.

In fact, completely unbeknownst to Washington at the time, there are more spies around him than just Dr. Church. One enemy agent has infiltrated the Cambridge camps with pro-British informants including a blacksmith and a butcher who serve undercover in a Continental artillery company. Likewise, Washington has no idea that a Boston artist named Henry Pelham has been surveying and sketching the Continental army's encampments in Cambridge and the surrounding areas. He was commissioned by British generals to secretly observe Washington's forces and create a detailed geographical map showing the Continental army's positions.

So, the lesson from Dr. Church and these other spies is obvious.

Espionage is important; but so is *counter*espionage.

Intelligence is important; but so is *counter*intelligence.

This is the defensive side of spycraft—and it isn't easy.

To be clear, there was no such word as "counterintelligence" in the colonies of the late eighteenth century. The term didn't emerge until the early World War II era, when American intelligence agencies matured and modernized. By this time, the notion of counterintelligence as a distinct discipline is codified within the larger umbrella of the intelligence services.

However, even if the term didn't exist in the North American colonies in 1775 at the onset of the war against England, the *need* for counterintelligence was dire, as much so as during any other war.

Just as the Continental army itself had to be created almost from nothing, Washington and his men will have to devise a whole new set of methods and tools to win the complicated intelligence war against their enemies. Working from scratch, they will adapt and devise new systems that will pioneer a brand-new field of intelligence warfare.

For now, in the fall of 1775, Washington's army is so deficient in counterespionage that they don't even have someone on staff who can break the code on an intercepted letter, let alone a team to combat the widespread and sophisticated espionage efforts of the British in and around Boston.

But Boston isn't the only place where spies are on the move.

A few hundred miles south, in New York City, another ring of spies is also at work, led by a man with a set of motives all his own.

15

———— · ————

New York, New York

October 1775

Although Boston is the epicenter of British military command in the colonies through the fall of 1775, the besieged city is far from the only place where British and Loyalist spies operate.

All over the colonies, in every major city, British officials recruit or cultivate Loyalists who can pose as Patriots and infiltrate rebel organizations. Whether it's a prominent citizen like Dr. Church, or a local tavern keeper or blacksmith who is likely to overhear rebel gossip, spies are everywhere. Some are paid for their service; others do it out of political conviction.

In particular, a web of informants pushes information up and down the northeast coast, using a network of British ships and Loyalist merchants who control many harbors and docks. The spies pass documents, intelligence, and contraband along trade routes from Philadelphia to New York City to Boston to Providence.

One person in particular is a key player in this operation: William Tryon, the Governor of New York. Based in one of the busiest trading hubs in the colonies—New York City—Tryon follows the flow of information as well as anyone.

The Patriots may now control many legislative bodies and local committees in New York, but this hasn't stopped the Governor from wielding power and influence in the city. Tryon conducts business from the Governor's residence inside the fort at the southern tip of Manhattan, and in City Hall meets regularly with his council—an appointed group of close advisers—and with other prominent Loyalists on how to save New York from further rebel influence. He still controls much of the commerce so essential to the city's fortunes, and his spies keep him informed on enemy activity throughout the city.

Then, on October 13, one of Tryon's spies provides him with a piece of intelligence that will alter the fate of the colony.

According to Tryon's spy, the Continental Congress in Philadelphia just sent a secret authorization for the rebel governments in each colony—to kidnap or seize royal officials or private citizens whom they suspect are unfriendly to the American cause. In the words of the Congress:

> *Resolved*: That it be recommended to the several provincial Assemblies or Conventions, and councils or committees of safety, to arrest and secure every person in their respective colonies, whose going at large may, in their opinion, endanger the safety of the colony, or the liberties of America.

These words would be alarming for any British sympathizer in the colonies. But according to the spy, that's not all. While the Congress was passing the resolution, they brought up one name in particular. William Tryon.

Tryon understands immediately that he is now in danger.

Given the chaos engulfing his city, Tryon has no doubt that local Patriots would take the Continental Congress's words as justification to seize or kidnap him. They could put him in jail, hold him for ransom, or simply murder him on sight.

In a panic, Tryon tries to enlist protection for himself. That day, he sends a written message to New York City's Mayor, Whitehead Hicks, demanding that the City Corporation—the city governing body—guarantee Tryon's unequivocal safety, or he will flee the city. He makes a stark threat that should any harm come to his person,

British warships in the harbor will retaliate against the city with the full force of their cannons:

> The Continental Congress have recommended it . . . to seize or take up the officers of this Government, and particularly myself, by name. I am therefore to desire you will inform the Corporation and citizens of this city, that I place my security here in their protection; that when that confidence is withdrawn, by any seizure of my person, the Commander of His Majesty's ships of war in the harbour will demand that the inhabitants deliver me on board the fleet; and on refusal, enforce the demand with their whole power.

Tryon's message begins a chain reaction around the colony. Mayor Hicks convenes an emergency council of city officials, and then writes back to Tryon the next day, hoping to reassure the Governor that they will support him.

> The Members of the Corporation unanimously expressed themselves, upon this occasion, in terms of the strongest affection and confidence respecting their Governor; and I am persuaded, Sir, that their fellow-citizens . . . are utterly disinclined to your removal from the capital of your Province.

The letter continues:

> The citizens . . . earnestly desire you will still continue your residence among us; and, from the declarations and temper of the people at large, I have not the least doubt of your enjoying the most ample protection.

As Governor Tryon reads between the lines, he sees that the letter lacks any concrete guarantee to keep him safe. The local officials are seemingly trying to chart a neutral course and not take sides. Tryon doesn't trust their tone—he wants a full-throated promise to defend him at all costs.

That same day, October 14, Tryon sends a note back to Mayor

Hicks, threatening to abandon the city if the local officials won't come to his aid: "As they have not authorized you to pledge to me their assurances of security in either case, my duty in this hour of alarm will not justify me to my Sovereign in staying longer on shore, without positive declarations of their full protection, under every circumstance." He repeats the threat of nearby British warships, prepared to retaliate against the city if he is harmed.

As the Governor awaits the response, a spy on the Patriots' side—a confidant of John Adams's known only as "the Intelligencer"—learns about Tryon's letter to Hicks, obtains a copy, and secretly sends it to Adams in Philadelphia.

He warns Adams that Tryon has heard of the Congress's resolution and is now threatening to call in the warships. The Intelligencer's letter adds: "be assured that Mr. Tryon is most assiduously stirring up every coal that will catch. . . . If something be not done very speedily he will give you some trouble, or I am greatly mistaken."

Ironically, Tryon's intelligence that the Continental Congress has targeted him for seizure is not entirely accurate. Although the Congress had indeed raised Tryon's name in the session that led to their new resolution encouraging the seizure of prominent "enemies of America," they had specifically declined to pursue action against Tryon. They were much more focused on kidnapping Virginia's Governor, Lord Dunmore, who they considered a greater threat at the time.

Nonetheless, the fact that Tryon now *thinks* that the Congress wants him seized creates new dangers for Patriots and Loyalists alike in New York—for example, if Tryon orders the British warships to fire on the unprotected city in retaliation.

As Adams and the others in the Congress contemplate their next move, Tryon receives a follow-up letter from Mayor Hicks, dated October 18. Hicks says that the city officials deliberated on the matter again, and everyone spoke warmly of the Governor: "the friendly and respectful terms in which people of all ranks express themselves concerning your Excellency on this occasion, and their anxiety at the thought of your retiring from the Capital, are very satisfactory."

Once again, some nice-sounding words with no promise of protection.

To further complicate matters, one of the city officials has meanwhile leaked Tryon's original letter requesting help to a local newspaper, which immediately publishes it. Suddenly the whole city is aware that Tryon is vulnerable and asking for protection.

Now there's practically an invitation for Tryon's enemies or some rebel mob to come after him, knowing he is unprotected. Tryon must take drastic action, or every passing hour could be his last.

On the night of October 18, 1775, Tryon packs his most important papers and belongings and, with the help of his aides, sneaks out of the downtown Governor's residence.

They travel in darkness to the Manhattan shore, and escape by boat to Long Island, landing in today's borough of Brooklyn. Tryon spends the night in the town of Flatbush, at the home of William Axtell, a member of the governor's council, where they make further arrangements.

The next morning, the little group travels back to the East River, where a small boat is waiting. The boat ferries Tryon and his belongings to a British transport called the *Halifax*, anchored in New York Harbor.

Here, Tryon can at least sleep without fear of waking up to the point of a bayonet.

From the safety of the ship Tryon sends one more message to the Mayor:

> Finding your letter of yesterday insufficient for that security I requested . . . my duty directed me, for the present instant, to remove on board this ship, where I shall be ready to do such business of the Country as the situation of the times will permit. The citizens, as well as the inhabitants of the Province, may be assured of my inclination to embrace every means in my power to restore the peace, good order, and authority of Government.

Alas, Tryon's movements aren't quite over. A few nights later, he is shuttled around once again, this time to a British merchant ship in the harbor called the *Duchess of Gordon*. On this larger ship there will be space enough for him to set up a headquarters with his meager papers and belongings, a place where he can conduct business. The *Duchess of Gordon* is also anchored right next to the sixty-four-gun British warship *Asia*, providing protection for the governor and his entourage.

On his first morning aboard the *Duchess of Gordon*, Tryon wakes up to the view of Manhattan across the water, less than a mile away. Here, the Governor takes stock of his new circumstances.

The city officials in New York, once his allies, have fallen under the sway of the rebels—or at least won't stand up to them.

The Continental Congress has officially authorized local Patriot committees to kidnap prominent Loyalists and Crown officials throughout the colonies—including, Tryon believes, himself.

Tryon has been forced to flee his own city by dark of night and take refuge indefinitely in the cramped quarters of a British ship. He has only a chest of important papers and a few changes of clothes.

The Governor's residence, full of his artwork and furniture, is left unoccupied and will likely be ransacked or destroyed by mobs.

However troubled New York City had seemed to Tryon when he first returned from England a few months ago, the current reality is far worse. The radicals are taking over his colony and have forced him into exile.

It all started on that day when the officers of the Continental army marched through the city, right under his nose, led by their Commander, George Washington.

Though the Patriots may think they're rid of their Governor, they couldn't be more wrong. Tryon isn't going anywhere.

In fact, he'll soon have a brand new plan—a plan designed to change the course of history.

16

Cambridge, Massachusetts

November 1775

Only his brother can save him.

As George Washington and his troops face the winter of 1775 outside Boston, the condition of his army grows worse.

Now sleet, snow, and freezing rain create a new level of suffering in the ragged outdoor camps. Lack of proper clothing and blankets becomes fatal rather than just uncomfortable, and the troops are short on both. Frostbite and hypothermia are constant fears. As the officer Nathanael Greene describes it, the freezing troops don't even have the essentials to build fires:

> We have suffered prodigiously for want of wood. Many regiments have been obliged to eat their provisions raw for want of firing to cook, and notwithstanding we have burned up all the fences and cut down all the trees for a mile around camp. Our suffering has been inconceivable.

The morale of the young army is low, and getting lower. The common soldiers, most of whom signed up looking for valor or quick money, are receiving neither. The drawn-out stalemate outside Boston means long days digging trenches, building fortifications, or standing sentry in miserable conditions. Meanwhile a constant lack of funds from the Continental Congress means soldiers' pay is deferred for months, and many worry that the pay may never come at all.

Desertions become frequent, and spirits are sinking.

Great Britain, on the other hand, shows signs of bolstering its military efforts in the colonies. On October 10, the British had replaced their current commander in Boston, Gen. Thomas Gage, with a new general, William Howe.

General Howe is one of the most respected current military leaders in England, and his appointment makes a strong statement. In addition, William Howe's brother Adm. Richard Howe is in charge of North American operations for the British navy. Together, the brothers represent a formidable threat. While the nascent Continental army struggles and shrinks, the British army grows and shows new resolve.

Yet, for all the challenges that Washington and his officers face at the onset of winter, another crisis is more frightening than the rest.

By a stroke of terrible luck, in early 1775, a deadly smallpox epidemic had begun to sweep through the colonies—and by summer and fall, just as the Continental forces assemble outside Boston, the epidemic spreads through the Northeast. This highly contagious disease, carried by the variola virus, is fatal in about a third of cases, and in others can lead to blindness or dementia.

For those who contract the disease but eventually return to health, the range of symptoms—fever, exhaustion, and painful running sores on the skin and in the mouth and throat—can be incapacitating for weeks. The disease is ravaging towns and cities throughout the northeastern colonies, and causing widespread panic as it spreads, particularly at a time of impending war.

"The Small Pox is an enemy more terrible in my imagination, than all others," as John Adams will write. "This distemper will be the ruin of every army from New England if great care is not taken."

Indeed, the Continental army camps, with unsanitary conditions and men living in close quarters, create a uniquely rich environment for the virus to spread. As evidence grows of a potential epidemic,

Washington sends a series of urgent letters to Congress: "If we escape the Small Pox in this camp, & the country round about, it will be miraculous—Every precaution that can be, is taken to guard against this evil."

Working frantically with local doctors, Washington helps to administer a system to separate contaminated soldiers and quarantine them in a special hospital. He contemplates an inoculation program for the entire army, but the only available vaccine has sometimes debilitating side effects—including the terrible running sores—and any soldier receiving it would become contagious during the vaccination period, leading to further risk of the disease spreading. While some officers and prominent citizens do take the vaccine, trying to administer it to the whole army at this point is too risky.

So Washington and his doctors must try to control the spread of the deadly virus. With some fourteen thousand troops fanned out in dozens of camps spanning several miles, the logistics of containing the disease are incredibly complex.

In early December, already overwhelmed by dealing with this crisis, Washington hears some shocking intelligence from within the city of Boston, where the disease is also spreading. A sailor working on the Boston docks learns about a plan on the part of the British, and shares the information with rebel officials: "Several persons are to be sent out of Boston, this evening or to-morrow, that have been lately inoculated with the small-pox, with design, probably, to spread the infection, in order to distress us as much as possible."

In other words, the British plan to send out of the city individuals who are known to be afflicted with smallpox, with the purpose of spreading the virus through the Continental army's encampments.

On December 4, Washington sends this letter to John Hancock at the Continental Congress:

> By recent information from Boston, General Howe is going to send
> out a number of the inhabitants. . . . A sailor says that a number of
> these coming out have been inoculated, with design of spreading the
> Smallpox through this country & camp. I have communicated this
> to the General Court & recommended their attention thereto.

This is a crude but ruthless form of early biological warfare—and the Continental officers have difficulty proving that the British are really doing it intentionally. But they do find evidence to support the claim. Several civilians emerging from the city in the next few days are in fact contagious. Now the Continental army must set up a system to monitor every person coming from Boston who might come within range of the soldiers' encampments.

Throughout the trials of handling the smallpox crisis, one potential outcome is so terrifying as to be almost unthinkable: that George Washington himself will be afflicted with the disease.

For Washington even to be inoculated would pose an enormous risk. The side effects of the vaccine can be terrible, and the process is risky. Moreover, for the Commander to be quarantined for several weeks at this juncture, when the army is fragile and a confrontation possibly imminent—well, simply put, it would be devastating.

That's where George's older half brother, Lawrence Washington, comes in.

Almost twenty-five years earlier, when Lawrence was suffering from tuberculosis, doctors had urged him to spend the winter of 1751 in Barbados, where the climate would be more favorable to his lungs.

Only one person accompanied Lawrence on this trip: his loyal younger brother, George, who was then nineteen years old. This trip, the one and only time George Washington left the colonies in his entire life, would be fateful in the most unexpected way.

Although the warm Barbados climate did little to improve Lawrence's lungs, the journey had a profound impact on young George's health. While on the island, he contracted smallpox, probably from a family friend the brothers visited in the village of Bridgetown, the island's capital.

At the time, the virus, still fairly uncommon in the North American colonies, was prevalent in the islands of the tropical West Indies. For more than a month on the island, Washington suffered from the terrible symptoms of the disease—including the gruesome sores—but he eventually recovered to full health, with only some of the trademark pockmarks on his face.

When nineteen-year-old George returned to Virginia in March 1752, he bore an unusual distinction: Having already suffered from smallpox, he was one of the few people in the colonies totally immune to the disease.

Now, some two decades later, as the smallpox epidemic sweeps through the colonies, killing tens of thousands of people just as the Revolutionary War is beginning, George Washington, the army's Commander-in-Chief, is protected.

Those several weeks that George Washington spent in Barbados were among the last he spent with his childhood hero and mentor. Lawrence died two months later. Thanks to those final months together with his brother, George Washington is shielded from a deadly scourge that will take many lives in his army, at a critical time when his sickness or absence would be devastating. Without fear for his own health, he can work tirelessly to set up the army hospital to care for the sick, establish a quarantine system for the contagious, and manage a public health emergency while also running an army.

Later, a rumor will circulate among the soldiers that their Commander is physically invincible—whether in battle or from disease—saved as he has been from death on multiple occasions. George Washington isn't invincible, but he does have something very powerful on his side—an older brother to protect him, even from beyond the grave.

17

As the Massachusetts winter continues, cold and sickness combine to create yet another problem for the Continental army: Their ranks are shrinking.

Desertions and illness deplete the troops' original numbers—numbers that were already lower to begin with than what Washington hoped for.

The army anticipates another potentially catastrophic loss of men in the new year, when the initial six-month enlistment period for many soldiers will come to an end, and officers fear many will choose not to reenlist.

In late November 1775, Washington is presented with a decision to potentially ease this problem. It's a decision that will force him to reassess his plan for the army—and to redefine who can be an American soldier.

The question, raised by his war council, is this: Should freed blacks be allowed to enlist in the army?

George Washington, a man raised in the planting classes in Virginia, has lived in proximity to slavery his whole life. In 1759, at the age of twenty-seven, when he took the hand of the wealthy young widow, Martha Custis, in marriage, he gained ownership of her late husband's land and property, including a total of eighty-five slaves. Over the next sixteen years, as Washington accumulated more wealth and land, he acquired several dozen more slaves.

There is no particular indication that during those years Washington ever seriously questioned the institution of slavery. He seemed to have no problem profiting from a practice that we now regard as a moral atrocity. As a Virginian landowner, and as a man who embraced the ethical codes of his privileged social position, Washington probably never even considered that black men and women are or should be equal to whites, either legally or morally.

But as with so many others, the war forces George Washington to reevaluate his beliefs.

For one thing, by traveling to northern cities like Philadelphia and Boston, Washington becomes aware of the burgeoning antislavery movement. In these cities, free blacks—some of them educated and interwoven into the fabric of society—are far more common. Some of the most prominent northerners in the revolutionary movement—people like John Adams, his wife, Abigail Adams, and their friend the influential Philadelphia political thinker Benjamin Rush—are opposed to slavery, and even link the cause of liberty in the revolution to the broader cause of liberty for enslaved peoples.

Washington, simply by being in proximity to people like Adams and Rush—and because he is otherwise deeply aligned with them in the mission of the war—is now at least exposed to the ideas of the antislavery movement, although he does not immediately embrace them.

In fact, when the possibility of enlisting black soldiers is first presented to Washington in late November 1775, he maintains his prejudice. Although some black soldiers had served in the Massachusetts militia and fought bravely in the Battles of Lexington and Concord and Bunker Hill, Washington initially holds to a Virginian's narrow view of what sort of soldier he wants in his new national army.

"Neither negroes, boys unable to bear arms, nor old men unfit to endure the fatigues of the campaign are to be enlisted," he codifies in the army's general orders of November 12. In this characterization, he crudely ranks potential black recruits in the same low category as whites too young or too old to fight. Even those black soldiers who have fought in the previous battles will not be eligible.

Soon, however, circumstances force a change.

In late December, an unusually fierce snowstorm bears down upon the sick and ill-equipped troops in the camps around Boston. More soldiers drop out or are incapacitated by cold and illness. Even more than before, the officers expect low reenlistment numbers.

The situation is dire. Washington needs more men—and he needs them fast—if he wants his shrinking army to survive in the coming year.

Washington's northern generals impress upon him the practical wisdom of allowing blacks to serve in the army. As Massachusetts General John Thomas puts it regarding black soldiers he led at Bunker Hill: "I look upon them in general [as] equally serviceable with other men . . . many of them have proved themselves brave."

Washington also learns that the black soldiers who served so well in the Massachusetts militia are now resentful that they can't join the new Continental army. As a result, officers worry that these black fighters will now go straight to Boston and offer their services to the British.

Just before the end of the year, Washington does what he must often do during the war. He adapts. With little ceremony he writes this simple note to John Hancock at the Continental Congress: "it has been represented to me that the free Negroes who have served in this army are very much dissatisfied at being discarded. As it is to be apprehended that they may seek employ in the [British] army, I have . . . given license for their being enlisted."

The Continental Congress immediately ratifies Washington's decision. From that day on, just like that, the Continental army is integrated.

Within a few months, hundreds of black soldiers are training and serving in Washington's army. That number will keep growing, and throughout the course of the long war black enlisted men will varyingly comprise between 6 and 12 percent of the Continental troops. Washington never reconsiders his decision, and black soldiers fight bravely in every major battle of the war.

Remarkably, the Continental army remains the most integrated fighting force in American history until the Vietnam War.

Later, after the war, Washington will return to his position as a slaveholder in Virginia. But his thinking on the subject is never the same. Within a few years, he comes to believe that slavery is morally incompatible with the American ideals he and so many others fought for. He writes of slavery that "there is not a man living who wishes more sincerely than I do, to see a plan adopted for the abolition of it." In his will, he grants freedom to his own slaves.

Make no mistake, Washington's transformation on slavery took decades, and it happened gradually. But it's pretty clear where this transformation began: in the cold, cold trenches outside Boston, on the eve of the first full year of the Revolutionary War.

18

Cold Spring Harbor, Long Island

January 1776

At the start of 1776, the world is about to change. Some of the most powerful men in the colonies are working to shape the massive forces of history.

Yet not every facet of history is decided by persons who hold positions of power. Sometimes ordinary people—farmers, laborers, servants—can alter the course of world events.

Indeed, in some ways the fates of George Washington and William Tryon, two players on the world stage, will be determined not by fellow politicians or generals, but by a team of largely forgotten small-time crooks.

Their criminal operation begins neither on the battlefields around Boston, nor in the heated political cauldron of New York City. It starts somewhere else, a place where small-time criminal operations are known to thrive.

Long Island.

This particular operation begins during a cold winter week in early 1776 when a man named Henry Dawkins travels from Manhattan to the small town of Cold Spring Harbor, in Nassau County, Long Island.

Dawkins is an artisan. For years, he worked as a silversmith and engraver of some reputation. Originally from London, he moved to the colonies in 1754, and settled in Philadelphia. After apprenticing for a silversmith for a few years, he opened his own shop in the city and ran this advertisement in the 1758 *Pennsylvania Journal*:

> Henry Dawkins, Engraver from London. . . . Engraves all sorts of maps, shopkeepers bills, bills of parcels, coats of arms for gentlemen's books, coats of arms, cyphers, and other devices on plate; likewise seals, and mourning rings cut after the neatest manner and at the most reasonable rates.

Dawkins's shop was busy, at least at first. His work became respected in the field, and his name appears on some prestigious work. Dawkins is credited with engraving the first-ever representation of the College of New Jersey—later known as Princeton University—and he crafted ornamental silver for some of the wealthiest families in Philadelphia and other cities in the region.

However, like many colonists at the time, Dawkins's career suffered when the colonies' disputes with England began. The various trade embargoes of the early 1770s hurt the economy, stripping wealthy citizens of disposable income. Artisans struggled to survive. Sometime during this period, Dawkins left Philadelphia and came to New York, perhaps to try his luck in a new city.

If luck was what Dawkins was looking for in New York City, he didn't find it. We don't know exactly why, but by the end of 1775, Dawkins was locked in a city jail. How long he spent there is also a mystery, but shortly after spending New Year's Day of 1776 behind bars, he was released.

Now he's on his way to Cold Spring Harbor, Long Island.

Accompanying Dawkins on the journey is another person, by the name of Israel Young. These two men are recent friends—or at least acquaintances. They first communicated while Dawkins was in jail. Young had apparently sought Dawkins out because he heard of the prisoner's trade skills. He visited him at the prison to discuss his work. That's how Dawkins later remembered it, anyway. At some point during these conversations between Dawkins and Young at the jail, the two men hatched a plan.

Now, with Henry Dawkins a free man, Israel Young has invited the engraver to stay at his house on Long Island, where he lives with his wife, and which he also shares with his younger brother Isaac Young.

The Young brothers' wooden house in Cold Spring Harbor is small and unremarkable, but the dwelling has one important feature: a private attic. Not a large attic, but just big enough to house a machine that the Young brothers recently acquired in New York City and transported to their home.

The machine is a printing press, purchased by Young for the price of twelve pounds and four shillings. On Dawkins's advice, Israel had selected what's known as a rolling press, comprised of a cylindrical drum that rolls paper under changeable engraved plates.

These men didn't acquire a printing press to print pamphlets, or books, or signs. They acquired the press for one reason.

Counterfeiting.

Here in this attic, Henry Dawkins and the brothers Young hope to strike it rich by mass-producing replicas of the colonial paper currency. With Young's new press, Dawkins's engraving and printing skills, and a private attic in which to work, they believe there's almost no limit to the number of counterfeit bills they can create.

This team of Long Islanders has reason to be optimistic about their plan. Counterfeiting is widespread all over the colonies at this time, and difficult for authorities to monitor.

Previously the Crown had controlled the currency and printed all the money. Counterfeiting was difficult. But recently, as discord grew between the colonies and the mother country, the new colonial governments decided to create their own paper money, distinct from the Crown's, to exert more control over their own economies. Each colony created a unique currency, with a distinct design and numbering system. So now there are a dozen paper currencies floating around; all of them are different, and most are poorly made.

For counterfeiters, it's a boom time. One common rule of thumb in the trade is to actually avoid making the fake bills look too clean or professional, because it will then stand out from the real stuff, which is so shoddy. What's more, because law-enforcement authorities are preoccupied with preparations for a potential war, the pursuit of counterfeiters is a low priority.

For all these reasons, in the cold early months of 1776, as Dawkins and the brothers Young begin their scheme, they have no reason to think they'll get caught, so long as they keep the operation to themselves.

In preparation, Israel Young has acquired some official forty-shilling notes from Connecticut, issued by the Connecticut Provincial Congress. This will be their first bill, and then they'll proceed to other denominations and currencies from other colonies. Once they engrave

Sample Connecticut forty-shilling note from 1775, as issued by the Connecticut Provincial Congress. Continental currency of this era was often so poorly made that counterfeiters intentionally added flaws and imperfections to fake bills to make them more realistic.

the plates, the free money will flow. As Isaac Young brags to his neighbor, he plans to "pay all his debts this summer in Congress money."

Within days, Dawkins sets up the rolling press in the attic. He puts his stool near a small fireplace to fight the frigid temperatures, and then gets to work engraving a plate that can be used to create a nice new stack of Connecticut bills.

As the operation begins, a key rule for the brothers is to keep the goings-on in the attic discreet, so that Dawkins's work, and even his presence in the Youngs' home, can stay secret. "No person was permitted to go into Dawkins' chamber," as one visitor later explained, "and Israel Young himself split the wood for fire and carried it up himself."

They allow only a few close friends in the home at all, and keep the attic operation as tight-lipped as possible. In fact, the door that leads to the attic is hidden behind a movable bed, so that even the existence of the attic remains mostly secret.

As these three Long Island small-timers get to work, they have no idea that their little criminal ring will soon intersect with the epic political events of the day, and in a way that none of them could ever expect.

19

Cambridge, Massachusetts

January 1776

Trust no one.

At least, that's what George Washington begins to think as he tries to protect intelligence and conceal information from the British army and its spies.

If nothing else, the Benjamin Church affair proved that even the most trusted confidants, people with spotless records, could be traitors in disguise.

"There is one evil I dread, and that is their spies," Washington soon writes, expressing the constant, nagging feeling that his army could be infiltrated at any moment by a secret enemy. It's as if he walks around with the feeling that no one, either figuratively or literally, has his back.

In a series of letters to his former aide Joseph Reed in the early weeks of 1776, Washington uncharacteristically unloads his deepest worries. There is almost a sense of panic, that he is shouldering too much, has no one to rely on, and that the army could be facing ruin. These fears sometimes keep him up at night. "The reflection on my situation, and that of this Army, produces many an unhappy hour, when all around me are wrapped in sleep."

These dark nights of the soul reflect a genuine feeling not just in

Washington himself, but among his aides and allies, that the General is bearing too much responsibility, and that the army has placed too much reliance on one man.

There is a growing sense, in the army's ranks and among the public alike, that the Continental army will live or die solely with George Washington.

This circumstance raises the terrifying question of what might happen should Washington's safety not be protected. With the army surrounded by enemies, the fear is real that George Washington could somehow be seized or stabbed in the back at any time.

What the Commander needs is safety, security, and loyalty from a few carefully selected men.

In his general orders for March 11, 1776, Washington sends out a special request to the commanding officers of each regiment: to deliver him four handpicked soldiers. He doesn't want just any four soldiers; he offers specific instructions for who can qualify.

> His Excellency depends upon the Colonels for good men, such as they can recommend for their sobriety, honesty, and good behavior; he wishes them to be from five feet, eight inches high, to five feet, ten inches; handsomely and well made, and as there is nothing in his eyes more desirable, than cleanliness in a soldier, he desires that particular attention may be made, in the choice of such men, as are neat, and spruce.

He further specifies that they must be "drill'd men"—meaning experienced soldiers instead of newcomers. In short, he wants the colonels to send him the very best soldiers he's got.

According to Washington's instructions, the men arrive outside his headquarters at twelve noon sharp the next day, standing at attention. Then, from these assembled soldiers, Washington personally selects a smaller number, about fifty, of those who meet his standards.

His goal is to create a superior new unit of the army.

These men will be only the elite. They will receive unique training and be given unusual privileges. They will travel personally with the Commander-in-Chief and other top officers, and they'll be trusted to guard the army's cash and other critical documents. They will carry out special duties that require skill and discretion.

Above all, they have one absolutely critical responsibility: to protect the life of George Washington.

Washington's idea for this new unit is likely modeled on European armies, many of which contain some sort of special honor guard entrusted with the most critical tasks connected to their high-ranking generals. The French have the elite Gardes Françaises, and the British army has the Royal Horse Guards to attend to top officers and to the king himself.

Although inspired by European examples, Washington's version will have a uniquely American flair. They'll have a special uniform in the Continental colors of blue and white, and carry their own distinct

Banner created for George Washington's personal unit of bodyguards, formed in March 1776. The banner bears the unit's memorable motto: "Conquer or Die."

banner. The banner depicts a revolutionary soldier holding the bridle of a horse; next to the soldier stands Lady Liberty, bearing a flag and flanked by an eagle and a shield.

The banner also displays the elite unit's special motto. "Conquer or Die."

In official army documents, this group of soldiers is given the name "the Commander-in-Chief's Guard." Sometimes they are also referred to as "His Excellency's Guards," the "Generals' Guard," or "Washington's Bodyguards." Among the soldiers, however, one simple appellation soon becomes most common: the Life Guards.

The nickname is apt. After all, for all of their other special duties and unique training, these soldiers' greatest responsibility is to protect George Washington's life.

For a fragile young army whose success rests almost entirely on the shoulders of its Commander-in-Chief, no obligation could be more sacred.

Soon, the Life Guards' hallowed duty to their Commander will be put to the ultimate test.

20

Intelligence. Cunning. Secrecy.

George Washington is about to learn once again that these are the keys to success in this war.

Outside Boston, the winter had seemed never to end. For months, the stalemate between the armies had continued, with Washington and his cold, disease-ravaged officers and troops living in a state of constant anxiety.

At one point, out of sheer frustration, and because he was about to lose thousands of soldiers whose enlistment was coming to an end, Washington even contemplated sending a mass of troops led by soldiers on ice skates across the bay in the middle of the night, to conduct a sneak attack and try to seize back the city. Fortunately his generals convinced him otherwise.

For both sides, the tense months-long standoff has been broken only by occasional skirmishes at the margins, as one side or the other hijacks a supply cart or tries to better its position by gaining another small field, barn, or hilltop.

Then, in March 1776, just as the Continental troops' purgatory seems truly interminable, the dynamic between the two armies changes abruptly thanks to the efforts of an unlikely young soldier.

Henry Knox was a working-class kid from Boston who had joined the Continental army the previous summer. He was a specialist in artillery—a subject he had mostly learned about by reading military books in his parents' bookstore growing up—and due to this specialized knowledge, he soon earned an officer's commission.

The generals liked him, and back in early November, Knox got up the nerve to propose to Washington an unusual plan that he thought could finally alter the stalemate in Boston.

It was a plan based on intelligence and deception.

Knox had received information that an empty fort in upstate New York contained a set of cannons not currently in use. Knox suggested that if the Continental army could somehow retrieve and transport these cannons without British knowledge, it could potentially bombard Boston from south of the city, and the British warships in the harbor wouldn't have an angle to fire back.

Washington met with his council of war to discuss the possibility. Some senior officers thought the logistics of transporting the cannons from the middle of upstate New York to Cambridge would be impossible, and therefore to attempt it would be a waste of men and resources.

Despite these objections, Washington was intrigued enough to take a chance on this enterprising young officer.

On November 16, 1775, Henry Knox embarks, accompanied at first only by his nineteen-year-old brother, on what will be an extraordinarily complex mission. After a trip down to New York City to procure transport supplies, the brothers make a weeklong trek north through New York State, hiring dozens of able-bodied men en route to man sleds and carts. Eventually they make their way to Fort Ticonderoga at the base of Lake Champlain.

Knox's information was correct. The brothers and their party find that most of the abandoned fort's cannons are intact and sit unused. In total, they gather more than fifty usable cannons and mortars of various sizes—some of which weigh more than a ton—and use a system of ropes and pulleys to load them on a series of carts.

With their team of hired men, Knox and his brother embark on an epic journey in the middle of winter hauling the cannons and mortars, first via boat over Lake Champlain, then via ox-drawn sleds through blizzards and across tundra, and finally over a series of mountain ridges in several feet of snow.

In all, Knox's team hauled roughly 120,000 pounds of artillery (to put it in perspective, that's about thirty modern full-size sedans) through mostly untamed wilderness over three hundred miles in the dead of winter, an eight-week journey the likes of which has never been undertaken before or since.

When the caravan arrives back near Cambridge on January 18, 1776, Henry Knox is a hero. George Washington promotes him on the spot.

The Continental army has a major new asset with all this artillery; just as important, the British know nothing about it. Now, it will take a clever and deceptive strategy for Washington to use these new weapons to gain the upper hand.

According to Knox's original idea, the key to the strategy is a series of hills and bluffs called Dorchester Heights, just south across the bay from Boston. Knox had predicted that from this elevated expanse, the cannons could fire down on British ships in the harbor, and at the city itself, at such an angle that the ships' artillery cannot answer back. If Washington's army can occupy and fortify Dorchester Heights without British knowledge, they will suddenly hold the upper hand over the enemy.

Secrecy is critical to the mission. If British sentries or spies detect the plan, the British troops will simply occupy the heights first, or set up defensive positions to block access.

After weeks of clandestine preparations, on March 2, 1776, Washington embarks on the carefully planned maneuver.

First, to create a diversion, the Continental army begins shelling Boston from artillery positions to the west of the city. The British army responds in kind, assuming this will be one of many harmless back-and-forth artillery volleys both sides have engaged in over the winter.

While the volleys continue, just after nightfall on the night of March 3, several hundred Continental soldiers stealthily travel along the perimeter of the water from their base camps to Dorchester Heights, joined by several ox-pulled sleds carrying the heavy cannons.

Earlier, a long line of hay bales were carefully placed along the route, designed to conceal the mile-long march of soldiers from the eyes of British sentries across the water. The soldiers had also prebuilt several fortifications in the camp, and these are hauled up to Dorchester alongside the cannons.

That night, under the cover of darkness, a total of more than three thousand men, accompanied by eight hundred oxen and dozens of carts and sleds, quickly and stealthily occupy the heights. Under the night sky, the soldiers build barricades, set up the premade fortifications, and carefully place the heavy cannons. Washington himself, on horseback, leads the moonlit operation, anxiously circling the men and directing the process.

By the first light of dawn, after an efficient ten hours of labor, a few thousand Continental soldiers have fully occupied the heights, complete with parapets, trenches, defensive barrels, and more than twenty massive cannons from the two forts at Ticonderoga.

As the sun rises, when British officers in Boston look through their spyglasses, they are greeted with an incredible surprise: the Continental army has occupied and fortified Dorchester Heights just across the harbor with about two dozen long-range cannons trained directly at them.

"My God, these fellows have done more work in one night than I could have made my army do in three months," the British commander, General Howe, is reported to have said. He estimates to his aides that it must have taken fourteen thousand troops to execute such a feat so fast; in reality the number was less than a third of that.

Suddenly, General Howe and the British are in a bind. For Howe to send troops by boat to storm and conquer the heights would be a massive undertaking, proceeding from an unfavorable position below the enemy. To have any chance of success, he would have to send so many troops southward across the bay that he'd leave the city highly vulnerable to an attack from another direction. Indeed, Washington has prepared forty-two flatboats with an amphibious force of four thousand soldiers to attack the city from the west, should Howe send his soldiers southward toward Dorchester.

However, if Howe *doesn't* launch some sort of attack, the British forts in the city and their ships in the harbor are sitting ducks, with the rebels able to fire their cannons from Dorchester Heights almost at will.

These are terrible options. At first Howe starts loading boats to storm the heights, despite the risks. When a sudden storm over the harbor delays the assault, Howe rethinks his weak position, meets with his top officers, and decides to call off the attack.

On March 8, 1776, Howe sends a message to the Continental army that would have been unimaginable only a few weeks ago: All British troops will now evacuate Boston. They'll leave without harming the city if the Continental army allows them to retreat peacefully.

Just like that, the British are evacuating Boston.

After eight long months of a tense and often grueling stalemate, the Continental army has just liberated Boston practically overnight. In the five days since the Continental army began its move toward Dorchester Heights on March 3, not a single soldier has been lost.

This wasn't achieved through force and greater numbers, but by deception and trickery—and by keeping the operation completely secret.

Intelligence. Cunning. Secrecy. These are the tools of war.

21

—·—

Cold Spring Harbor, Long Island

March 1776

Some three hundred miles away from Boston, a very different operation is simultaneously under way.

Here, in the small town of Cold Spring Harbor, Long Island, the counterfeiting team of Henry Dawkins, Israel Young, and Isaac Young is planning ambitious next steps from its headquarters, which happens to be the cramped, cold private attic of the Young brothers' small wooden house.

Unfortunately, despite the team's grandiose plans, its counterfeiting scheme has run into an early snag.

At first, everything was going well.

Dawkins, the experienced engraver and silversmith, had painstakingly created a metallic plate for their printing press, engraved with the design and wording of the paper currency from the colony of Connecticut. He copied the design and lettering perfectly from existing bills, also allowing for some irregularities to be consistent with the poor craftsmanship of colonial money.

Following Dawkins's directions, the Young brothers also acquired the necessary ink and, of course, the correct printing press, now set up and operating in the attic where Dawkins secretly works.

Unfortunately, the team learns there is something they *don't* have:

the correct paper to make the bills. The printing parchment they had obtained doesn't, it turns out, match that of the existing currency. No one had double-checked this in advance.

Now, here they are in their little attic, with a nicely engraved printing plate, a working press, and rolling drum, and no paper to print the bills on.

For the aspiring counterfeiters, the news soon gets worse. After doing some research on the matter, they learn that not only do they not have the correct paper, but that the paper is available only in one place: Philadelphia. When the Continental Congress established the protocols for colonial currency, it created a unique paper that only it, the Congress, could send to each colony. The paper is made and sold only in Philadelphia, so the Congress can regulate the volume of currency being tendered.

Presented with this unfortunate setback, many other counterfeiters might give up.

Not these counterfeiters.

Neither Dawkins nor the Young brothers are in a position to make the trip to Philadelphia to acquire the paper. However, the Youngs happen to know someone who is. They have an acquaintance who, by chance, is already planning a trip to Philadelphia to sell a couple of horses. Maybe, for a piece of the action, he will also procure them some counterfeiting paper.

The friend's name is Isaac Ketcham. He is also a Long Islander, from the larger neighboring town of Huntington. Ketcham, at least by his own admission, is not, in fact, a criminal. As he later describes himself, he's an honest man, a family man. However, like many other ordinary folk during the chaotic early years of the revolution, he's out of work, short on money, and needs to put food on the table for his family. To make his situation worse, Ketcham's wife died recently—leaving their six children entirely reliant on their father for care and support. Isaac Ketcham is not in a position to turn down an opportunity.

The three-person team is now a four-person team.

They agree on a plan. On April 19, Ketcham will leave Long Island and travel to Philadelphia with instructions on what kind of paper to buy, and where to buy it. The Youngs give him some funds to make the purchase.

Of the members of the Cold Spring Harbor counterfeiting operation, Isaac Ketcham is, by any measure, the least involved and least criminally motivated of the team. But ironically, it is Isaac Ketcham who will cause this little band of criminals to intersect with the most seismic events of the day—and possibly alter the destiny of a continent.

22

———·———

New York Harbor

March 1776

The *Duchess of Gordon.*

Governor Tryon had spent the entire winter, through freezing temperatures and snowstorms, exiled on this British ship. He was often cold, often angry, often bitter—but always busy.

Tryon has spies and agents posted at wharves, docks, and inns all over the New York area. His men regularly gather Patriot correspondence and information, and then ferry the goods to him at night on the *Duchess of Gordon.* Tryon can then forward his intelligence to British officers or his Loyalist allies in New York, New Jersey, Connecticut, and other colonies.

Patriots in the region have learned to respect and fear Tryon's ring of spies and his intelligence capabilities. In December, a New York City Patriot publication called *The Sentinel* distributes a broadside specifically alerting citizens to the Governor's spying from the *Duchess.* The proclamation begins with this exhortation: "To the inhabitants of New York . . . WARNING THEM OF THOSE WHO TRANSMIT INTELLIGENCE TO GOVERNOR TRYON."

The proclamation goes on to call the *Duchess of Gordon* an "Intelligence Office" for the enemy, and continues with this warning: "Believe me my friends, the Governor never meant any thing else by going on board that vessel, but to collect intelligence for our merciless enemies, which he has been but too successful in obtaining." And finally, "What in the name of Heaven have we to do with the wretches on board that ship?"

In February, Tryon also makes an important move to consolidate his power. Whitehead Hicks, the aging New York City mayor, has resigned to take a position as a provincial judge. The mayoralty is now open, and Tryon seizes the opportunity to appoint a new mayor who is more sympathetic to his cause: a former lawyer by the name of David Mathews.

Although born and raised in New York, David Mathews is a Loyalist through and through, firmly against the rebellion. He is also a man who understands how to skirt rules to get things done. Known for living an extravagant lifestyle above his means, Mathews has a reputation for slippery morals.

Even Mathews's supposed political allies speak poorly of his character. According to the prominent Loyalist judge Thomas Jones, Mathews is "a person low in estimation as a lawyer, profligate, abandoned, and dissipated, indigent, extravagant, and . . . over head and ears in debt." One of Mathews's former peers refers to him outright as a "villain" and accuses him of embezzling goods that were donated through charity to poor children.

Most important for Tryon, Mathews is a man who will serve to protect his own power and money, which also means protecting and serving the man who appointed him. Through Mayor Mathews, Tryon will have a right-hand man on the ground to help serve his political agenda, and someone who has the powers of the mayoralty at his disposal to combat the increasing Patriot control of the local institutions of government. Mathews quickly becomes a regular visitor on Tryon's ship, where the Governor conducts his clandestine meetings.

Much of Tryon's efforts become focused on what he sees as a critical goal: creating and overseeing a Loyalist network in and around the city. He believes they need to fight back against the rise of rebel power in the region. He still believes that the majority of people are on his side—they just need better organization.

Of course the Loyalists also need to raise arms, and for this they must have new supplies of weapons. Over the winter, Tryon had bribed New York gunsmiths to offer their services only to Loyalists and to the royal army. At one point he bragged to a British official that three out of the four major gunsmiths in New York would now make weapons only for friends of the Crown.

In early March, Tryon decides to use his platform as Governor to send a message to the city. The rebels need to be humbled, and the Loyalists need some support. The Governor will issue a public proclamation reasserting the Crown's—and therefore his own— preeminence in the colony.

He spends several days writing the proclamation and, on March 16, sends the document ashore to his new mayor, David Mathews, with directions for Mathews to distribute it to prominent citizens, and also to "have it inserted in the several Gazettes published in the City of New York."

On March 21, multiple New York City newspapers carry the Governor's message, addressed "to the inhabitants of New York."

Tryon's proclamation begins by decrying the "prejudice, delusion, and faction" that have overtaken the city as a result of the rebellion. He reminds the public that contrary to what these radicals have been advocating, "It is in the clemency and authority of *Great Britain* only, under *God*, that we can look for happiness, peace, and protection." He regrets that some "deluded people" have been subverting the rule of law, but he wants to send a very clear message to those who stay loyal that they can rely on the full "weight and force" of Great Britain to fight for them. Whereas for its enemies, England demands a "timely and dutiful submission."

Tryon had hoped that his forceful words would embolden the Loyalists in the city and intimidate the rebels. Unfortunately for the Governor, his message has the opposite effect.

Within hours after the newspapers publish his words, a crowd gathers in the city to mock and curse the proclamation—and soon they're marching loudly through the streets. The crowd stops at Bowling Green and, shouting jeers and insults, raises an effigy of Tryon with a placard around its neck reading: "William Tryon, late

Governor of this Province, but now a . . . traitor to its dearest rights." Around nightfall, the mob raises and hangs Tryon's effigy on a fake gallows, then burns it and kicks it around the streets until it disintegrates.

Meanwhile the remaining Loyalists in the city, far from being emboldened by Tryon's proclamation, cower in their homes with their doors locked, afraid the angry mob could come after them next.

Tryon learns of this outrage in the dark, cramped quarters of his ship. There is nothing he can do to stop the spectacle. All he can do is reflect on the cursed state of his colony.

Two years ago, he was a strong and popular Governor who commanded the respect and admiration of the public. Now, thanks to the rebellion, his name and likeness are literally being dragged through the street.

Tryon doesn't have long to stew over the newest outrage that has befallen him. A few days later, he hears the remarkable news that has changed the world: The Continental army just chased the British forces out of Boston. All over the colonies, George Washington is being lionized as a hero.

Like other Loyalists in the colonies, Tryon's first reaction is shock and horror. The Governor literally can't find words to express his outrage. "My feelings on this occasion," he writes to the British Secretary of State, "are not to be expressed." It's almost unthinkable that the British army would allow itself to be humiliated on the world stage by the ragtag colonial forces.

Surely the mighty British must retaliate. Surely they will now unleash their full power against the colonies and crush the rebellion for good. But the question remains: Where and when will the British strike back?

Tryon is one of the first to learn the answer. New York City. The British will now send the full force of their army and navy with a plan to occupy Manhattan and make it the new seat of war. The colonial army will try desperately to defend it.

That means something else. George Washington will be coming back to New York City.

It's around this time, and soon after this realization, that Tryon, in the dark underbelly of his ship, begins to formulate a plan.

For this plan to succeed, the Governor will need to marshal all his resources, all his spies, and all his men.

It's a complex scheme and a *deadly* one.

Everything about it must be secret.

It's a plot against the Continental army. Against the army, and against the army's leader. It's a plot against George Washington.

23

---·---

Boston, Massachusetts

March 1776

The public is stunned.

The British are retreating from Boston.

For the next few days following General Howe's surrender to the Continental army on March 8, the city is thrown into chaos as roughly ten thousand British soldiers empty their forts, abandon their lodgings, haul belongings through the street, and throw fortifications and artillery into the harbor rather than leave them for their enemies.

Among the civilians in Boston, no one is more terrified than the Loyalists. Now that Washington's army is about to move into the city, these civilian British sympathizers fear imprisonment or worse for themselves and their families.

They "carry'd death in their faces," as one onlooker wrote of the Loyalists, and a few supposedly committed suicide by throwing themselves in the harbor. Many more of them, over a thousand, pack their belongings and board the British ships, ready to leave their birthplace and homes for an uncertain future in England or whichever British colony the Crown is willing to relocate them.

By March 17, 1776, the last of the British troops board their ships. Washington, ever the gentleman, allows his Boston-born general Artemus Ward to make the first grand entrance into the city, while he himself stays back. He carefully monitors that any soldiers who enter be inoculated for smallpox, for fear of vulnerable soldiers catching the disease and further spreading it. He gives instructions that his soldiers are forbidden to attack any straggling British troops, forbidden to loot buildings, and forbidden to harass any citizen regardless of allegiance.

Meanwhile, the remarkable news spreads around the colonies. Against all odds, the Continental army just forced the British out of Boston. For those who support the Patriots, the response is jubilation.

More than ever, the praise and glory are bestowed on one man: George Washington, the Commander-in-Chief, who led the new army to this unexpected success.

The "Glorious Cause," as the rebellion is now sometimes called, needs a public face; Washington, whether he wants it or not, is now the official embodiment. Washington's image, in portrait or on horseback, is printed in newspapers and pamphlets in every colony. Two new merchant schooners in Massachusetts are christened the *George* and the *Martha* in honor of the Commander-in-Chief and his wife. One of Washington's favorite officers, Nathanael Greene, names his newborn son George Washington Greene. In an elaborate ceremony, Harvard College bestows on Washington an honorary degree. In Philadelphia, the Continental Congress creates a special medal for Washington, to reward the Commander's achievement.

One person, however, is not sharing in all the joy and adulation: George Washington himself.

Washington knows, in a way the public does not, that he has so far faced only a tiny fraction of British power. The British troops in Boston were originally sent there to quash a local rebellion—they were not outfitted to wage a proper war. There has still been no actual battle in which the Continental army has had to face the might of the British army. Boston had been merely a standoff, a staring contest, with one clever strategic move that suddenly ended it.

Now, everything is different. The British army has just been officially humiliated on the world stage.

There is no longer any ambiguity. This means all-out war. The British Empire wields the greatest military force on the planet, and there can be no doubt that they will send the vast might of their navy and army across the ocean to destroy the Continental army and subdue the colonies once and for all.

Where will they attack next?

All the intelligence points in one direction. New York City. Washington knows he must go there.

It's a hostile and unfamiliar place, full of intrigue and treachery.

In George Washington's mind, the greatest danger in the city is from the British army.

But what he can't possibly realize is that the true greatest danger may be posed by a very different enemy—an enemy now aboard a ship floating in New York Harbor.

PART III

A Bloody Summer

24

---·---

New York, New York

March 1776

The British are coming for New York City. Everyone knows it.

Centrally located along the Atlantic coast, surrounded by waterways, and with a massive harbor sufficient to house even the largest navy, New York City seems the ideal seat of operations for England to launch a full-scale attack against the colonies.

Furthermore, if the British can capture New York City, they will also control the Hudson River due north of it. Once the British control the Hudson, the colonies are essentially bisected, with New England cut off from the rest. "The Hudson naturally presented itself as a very important object," the British general Henry Clinton writes in his journal. If the Crown's forces can control it, "communication between the colonies to the north and those to the south would be effectively severed, making it impossible for them to join forces, or even for the northern colonies to feed their troops."

The colonists understand this too. As John Adams puts it, New York City is "a kind of key to the whole continent," and therefore "No effort to secure it ought to be omitted."

In short, the British desperately want to occupy New York City and the Americans desperately want to defend it from them. The problem for the Continental army is that New York City, encircled as it is by water, is essentially indefensible against a naval attack—and the Royal Navy is the largest in the world.

For Washington and his generals, New York City has long been, truly, the stuff of nightmares. Back in early January, Washington's second-in-command, Gen. Charles Lee, wrote to Washington:

> The consequences of the enemy's possessing themselves of New York have appear'd to me so terrible that I have scarcely been able to sleep from apprehensions on the subject—these apprehensions daily increase.

New York City had also occupied Washington's mind, for reasons beyond just military strategy.

For one thing, there is the Governor, William Tryon.

Even up in Boston, Washington had heard reports about Tryon's activities in New York City. Rumor had it that Tryon was running spies from his ship, ferrying intelligence up and down the coast. Washington was frustrated to learn that the exiled Governor still wields so much power—"The city seems to be entirely under the Government of Tryon," he complains to Joseph Reed—and he recognizes the danger in allowing an enemy to control such a critical city.

Washington's concern about Tryon's influence extends to a broader fear that Loyalists in the New York City region present a major threat. While in Boston, Washington had heard reports from the New York Provincial Congress—the colony's governing Patriot body—that the region around New York City was full of Loyalists secretly and not so secretly plotting against the Continental army, especially in Staten Island, Queens County, and other parts of Long Island.

As one contemporary said of Long Island in particular: "It was well wooded, well stocked with foxes, and of good reputation for apples, mutton, and Loyalists."

In general, Washington feared that these "internal enemies," as he calls the Loyalists, could be just as dangerous as the British army. Whether by operating as hidden spies, or themselves raising arms, Loyalists are a constant menace. The New York City region, it seems, is a hub of this activity.

By January, while Washington was in the midst of planning to seize Dorchester Heights outside Boston, he decided to take preemptive measures to protect New York City. On January 8, he sent Gen. Charles Lee—the one having nightmares—on a mission to monitor the city and its surrounding counties.

"Knowing it to be of [great] importance to the interest of America, to prevent the Enemy from getting possession of these places," Washington wrote to his officers, "I have dispatched General Lee with orders to repair to New York with such volunteers as he can raise on his way . . . to put the city & the fortifications up the river in the best posture of defence."

Lee's mission is threefold: to try to fortify the city militarily, to suppress the Loyalists in the surrounding areas, and, last but not least, to attempt to put a stop to Governor Tryon's activities.

Washington becomes especially alarmed when he hears that Tryon might be trying to raise his own army to control the colony by force. Just after Lee departs from Boston, Washington writes him a letter to update him on this development:

> There is good reason to believe that Tryon has applied for some troops . . . so that you will see the necessity of your being decisive & expeditious in your operations in that quarter—the Tories should be disarmed immediately . . . you can seize upon the persons of the principals. . . . And happy should I be, if the Governor could be one of them.

Unfortunately, as much as Washington or Lee might like to "seize" Governor Tryon, the task is now impossible. Tryon's ship the *Duchess of Gordon* is anchored right next to the massive British warship *Asia*. The colonies have no warships of their own, so if any vessel even so much as approached the *Duchess* to try to grab Tryon, the *Asia* could blast it out of the water. The Continental army will have to find other ways to challenge the Governor's power.

Charles Lee is an inspired choice to carry out Washington's multipronged mission. Although he is British by birth and background, and only emigrated from England to the colonies a few years earlier, Lee

has since become one of the fiercest and most outspoken Patriots—
and one of the first to argue for full independence from England.

Lee is so famously hot tempered that during his service as a British
officer in the French and Indian War, one of the Native American
tribes who fought beside him gave him the nickname "Boiling
Water." Disheveled in appearance and prone to profanity, Lee often
said he loved dogs more than people, and rarely traveled without a
pack of canines, including a Pomeranian named Spada, a dog that
from a distance was sometimes mistaken for a bear.*

Lee's aggressive personality could also get him into trouble. Once,
he became so frustrated with the pacifist wing of the Continental
Congress, he declared publicly that even if these congressmen
found their wives with the Howe brothers *in flagrante delicto*—that
is, having sex with the two British commanders—they would be too
indifferent to interfere.

Lee arrives in New York City on the afternoon of February 4, 1776,
accompanied by close to fifteen hundred militiamen he has recruited
in Connecticut along the way. The news of his arrival causes quite a
furor in the city, sparking widespread panic that the British man-of-
war *Asia,* already anchored in the harbor, will fire on local homes in
retaliation.

Lee tries to assuage these fears by publicly insisting that the warship wouldn't dare do so while he has an armed militia in the city.
As one newspaper prints on February 6, "Lee says he will send word
aboard the man-of-war, that if they set a house on fire in consequence of his coming, he will chain one hundred of their friends
together by the neck, and make the house their funeral pile."

Not exactly mollified by these words, many citizens start evacuating Manhattan, creating a sense of confusion and upheaval that will
become the new norm for New York City in the weeks and months
ahead.

Once General Lee is in the city, he quickly assesses the profound

---

* Pomeranians are today a smaller breed of dog, usually with a maximum size of
eight pounds. In the eighteenth century, however, the average size of the breed was
significantly larger.

difficulty of defending New York City without a serviceable navy, an asset the rebels have no hope of acquiring in the near future. Without any Patriot ships to defend against it, a foreign fleet could flow into the harbor and surround the city with cannons.

In a letter to Washington, Lee concedes: "What to do with the city, I own, puzzles me; it is so encircled with deep, navigable water, that whoever commands the sea must command the town."

Nevertheless, Lee devises and embarks on an ambitious plan to build fortifications, redoubts, and other defenses all over Manhattan, Brooklyn, Queens, and Long Island, to prepare the city as well as he can against a potential future naval attack.

While Lee oversees the physical labor of erecting these elaborate fortifications, he also begins to grasp the depth of the Loyalist plotting in the region. For example, in January some three hundred cannons that the colonial militias had collected and stored in gun parks in Westchester County were secretly "spiked"—that is, steel-pronged plugs had been driven into their touchholes, and their firing mechanisms smashed—making them unusable without extensive repair.

A body called the City Watch was supposed to be guarding this huge cache of critical weapons, but according to the Town Major, many of the City Watch were secretly Loyalists, or had been bought off by Loyalists, and therefore sabotaged the very cannons they were supposed to be guarding.

Around the same time as the cannon incident, the New York Provincial Congress was closely monitoring the activity of the Loyalist population on Long Island, defined loosely by the Congress as those who refused to sign a pledge of support for the local colonial governments. Of even more concern than their political opposition are rumors that these Long Island Loyalists are secretly stashing firearms with plans to start an uprising.

In response, the Provincial Congress requested some nine hundred volunteer militiamen from neighboring New Jersey to disarm the offending Loyalists. This militia, led by Brig. Gen. Nathaniel Heard, conducted a raid on several Long Island towns, disarming hundreds of citizens and arresting nineteen of the alleged ringleaders.

Seemingly in every direction around the city, there are Loyalists afoot: on Staten Island; in Kings and Queens Counties on Long Island; in Westchester and Dutchess Counties; and in New Jersey and southern Connecticut.

Such was New York City in the early months of 1776: full of dark plots and schemes—with rumors of yet more to come. While the rebels may control the local political bodies and governing committees, on the ground there are "internal enemies" all around, conspiring against them.

True to form, General Lee takes aggressive action in the city, ruffling feathers at every turn. Needing a right-hand man, Lee appoints a controversial local rebel radical named Isaac Sears—known for raising mobs, tarring and feathering Loyalists, and smashing Tory printing presses—to lead additional raids on Long Island.

Sears's method is to go into towns with suspected Loyalist operatives and force them to take an oath supporting the rebellion. Those who refuse are disarmed or arrested. Sears writes a report to Lee after one of these raids:

> I . . . tendered the oath to four of the great Tories, which they swallowed as hard as if it was a four pound shot, that they were trying to git down. . . . I can assure your honor they are a set of villains in this country, and believe the better half of them are waiting for support and intend to take up arms against us. And it is my opinion nothing else will do but removing the ringleaders to a place of security.

Sears makes a few arrests. However, General Lee begins to sense that arresting scattered farmers and townspeople in Long Island isn't getting to the real root of the problem.

There seems to be something bigger afoot in New York, a greater organization that is tying these schemes together.

Lee begins to suspect that all signs point to one person as the mastermind: the exiled Governor, William Tryon, who haunts the city from the *Duchess of Gordon* in the harbor.

Much like Washington, Charles Lee has always distrusted Governor Tryon. Lee was one of those who had advocated seizing Tryon back in the fall, and was frustrated when the plan was not pursued. This lack of resolve by Congress had allowed Tryon to escape to the safety of his ship. Now, according to rumors swirling around the city, Tryon is masterminding many of the Loyalist plots from his floating headquarters.

Lee is frustrated to find that local authorities are currently doing little to stop the exiled Governor from operating. In particular, Lee is outraged that boats are going to and from shore to Tryon's ship at will, providing him with all the provisions and communications he needs to run his spy network and control the city.

Although powerless to harm Tryon physically, Lee is determined to thwart him. He urges the New York Provincial Congress to prohibit any further contact or ferrying of goods between persons on land with the "King's Ships"—specifically the *Duchess of Gordon*—without their express permission.

The Continental Congress in Philadelphia supports Lee's new rule, and the New York Provincial Congress puts it into effect.

Lee writes George Washington to inform him that when it comes to Tryon, Lee has made sure "to stop all provisions from the city and cut off all intercourse with him—a measure, which has thrown the Mayor, Council, and Tories into agonies." Lee makes a further sarcastic jab at those in the city who still maintain loyalty to Tryon:

> The propensity or rather rage for paying court to this great man, is inconceivable. They cannot be weaned from him. We must put wormwood on his paps or they will cry to suck, as they are in their second childhood.

(Lee's analogy refers to the farmer's technique of putting a foul-tasting substance on a sow's teats, to force her piglets to find their own food.)

As it happens, Lee's effort to prohibit all communications between Tryon and the shore is only partially successful. The New York Provincial Congress worded its resolution in such a way that Tryon can still receive boats delivering food and other provisions to his ship, so long as there are no overt "communications" between the parties.

But this caveat is unenforceable; once a boat has ferried provisions to Tryon's ship, there's no way to monitor whether anyone boards the ship to meet or conspire with the Governor.

Within days of the Provincial Congress implementing the new resolution, Lee learns that Tryon is bringing gunsmiths from town aboard his ship to solicit their help in arming Loyalists on Long Island, while discouraging them from doing business with Patriots. Lee quickly writes another angry letter to the Provincial Congress:

> I have received intelligence that Mr. Tryon has been guilty of most grossly abusing the indulgence shown to him; that he has inveigled some of the gunsmiths on board his ship; and that he is endeavouring to seduce as many as he can, with the view, undoubtedly, of distressing us in the article of arms.

Lee further urges the Provincial Congress, more generally, that Tryon should be closely watched so that "he will not intrigue, cabal, or machinate mischief of any kind to the Continent or Province."

Lee surely wants to find other ways to disable the governor. However, before he can do so, the General's tumultuous New York visit comes to an end. After barely a month, the Continental Congress, with Washington's blessing, chooses to send Lee to the southern colonies to oversee urgent new missions brewing in Virginia and the Carolinas.

To Tryon's benefit, on March 4, Lee departs New York. Yet just as Lee is walking out the door, an even more disturbing report from New York is about to arrive.

25

General Lee is not the only Continental officer who finds evidence of Governor Tryon's clandestine schemes in New York City.

After Lee's departure for the south, and while Washington remains with his army in Boston, he puts another top officer, Gen. William Alexander, known more commonly as Lord Stirling, in charge of fortifying New York City and picking up where Lee left off.

Stirling is not a firebrand like Lee, but he is a native New Yorker and understands the region. By early March, Stirling is raising more troops for the city, and putting soldiers and civilians alike to work, building the fortifications that Lee had begun.

Working with the New York Provincial Congress, Stirling calls on "all male inhabitants . . . as well as all the Negro men in the city and county of New York" to help in the massive physical labor involved in building fortifications.

Soon Stirling, like Lee before him, is also busy trying to suppress clandestine Loyalist plots in the region. He writes letters to Congress and to George Washington, describing his discovery of various uprisings in New Jersey and Queens, and his efforts to arrest the leaders.

Of these reports, the most troubling points in one direction: to Governor Tryon's ship.

On March 11, Stirling learns in particular about two men arrested for ferrying goods to Tryon aboard the *Duchess of Gordon*. With this arrest comes some of the most important intelligence anyone will find.

As the two captured men are hauled before the local authorities, they point the finger at a third man, someone named Thomas Vernon, whom they insist is the ringleader.

Vernon, it turns out, is a hatter. Based on Long Island, he's apparently been leading excursions to and from the British ships in a small boat he owns, and on several occasions, has transported supplies. Among other provisions, he's delivered two thousand oysters to the warship *Asia*, and two thousand to the *Duchess of Gordon*.

Trafficking such as this with the British ships is now forbidden. It's a punishable offense. Still, this infraction alone would not normally warrant Stirling's personal attention.

The problem expands, however, when one of the men confesses that he and Thomas Vernon didn't just deliver goods to the ships—they actually went aboard the *Duchess of Gordon* and had a meeting with the Governor.

From the man's account, it becomes clear that Vernon's connection to Tryon is about more than just oysters. In fact, Governor Tryon has being paying Vernon to carry out various secret tasks for him, all around the region.

Vernon had hired the other two men "to rig out a sloop the said Vernon had lately purchased by order of Governor Tryon, to be employed by the Governor as a tender or cutter, and occasionally to cruise in the north and east rivers."

In other words, Tryon had given Vernon money to purchase a boat, on which Vernon could carry out the Governors' orders by traversing the waterways around the city. The Governor also provided money to outfit Vernon's sloop with swivel guns, making it an armed vessel.

According to the men, Vernon's primary mission from Tryon is to seek out Continental soldiers or militiamen whom he can induce, by either force or persuasion, to switch sides to the British. One of the prisoners provides more details:

[Vernon] went on board . . . the *Duchess of Gordon*, and there conversed with the Governor . . . who urged him to be active in procuring as many men as possible . . . ; that above fifty or sixty soldiers now in town in the Continental service were engaged by the said Vernon for the service of the Ministry.

Read that part again. Some *sixty* soldiers from the Continental army have secretly joined the British.

If true, this is a shocking admission: Governor Tryon is bankrolling a scheme to bribe Continental soldiers or militiamen to betray their army and side with the British forces. According to the testimony, Vernon has already coerced dozens of former Continental soldiers—probably militiamen raised in New York, or perhaps some of the troops General Lee brought with him—into switching sides.

At a time when the Continental army is desperate to raise and maintain soldiers, this isn't just troubling. It's a potential disaster.

If these American soldiers have been compelled at gunpoint to work for the British, this would be called "impressment"—when an army or navy forces men to join against their will. The fact that Vernon's sloop is outfitted with swivel guns suggests that this is a possibility.

However, for Stirling and the other Continental officers, the more worrying prospect is that Tryon and Vernon bribed or otherwise lured several dozen men to betray their army voluntarily.

On the eve of what looks to be a massive battle for the future of the colonies, a wave of traitors going to the other side could be cataclysmic for the Continental army. Sadly, it's not hard for the officers to imagine. They know that morale among their troops has often been poor, due to the deferred pay, lack of supplies, and poor living conditions.

On top of that, another basic calculation is made by civilians and soldiers alike: They want to be on the side that wins. If Continental soldiers genuinely fear that the British will destroy Washington's army and win the war, the choice to switch sides becomes a choice to save oneself from later imprisonment or death.

The testimony about Thomas Vernon also contains one final interesting detail. In addition to Governor Tryon, two other men were apparently also on the *Duchess of Gordon:* the "Attorneys General Kempe and Skinner."

"Skinner" is New Jersey attorney general Cortlandt Skinner, a prominent Loyalist who had recently fled New Jersey under threat of arrest by the colonial authorities. Thanks to this new testimony, colonial authorities now know that Skinner is on board the *Duchess of Gordon*, consorting with Governor Tryon.

"Kempe" refers to New York's attorney general, John Tabor Kempe. Kempe is likewise a Loyalist who's wanted by the authorities, and is now apparently part of Tryon's cabal on board the ship.

What all this means is that Tryon is running a sophisticated operation from the *Duchess.* He's accompanied by powerful men, he operates a paid network, and is organizing missions all over the region.

Finally, and most distressing of all, Tryon is actively luring soldiers from the Continental army to join the enemy.

Two days later, Stirling writes a letter to John Hancock and the Continental Congress, summarizing what he's learned:

> By some prisoners taken into custody, there is great reason to believe that Governor Tryon has his emissaries in several parts of the Province, engaging men to serve both by land and water. One tells that he is engaged, with fifty others, under a certain Vernon. . . . I have referred some others . . . to be examined; and, I doubt not, we shall find out and defeat their machinations.

After all the testimony is heard, local authorities arrest Vernon and order him put in prison. Naturally, they confiscate his armed boat. The other men are also jailed, with lesser sentences.

The good news is that they've now captured and locked away one of Tryon's lackeys. But the questions remain: How many Thomas Vernons are out there, secretly carrying out the Governor's designs in the region? How many Continental soldiers have already deserted and switched sides? And what other "machinations" might Governor Tryon be plotting?

The generals will soon learn that when it comes to uncovering Tryon's schemes, they've barely scratched the surface.

26

---·---

Boston, Massachusetts

March 1776

Within days of the British evacuation of Boston, George Washington begins sending regiments to New York City.

He's anxious to get there himself, but he's held back by a strange development. Although the British troops all left the city and boarded their ships, initially the ships themselves didn't leave the harbor. As if to confuse Washington, the large transports and warships remained in the waters near Boston for almost a week, some still visible from shore.

For all Washington knows, the entire evacuation might be a feint, and the second he leaves the region, the British could retake Boston.

In reality, the British are simply figuring out where to go. While there is some incentive for the British troops to get to New York as fast as possible, General Howe instead determines that his army will be better served by regrouping, loading up on provisions and supplies, and waiting for reinforcements.

Therefore, when the British ships finally leave the harbor, they are bound not for New York, but for Halifax, Nova Scotia—another British colony at the time. In Halifax, they will resupply, wait for reinforcements, and prepare for their coming invasion of New York City.

For General Howe and the British, this time there can be no error.

They have the vastly superior military force; it is now time to marshal it, focus it, prepare it—and send everything they have to devastate the colonial army or cow it into submission with the sheer size and strength of their naval fleet.

Once the British ships depart Boston waters, Washington sends the rest of his army south, in staggered detachments. The officers mostly travel by horse or carriage, and a few companies secure transports to travel by water along the coast. But the majority of the approximately eight thousand troops who make the journey do so the old-fashioned way: They march.

The route is about 220 miles, mostly along the Boston Post Road, passing through southern Massachusetts, Rhode Island, Connecticut, and Westchester County, before reaching New York City.

This long journey by foot is accomplished by the troops walking twelve hours a day, every day, usually five or six miles before breakfast, for roughly two weeks. Most soldiers carry a thirty- or forty-pound pack, containing all of their clothes and supplies. Based on orders from the generals, the officers push the soldiers to march in an "extreme hurry" and "at great speed" regardless of temperature, and straight through rainstorms, hailstorms, muddy roads, and whatever else the elements can throw at them.

George Washington himself departs Cambridge on April 4, 1776, along with Adj. Gen. Horatio Gates and their top aides. Although Washington's horse-drawn transport is faster than the marching soldiers, he must endure the frustrating delay of stops at various cities along the way, to meet with local officials and be accorded due honors.

His party makes stops in Providence, Norwich, New London, and New Haven, among other smaller towns and villages. In Norwich, he confers with the Patriot Governor, Jonathan Trumbull; in New London he inspects the latest fortifications and defenses along the coastline, also meeting with prominent merchants and other citizens.

Washington endures these formalities, always polite, always gracious, dutifully shaking hands and exchanging pleasantries, even while his thoughts are consumed by the harrowing difficulties that lie ahead in New York City.

Also accompanying Washington on his journey, and never far from his person or his belongings, are several soldiers from his newly formed Life Guards. They guard the army's war chest—an actual wooden chest containing money and top-secret documents—and most important, they guard General Washington himself.

As their procession moves away from the Patriot stronghold of Massachusetts, Loyalist sentiment generally increases. After the seismic news of George Washington's success at Boston, he is now unquestionably the personal embodiment of the colonies' rebellion, and held in great awe on the Patriot side. But for Loyalists and other opponents of the revolution, George Washington is now enemy number one.

The members of Washington's entourage know that in any village, any town, or any farmhouse, an assassin or deadly enemy could be lurking. One musket, one bayonet, one dagger could instantly destroy their leader. The Life Guards' sworn duty is to prevent this. From here forward, one or more of them will accompany him everywhere

Finally, after a nine-day journey, on the night of April 12, Washington and his men travel through what is now the Bronx to reach the King's Bridge, which stretches across Spuyten Duyvil Creek to Manhattan's northern tip. While still on the mainland side, they spend the night. Then, on the morning of April 13, Washington and his men cross the bridge and officially enter the island of Manhattan.

At the time, the northern three-quarters of Manhattan is mostly woods and farmland, but a clear road passes from the King's Bridge straight down the island. After a few hours travel south, Washington's party begins to draw close to the northern line of New York City, which extends roughly to present-day Chambers Street. There they start to see the houses, buildings, and bustling streets of the city.

One thing is clear. New York City is not the same place it was when Washington last passed through nine months earlier, en route to Boston.

Today, New York is a city preparing for war.

For ordinary residents, the transformation began a few months earlier. With warships in the harbor, tarring and feathering in the streets, and news reports every day from Boston and overseas indicating nothing but more hostility between the colonies and England, many New Yorkers expected and feared that war would come to their city. As a result, many families started evacuating back in the fall, either to move permanently or to seek temporary residence elsewhere.

By the early months of 1776, a third or more of New York City's 25,000 residents have already left. For months now, many businesses have been closed, houses have been shuttered, and some buildings have fallen into disrepair.

Despite all the residents who have left, there are also many who have no choice but to stay. Moving tended to be an option for the well-to-do, who could secure transportation by horse or carriage, and make arrangements to have belongings shipped.

For those without means, this wasn't possible. Some poor and working-class families chose to leave the city on foot, physically dragging food, clothes, and belongings in carts down muddy roads, over bridges, or onto ferries out of Manhattan. Others remain, facing whatever dangers might come. Likewise, the sick and infirm had no way to leave. Still others had the means, but had nowhere else to go.

Of course, there are also many who stay in the city for their own reasons, despite the threat of violence. Sailors, seamen, mercenaries, and various laborers all know that war can mean a paycheck, so they come to the city upon news of the impending confrontation.

Other young men hang around, hoping to enlist with the colonial army now, or with the British troops when they arrive. City officials, politicians, and civil servants still run the city out of obligation, or because they can't abandon their work.

The buzz of war also means that political activists on both sides are marching in the streets or meeting in cafés, making the taverns loud with arguments and angry speeches. The printing presses still busily roll, churning out various newspapers and pamphlets.

Finally, the city's unusual condition brings in thieves, looters, cutthroats, and various other ne'er-do-wells, all looking for some angle to profit or thrive from New York's confused state.

However, in April 1776, by far the most prominent feature of the city is the arrival of thousands of Continental soldiers. Unlike outside Boston, where the army was spread out over wide encampments in fields and commons, here, many of the soldiers must board in tight city quarters. For the most part, they occupy the homes and buildings vacated by those who have left, sometimes sleeping several to a room.

This is how Washington finds New York City as he, his generals, and his Life Guards march into it. There are some crowds in the street cheering his arrival, to be sure, but in this complicated city there are both friends and enemies of the revolution—and at first glance, it can be hard to tell them apart.

When Washington first arrives in New York late on the morning of April 13, he goes directly to his new working headquarters at One Broadway, in the southwestern tip of lower Manhattan, just off a small park called Bowling Green.

There, Washington is greeted by a deeply unwelcome sight. Right in the middle of Bowling Green, and visible from the front door of his headquarters, is a massive statue of none other than George III, the King of England.

Set grandly on top of a huge fifteen-foot stone base, the gilded lead statue depicts his Majesty on horseback, wearing Roman garb like an emperor, and bearing a triumphant expression. It's a fitting introduction to the trials that await George Washington in New York City, the very embodiment of everything he is fighting against is almost close enough to cast an actual shadow on the place where he'll be working every day.

However, as Washington enters his new headquarters for the first time, King George isn't the only powerful enemy within dangerous proximity.

Less than a mile away, floating in a wooden ship anchored just south of the downtown docks where the East River meets New York Harbor, the exiled Governor of New York works feverishly. In his dark, cramped quarters, William Tryon is devising an increasingly elaborate plot against the rebel usurpers and their so-called Commander.

27

—·—

Huntington, Long Island

April 1776

It's all about the paper.

On the morning of April 19, 1776, Isaac Ketcham departs from his home in the town of Huntington, Long Island, and begins what will become a roughly four-day journey to Philadelphia.

Ketcham takes with him two horses. After all, selling these two animals to a Philadelphia-based buyer was his original reason for making this trip. Now, however, his mission is about something more.

Ketcham's extra assignment, as agreed a few weeks ago, comes from his Long Island acquaintances: the Young brothers, and their partner in crime, the engraver-turned-counterfeiter Henry Dawkins.

In Ketcham's personal bag, he carries a small sample of paper, of a very particular sort. It is the exact color and grade used to create the Continental currency. This paper is produced only in Philadelphia, and Ketcham's task is to find the paper that matches his sample, and purchase as much as he can. If Ketcham can procure a large quantity, the Dawkins/Young Long Island counterfeiting ring will be printing paper currency by the pile this summer—and Ketcham will be paid for his role.

Ketcham obtained the sample in his pocketbook by making a stop in a New Jersey town called Brunswick Landing, as instructed by the

Young brothers. There, he was told, he should find and talk to a man named Levi Lott, an acquaintance of the Youngs who has experience with paper mills and could offer more advice on how to find the right paper once in Philadelphia.

Ketcham found Levi Lott, but Lott didn't have any suggestion for where in Philadelphia to source the paper. However, Lott did give Ketcham a very small sample of the exact kind of paper the team will need to duplicate Continental currency.

Lott explained to Ketcham that in order to get this sample, he had obtained a full sheet of paper bills and cut out a few centimeters of the raw paper between them. Once in Philadelphia, Ketcham will be able to show the sample to paper sellers and inquire where he might find a batch of stock to match it.

From Brunswick Landing, New Jersey, the travel time by horseback to Philadelphia is just over a day. Given his original departure from Long Island on April 19, Ketcham probably arrives at his destination on the morning of April 22. Once there, he first takes care of his prior business with the two horses, making the intended sale.

Yet when it comes to procuring the currency paper, Ketcham's visit to the city doesn't go as planned. In fact, he never makes it to Philadelphia's paper mill. After asking a few merchants and shopkeepers in town, he's dissuaded from going there by a man he later describes only as a "Dutchman."

This Dutchman tells Ketcham that he knows where the paper is made—but that the makers will not sell him any paper because they are "sworn." Meaning that they have probably taken an oath that they will use this paper only for official purposes. Certainly, they won't give it to a stranger from Long Island like Isaac Ketcham.

Whether due to his conversation with the Dutchman, or for some other reason, Ketcham stops trying to acquire the paper. Maybe it's because he is, at heart, a family man and an honest one—and he has a crisis of conscience about being involved in an illegal operation. More likely, he starts to worry that he'll get caught. According to records of Ketcham's later statements on the matter, he was nervous that even if he did procure the paper, the large size of the sheets might be too conspicuous while he travels:

Though he at first intended to obtain paper at Philadelphia for the purpose of printing money, yet, on consideration, he thought it dangerous, and determined not to bring the paper, even if he could obtain it; that he considered if he got the paper it would not go into his saddle-bags, and that if he should carry it in a bag, it would be discovered, and therefore determined not to bring it.

In any case, on or around April 26, Ketcham departs Philadelphia with two fewer horses and no paper at all, beyond the small sample still in his pocketbook. Despite several weeks of buildup and planning, Ketcham's trip to Philadelphia has been a bust—at least from the counterfeiters' point of view.

Indeed, as he begins the trip home, Ketcham probably doesn't relish having to tell the Young brothers and their coconspirator, Henry Dawkins, about the inauspicious results of his mission. But tell them he must, because he has nothing to show for his trip.

During the journey back to Long Island, Ketcham's conscience may in fact be clearer than it was a few days earlier. After all, he is no longer actively participating in a secret illegal scheme. He can go back to his six children in Huntington, Long Island, and look for an honest way to make ends meet. The Young brothers can find some other way to get paper for their phony bills.

However, as Ketcham is about to realize, whatever sense of relief he may be feeling during the trip back to Long Island, it won't last long. When he gets home, Ketcham will find that separating himself from this band of outlaws is more difficult than he expects.

28

New York, New York

April 1776

It had been a long time since George Washington and William Tryon had crossed paths. The last time was back in June 1775, when Washington had passed through New York en route to Boston, on the very day Tryon had returned from London to resume his governorship.

Now, they are in the same city once again.

Much has shifted in those nine months, but one thing has not changed at all: Washington didn't trust Tryon then, and he doesn't trust him now.

Once in New York City, Washington learns more about the various Loyalist plots afoot in the region. Based on his generals' reports and rumors on the ground, Washington now strongly suspects that William Tryon is behind these plots, or at least behind some of them.

Back in February, Washington had fully approved General Lee's initiative to prevent boats from shuttling back and forth between shore and the "King's ships," specifically the *Duchess of Gordon* where the Governor resided.

However, now that Washington is here in the city, he learns quickly that the rules preventing communication between the ships and the shore are not being enforced. On a regular basis, small boats are ferrying information back and forth to the *Duchess of Gordon*, with apparent impunity. Clearly, this communication with the shore is how the Governor maintains his influence.

On April 17, four days after his arrival in the city, Washington writes a letter to New York's Committee of Safety, the local body tasked by the Provincial Congress with monitoring the safety and security of the city.

Regarding Tryon receiving visitors and supplies from shore, Washington complains that:

> a continuance of the intercourse which has hitherto subsisted between the inhabitants of this colony, and the enemy on board the ships of war, is injurious to the common cause. . . . I should be anxious to remove an evil which may contribute not a little to the ruin of the great Cause we are engaged in, and may . . . prove highly detrimental to this colony in particular.

Notice the words he uses to describe the actions of his enemy, Governor Tryon: "an evil." In the letter, he puts pressure on the local officials to enforce the rule:

> [I am] relying upon your zeal and attachment to the cause of American liberty for your assistance in putting a stop to this evil, and that you will cooperate with me in such measures as shall be effectual, either to prevent any future correspondence with the enemy, or in bringing to condign punishment such persons as may be hardy and wicked enough to carry it on.

The Committee of Safety receives the letter and convenes to discuss it. The next day, April 18, the committeemen pass a new resolution expanding upon their previous edict. In the resolution, they reinforce the existing rule that forbids any communication between "the ship in which Governor Tryon resides, on the one part, and all the inhabitants of the Colony on the other."

This time, the committee also clarifies that the delivery of any goods or other merchant activity between shore and the ships—even just the sale of food—will also be forbidden. The resolution ends with the strongest possible language:

> *Resolved and Ordered*, that no inhabitant of this colony, upon any pretense, or for any purpose whatsoever, either in person or in writing, directly or indirectly, do presume to have or maintain any intercourse whatsoever with any ship or vessel belonging to or employed in the service of the King of Great Britain . . . or with any person or persons on board of the same, upon pain of being dealt with in the severest manner, as enemies to the rights and liberties of the United North American Colonies.

In other words anyone who communicates in any way with Governor Tryon's ship is not just breaking the rules—but is committing a treasonous act.

The committee assures George Washington that it will impress upon the operators of every dock and wharf in Manhattan that no boat can disembark from the city bound for the *Duchess of Gordon* or any other king's ship.

For the most part, Washington is satisfied with the language in the committee's new resolution.

However, within only a few days, Continental officers learn of yet more instances of supply boats delivering goods to the *Duchess*. What Washington realizes, and what the city's committee is probably reluctant to say, is that the civilian authorities simply don't have the resources or ability to monitor every single boat in the city.

What's more, the offending boats have devised sophisticated schemes to trick, bribe, or evade the sentries on the docks to reach the *Duchess of Gordon* and the *Asia*. Many merchants in the city are still loyal to Governor Tryon and want to continue to curry favor with him. Others may have no loyalty one way or the other, but won't turn down the chance to sell their goods at healthy prices to the royal ships in the harbor.

As long as Tryon can ferry provisions, spies, and intelligence back and forth to shore, he can exert power and control over the city. Tryon is obviously not dissuaded by the rules put forth by the Provincial

Congress, so Washington decides he must contribute the force of his own voice and his own army.

A few days later, on April 29, Washington writes another letter on the matter, but this time not to the Committee of Safety. This goes straight to the one place where it won't be ignored: the newspapers, for the entire city to read. Washington specifically indicates the letter is "Given under my hand"—which means it's written by him personally, so it can't be misunderstood as just coming from an aide.

Washington's proclamation to the public appears in the *Constitutional Gazette* on May 1 and the *New-York Journal* on May 2. In the letter, Washington expresses outrage that some "base and wicked persons" in the city are disobeying the rules by maintaining contact with Tryon and his men "for the purposes of giving intelligence and furnishing them with supplies or provision."

In response to these crimes, Washington wants to make clear that violations will now be considered acts of treason and therefore punishable by his army:

> To the end that such evil and pernicious practices may be remedied and prevented in future, I hereby publish and declare, that if any person, or persons shall hereafter presume to have . . . any kind of correspondence whatsoever, or furnish and supply the said ships of war, and other vessels . . . they so offending will be deemed and considered as an enemy, or enemies to the rights of the said colonies, and if apprehended will be treated accordingly.

Finally, Washington makes clear that this law will be enforced not just by the civilian authority of the Committee of Safety, but also by his own soldiers who now occupy the city. The proclamation concludes: "I do hereby will and require all officers and soldiers in the army under my command . . . to use their utmost care and diligence for preventing the same, and apprehending and securing all persons who shall be guilty thereof."

Washington knows that everyone in the city will see this public proclamation—including, of course, Tryon himself. This should put some fear into those who have been manning the boats, and into the merchants who continue to do business with the Governor. If they do it again and get caught, they'll have to answer to General Washington's army.

In truth, Washington probably knows that there is only so much he and his soldiers can do to monitor every merchant vessel departing from or arriving at every dock in the city, at every hour of the day or night. He's short on men and needs to prepare the city's defenses against the massive British attack that's about to come.

Still, he needed to make this statement. He needs to show who makes the rules in this city. If someone like William Tryon punches, you have to punch back.

In fact, the fight between these two men over the fate of the city is just getting started.

29

During his first few nights in New York City, George Washington stays overnight at his workday headquarters at One Broadway. However, it soon becomes necessary for the Commander-in-Chief to find a less conspicuous location for his sleeping quarters.

In less than a week, Washington's aides move him to a less exposed lodging away from downtown. It's on an estate called Mortier's—also known as Richmond Hill—that lies roughly two miles to the northwest, in a wooded and secluded section of Manhattan's west side, at what is now roughly the corner of Charlton and Varick Streets.

Previously, the property was owned and inhabited by the wealthy royal colonial official Abraham Mortier, who fled the city to escape the coming battle. The Continental army had promptly secured it, as they did with many homes and estates left empty by fleeing Loyalists. With serene views of the Hudson River, the manor house and its estate will provide Washington a retreat from bustle and noise—as well as the safety of being farther removed.

On the night of April 17, 1776, Washington, accompanied by soldiers and aides on horseback, arrives at his new home in the woods. This manor will be both his lodging and a second base of operations as the army prepares for the coming attack.

A key member of this residence will be an official housekeeper, Mary Smith. A local woman who had previously served prominent New Yorkers, Mary will run the kitchen, manage the servants, and oversee Washington's daily living expenses.

Because the army's move to New York City is the first time the officers are conducting business in a new location after their initial set-up in Cambridge, new procedures must be put in place for how the Commander-in-Chief and his generals live and work.

Accompanying George Washington at all times, whether at his work headquarters on Broadway or at the Mortier manor house, are members of the Life Guards. Under the direction of their Captain, Caleb Gibbs, the guards establish a series of regimented routines to protect the Commander-in-Chief.

Two armed Life Guards always stand at attention at the front entrance of the residence. Two stand at the back. This guard duty runs in shifts, like the modern Secret Service, so sentries are posted around the clock. When Washington relocates at any time of day or night, the Life Guards relocate with him. In addition to monitoring his person, at least one guard is always in the immediate vicinity of the army's war chest, containing confidential documents and a stash of money.

The Life Guards run special drills to prepare for any potential harm to their Commander. At any sign of danger or hostile approach, the guards who stand sentry at each entrance run inside, barricade the door, and take positions by each window, muskets loaded and primed.

With the Life Guards becoming so interwoven with Washington's daily movements, Captain Gibbs becomes in effect the manager of the Commander-in-Chief's household operations. At the Mortier manor, Gibbs oversees the housekeeper, Mary Smith, and coordinates his guards with the daily comings and goings of every officer or acquaintance who interacts with General Washington.

Likewise, Gibbs's second-in-command, Washington's nephew George Lewis, is given special responsibilities unique to the position. Within a few weeks, Washington will issue a general order that "any orders delivered by Caleb Gibbs and George Lewis, Esquires—officers of the General's Guard—are to be attended to in the same manner as if sent by an aide-de-camp." In other words, the leaders of the Life Guards are part of Washington's innermost circle and have the authority to issue commands on his behalf.

Within the Continental army and the rebel militias, the renown and mystique of the Life Guards begins to grow. When a Continental captain stationed in Fairfield, Connecticut, intercepts and secures a small naval vessel from British sympathizers, he even brags in a letter that he has rechristened the boat the "Life Guard."

Today, history books are filled with stories that say that the Pinkerton Detective Agency, during Abraham Lincoln's time, was the inspiration for the Secret Service. But in some ways, it is Washington's Life Guards who should get the credit—an elite force, specially trained, and prepared at any moment to lay down their lives for their leader.

At a time of increasing danger in the war, when the Continental army is preparing to face a possibly devastating assault, the Life Guards are men in whom George Washington can place his greatest trust.

But that trust is about to be tested, in ways that Washington could never imagine.

30

$\underline{\quad\cdot\quad}$

With Washington and the Continental army now fully entrenched in and around Manhattan, residents and soldiers alike begin to face a new reality. New York City is on the verge of war.

The British, having been humiliated once, are now likely to strike back with the full force of their massive power. John Hancock describes England's position this way. "We have all the reason . . . from the rage of disappointment and revenge, to expect the worst. Nor have I any doubt, that as far as their power extends, they will inflict every species of calamity upon us."

From the point of view of Washington and the Continental army, the outlook is daunting at best and potentially catastrophic. As the army continues work to fortify the city, Washington learns that the Crown has just acquired additional mercenary troops from Germany— somewhere close to seventeen thousand—to augment their already superior forces.

These German mercenaries, generally known as Hessians, are seasoned and well-armed fighters. With these reinforcements added to their already vast army and navy, the British commanders—Gen. William Howe and his brother, Adm. Richard Howe—are preparing one of the largest and most powerful expeditionary forces in history.

All this immense firepower will be directed at one city, on a skinny island, surrounded by waterways, with no navy to defend it.

"I fear for you and my other New York friends," a London resident writes to an acquaintance in Manhattan, "for I expect your city will be laid in ashes."

The only defense and the only hope for survival is Washington's army.

In total, the Continental forces now stand at around eight thousand, combining troops from Boston with the newer militias recently raised within New York. Of this number, somewhere between 15 and 20 percent are inactive due to disease, injury, or other health-related causes.

Upon his arrival in April 1776, and in the weeks ahead, George Washington writes a series of urgent entreaties to Congress, begging for more soldiers to withstand the coming onslaught. In response, Congress orders neighboring colonies to send more troops to New York City, both new volunteers and existing militias, to reinforce Washington's army.

Soon, from all directions, several thousand new American troops stream toward the city to join the cause. These new men, however, are mostly unskilled, inexperienced, and unequipped recruits, not up to even the low standards of the troops Washington had back in Boston. These newcomers must be trained completely from scratch, a task demanding time and resources, all when the enemy could arrive at any moment.

The new wave of soldiers enter Manhattan by foot and by ferry, needing food, lodging, and clothing. The influx of men begins to overwhelm the residential and commercial buildings of the city, and almost every available structure is converted for military use. "We are a complete garrison town," one resident reports. Another civilian describes the "terror and confusion" as more soldiers inundate the already tense environment.

The Continental soldiers are quickly put to work doing the hard physical labor required to fortify the city. Starting in the early morning, soldiers tear up the streets to create blockades, cut down trees for lumber and firewood, and build crude walls and other defensive structures. Work commences on a new fort in northern Manhattan and another just across the Hudson in New Jersey. The new forts are called Fort Washington and Fort Lee, respectively, named after the Commander-in-Chief and Maj. Gen. Charles Lee—"Boiling Water" himself—who helped devise the plans during his short but memorable visit in February.

At the same time, some of the finest homes in New York City, abandoned by fleeing citizens, serve as the makeshift barracks for the incoming soldiers. As one onlooker relates, "Troops are daily coming in; they break open and quarter themselves in the houses they find shut up. Necessity knows no law."

In what were once the grand parlors and boudoirs of the city's elite, now the poor, unwashed, sometimes illiterate farmers' sons who comprise the common soldiery eat their daily food scraps and sleep several to a room, rarely if ever bathing, even after long days doing drills and laboring in the dirt and mud.

Sometimes, the quartered troops hack up the expensive furniture to serve as firewood. "Oh the houses in New York, if you could see the insides of them!" one resident writes. "Occupied by the dirtiest men on the continent . . . if the owners ever get possession again, I am sure they may be years in cleaning them."

As usual, Washington and his officers attempt to instill some discipline with new rules to prevent this destruction. In the general orders of April 17, Washington complains that "many houses taken up for barracks, are much abused by the Soldiers," and prohibits "any wood being cut upon the floors or any water or filth thrown out of the windows." By most indications, these rules are not particularly well enforced, if at all. Homes continue to be destroyed.

In fact, damaged houses are the least of the army's worries. The visiting troops quickly overwhelm the city's sanitation, sewage, and water systems. The same bad hygiene and lack of sanitation that plagued the soldiers' camps outside Boston now plague the New York City quarters, even more amplified by the tighter proximity of the soldiers in city buildings, as well as the prevalence of dust, soot, and garbage in the air and on the streets.

With no prior regional infrastructure in place to supply a national army, the Continental Congress and local colonial authorities have to scramble to accommodate the army's never-ending needs, rarely reaching them on time. As a result, the troops in New York City are in a constant condition of being insufficiently clothed, fed, armed, and supplied.

Even more troubling for George Washington is the growing ratio within the army of new soldiers who lack any experience or training. "To expect . . . the same service from raw and undisciplined recruits, as from veteran soldiers," Washington writes, "is to expect what never did and perhaps never will happen." Somehow, these "raw and undisciplined recruits" are supposed to stand up to the best-trained armies in the world.

George Washington soon summarizes his army's prospects in a candid letter to his brother John Augustine. "We expect a very bloody summer at New York," Washington writes, "and I am sorry to say that we are not, either in men or arms, prepared for it."

All the while the hulking British warship *Asia* sits anchored in the harbor, visible from shore, its massive array of cannons aimed at the city's homes. In the *Asia*'s shadow floats the smaller *Duchess of Gordon*. Inside, William Tryon and his allies meet and plan, with intentions impossible for Washington or his officers to know or fathom. Every evening after the sun sets, the dark silhouettes of these ships serve as a constant reminder to soldiers and citizens alike of the massive show of power that awaits when the British fleet arrives.

It's coming. It's just a question of when.

31

New York Harbor

April 1776

Washington's army is so close.

On many mornings when Governor Tryon wakes up aboard the *Duchess of Gordon*, he can see the waterfront buildings and docks of southern Manhattan, across the harbor from where his ship is anchored. From this visible shoreline, Tryon knows that George Washington's headquarters—the very heart of the Continental army—is only a few blocks away.

Here on his floating base of operations, Tryon is doing everything within his power to undermine that very army.

Not by force, of course. He's using other, more surreptitious means.

Throughout the months of winter and into the spring, Tryon's intelligence-gathering efforts have continued to improve, and his efforts are noticed by both sides in the conflict. When Tryon's ship had to spend a few weeks farther from shore due to ice patches in the harbor back in February, the British general Henry Clinton—one of the most astute officers in the Crown's forces—wrote to Tryon: "I lament much that this movement will put you at such a distance from intelligence, as Your Excellency is almost the only one on the Continent that can get any."

In his unusual role as floating spymaster, perhaps Tryon's most audacious feat of the season is to plant a mole at the Continental Congress in Philadelphia—a mole who can therefore deliver to him regular updates of the highest-level proceedings in all the colonies.

Tryon accomplished this by somehow arranging for his own former servant to be hired by an oblivious congressman, James Duane from New York, to serve as the congressman's valet and personal aide. While Duane employed the valet, Tryon simultaneously paid the young man to send him regular updates from the inside.

This bold scheme of Tryon's is eventually discovered. As one Philadelphian recounts the story, "At length a doubt arose in the breast of Mr. Duane . . . that his valet, who had formerly lived with Governor Tryon, had, at night, when he went to bed, taken his minutes out of his pocket, which he had copied, and sent to his late master."

Once the valet's cover was blown, he eluded capture and escaped from Philadelphia, after which Tryon had to arrange for the young spy's secret transport to England to avoid imprisonment or worse.

Somehow Tryon orchestrates this entire scheme, and others like it, from his small shipboard headquarters.

Naturally Tryon hasn't been doing all this work alone. In the past few months he's had a team of allies coming and going to support his efforts, including an inner circle of confidants. For a while he'd been able to conduct regular meetings with his Governor's Council, comprising seven men who served as his appointed governing body when he was still running the government.

Tryon has had to curtail these council meetings ever since Generals Lee and Washington cut off communications between shore and the king's ships; with these new regulations it's too difficult for Tryon to sneak the council on board.

Still, he has had other regular confidants, including David Mathews, the Mayor of New York City, who often comes aboard; Cortlandt Skinner, the attorney general of New Jersey, who, like Tryon, fled to the *Duchess* when the rebels threatened to seize him; John Tabor Kempe, the attorney general of New York, who also came aboard to avoid prosecution; and Edmund Fanning, Tryon's trusted secretary and top aide, who has been with Tryon since his North Carolina days. Edmund Fanning has a servant who is also another regular on the ship—a dark-skinned man often tasked with the risky business of ferrying sensitive information and goods back and forth from ship to shore in the dead of night.

For Tryon the spying and ferrying of information are now only part of the operation from his ship. Now that spring is here, and now that the British army is expected, his focus shifts from gathering intelligence to gathering something else: soldiers.

It starts with mobilizing ordinary citizens in areas where the Continental army does not exert control—finding small towns and rural areas where farmers and townsfolk will agree to secretly take up arms against the Continental forces.

In some cases Tryon also organizes the secret flow of guns from their ships to these areas surrounding the city. Once formed, the underground groups communicate with one another and create a secret network of Loyalist influence in the counties throughout the region.

For Tryon, creating new soldiers from citizens is good, but there's something else even better: luring Continental soldiers to switch sides.

What more devastating way to subvert the Continental army than to turn its own soldiers against it? Tryon has already demonstrated that soldiers currently fighting for scraps in Washington's army, often under terrible conditions, are susceptible to being "turned."

Tryon's underlying conviction, and one on which he has never wavered, is that most ordinary residents in the colonies—or at least in New York—remain devoted to England. The radicals and rebels may have temporarily scared them or bullied them into proclaiming their support for the revolution, but they can just as easily be persuaded back to their original allegiance. He believes this of citizens, and he believes this of soldiers.

Tryon's attempts to turn soldiers began with relatively small efforts, sending recruiters around—men like Thomas Vernon, for whom Tryon had purchased the armed sloop—with money in their pockets, hoping to lure or bribe suggestible soldiers or militiamen in the counties surrounding the city.

Once on the payroll, some recruits are sent aboard the British ships in the harbor, either the warship *Asia* or the Governor's own ship, the *Duchess of Gordon*. Others are sent to Long Island, where a growing number of Loyalists are banding together to organize against the rebels. Others remain where they are, but act as undercover agents, still outwardly allied with the rebels, but secretly communicating with Tryon's spies and recruiters, offering intelligence, and awaiting instructions.

Tryon's recruiting efforts in the spring of 1776—and evidence will later show that these efforts stretch from Long Island to New Jersey to upstate New York—become the foundation of a vast new operation.

If he can assemble a wide but secret web of followers, prepared to raise arms or otherwise act on his behalf, there is no end to the havoc he can wreak upon the Continental army.

Tryon's plan has many components, but one common thread is that he will wait for the perfect moment—the very moment when the British army arrives this summer—and then his secret web of recruits will rise up and take action.

For those Continental soldiers whom he has already secretly recruited on Long Island, in New Jersey, and in upstate New York, this could mean suddenly turning their guns on their fellow soldiers. For others, it could be acts of military sabotage: blowing up bridges, stealing weapons, or destroying supplies.

Through the months of April and May, Tryon's plans steadily take shape.

Still, he wants to do more.

Tryon can practically see George Washington's headquarters from his ship in the harbor. How can Tryon penetrate the real inner circle? How can he get closer and do even more damage?

Maybe, instead of recruiting Continental soldiers on the outskirts, Tryon can find a way to infiltrate the very heart of Washington's army. Not on Long Island, not in New Jersey, but right here in Manhattan.

Somehow, Tryon needs to get to someone on the *inside*.

32

New York, New York

May 1776

Gilbert Forbes is a gunsmith. This much is known.

Gilbert Forbes's shop is on Broadway, across the street from an ale-house named Hull's Tavern. He is a "short, thick man" who often wears a white coat, according to a few who know him.

These are the basic facts about Gilbert Forbes. After that, things get murky.

What's clear is that in the early months of 1776, there seems to be nothing unusual about Forbes, as a gunsmith or as a person. His first appearance in the public records that year is unremarkable. On March 22, he had gone before a local law-enforcement body, the New York Committee of Safety, for help settling a petty dispute with an-other gunsmith, who Forbes claimed was trying to steal his employee. The entire matter is contained in one paragraph in the Committee's records:

> Gilbert Forbes, of the City of New York, gunsmith, informs that he has lately had a certain William Clarke, a lockfiler by trade, and a useful mechanic, employed in his service; that a person named Winter, from Chester, in Maryland, has lately come here, and in-sists on taking the said William Clarke. . . . Winter now claims him

as a servant, and has threatened to apprehend the said Clarke, and to commence a suit against the said Gilbert Forbes.

That's it. The authorities side with Forbes, he presumably keeps his employee, and the other gunsmith goes back to Maryland. On just that single day at the Committee of Safety when Forbes pleads his case, there are probably a dozen matters of greater importance.

In ordinary times, that minor dispute might be all that history would ever record about a man like Gilbert Forbes.

These are not ordinary times.

In the spring of 1776, on the eve of the first large-scale battle of the Revolutionary War, one commodity is in an almost infinitely high demand: guns. The flintlock muskets and American hunting rifles of the era are not mass-produced, and the colonial army in particular is in constant, almost desperate need of more firearms.

In the vast annals of the Continental army's war papers and correspondence, few topics come up more frequently than the urgent need for more weapons and more gunpowder, requested by every regiment and in every colony, almost on a daily basis. During the army's stay in New York, the need for guns is so great that soldiers are sent door-to-door in the surrounding counties, asking farmers and ordinary citizens in small towns to donate or sell their guns to the cause.

While some do sell, most ordinary citizens, whether in rural areas, small towns, or cities, are more than ever inclined to keep their personal guns, to protect themselves and their families in violent and unpredictable times.

While the British regular army has no shortage of guns, their Loyalist allies in the colonies are just as desperate as the rebels to acquire weapons—all the more so because the rebel authorities often "disarm" suspected Loyalists by confiscating their firearms.

In other words, in the winter and spring of 1776, guns are bought, sold, stolen, traded, seized, collected, stored, hidden, and generally coveted far more than before.

For all these reasons, the formerly unexceptional work of a colonial gunsmith takes on greater prominence. For Gilbert Forbes, it is his work as a gunsmith that will thrust him unexpectedly into the center of the many plots and schemes swirling around the city.

In fact, he will soon be a key player in the greatest plot of them all.

It all starts quietly on a day in late April or early May. According to Forbes's own later account, on this day, he is talking to an acquaintance, a "burr-millstone maker" named Webb. In this conversation Webb tells Forbes that if Forbes has any extra firearms in his shop, Webb knows where they'll fetch a good price.

Okay. Where?

Aboard the British ship in the harbor, the *Duchess of Gordon*, where the exiled governor, William Tryon, is headquartered.

Tryon needs guns and is ready to pay. Forbes's ears perk up. He has a stash of nine rifles in his shop and some muskets too. He's looking for a buyer.

Shortly after this conversation with Webb, Forbes hears a similar story from another person, a "young man who lived with James Rivington." James Rivington is widely known for having operated a prominent pro-British printing press in New York City, before an angry rebel mob looted his shop and destroyed his press. Anyone who lives with James Rivington is likely to have good information from the British ships.

From two sources now, Forbes has heard that he can obtain a high price for his firearms from Governor Tryon, aboard the *Duchess of Gordon*.

The gunsmith is ready to make a sale.

Of course, however high a price Governor Tryon may be offering for rifles, many gunsmiths wouldn't even consider the transaction. With the Continental army stationed in New York, and with General Washington himself forbidding any communication or trade with Tryon or anyone else on the British ships, selling rifles to the *Duchess of Gordon* is to risk imprisonment or worse if caught.

So in the spring of 1776, is it just money that motivates Gilbert Forbes to take this chance?

Evidence suggests there's more to it than just greed. There are no concrete records of Forbes's political leanings before this time, but from this point forward, various accounts will place him inside a web of surreptitious Loyalist activity in the city.

Although most Loyalists fled the island of Manhattan at or before the arrival of Washington's forces, an underground network remains, whether to do business, spy on the rebels, or act as resistance.

Like much of what happens in New York City, Loyalist activity is often centered around taverns and other drinking establishments: alehouses like Houlding's and Lowry's are known as meeting places where the faithful can converge, conspire, share intelligence, curse the revolution, or raise a glass to the King.

Gilbert Forbes will soon be a known presence at these venues. He will be heard "talking Tory" with other colonists who maintain loyalty to the British. Still, it is difficult to know whether Forbes's Loyalist politics predate his decision to sell guns to the ships, or whether his convictions arose after he made his decision to do business with the Governor's ship.

Regardless of his innate political leanings, something else about Gilbert Forbes will emerge in the wake of his decision to sell rifles to Tryon. He seems to have ambitions beyond being just a gunsmith.

Indeed, events suggest that Forbes is looking for an opportunity to change his station, to take risks, and to accomplish bigger things. Like many others living through this moment in history, perhaps Gilbert Forbes sees in the chaos of the early war an opportunity to expand his life's ambitions—and the underground Loyalist movement happens to be the avenue that opens before him.

Whatever Forbes's true motivations, he is soon making arrangements to deliver his firearms to the *Duchess of Gordon*. Forbes's shipment will include nine rifles and eleven "smooth narrow-bored guns," otherwise known as muskets. These two types of firearms— the accurate but slow-loading American-made rifles, and the less accurate but faster and more powerful British-made muskets—are the most common weapons in the colonies, and the most commonly used by soldiers. It is no surprise that these are the weapons Forbes has in his shop.

Webb, the man who first suggested the idea of the sale, becomes the intermediary and confirms to Forbes that "Governor Tryon will

The most frequently used American-made weapons in the Revolutionary War are long-range rifles, like the Pennsylvania model pictured above (*top*). More common for both armies are British-made smoothbore guns, known as muskets (*middle*). Muskets are inaccurate but faster to load, and a bayonet (*bottom*) can be affixed for hand-to-hand fighting. In May 1776, Manhattan gunsmith Gilbert Forbes agrees to the secret sale of nine rifles and eleven muskets to Governor William Tryon, aboard the British ship *Duchess of Gordon*.

give him three guineas apiece" for the rifles and guns. Payment will be made after receipt. Exact comparisons across eras are difficult to make, but three guineas in 1776 comes out to the equivalent of around $550 in modern currency. So with twenty firearms in the shipment, Forbes will hypothetically make the equivalent of $11,000 if the deal goes according to plan.

But first, the delivery somehow has to get to the Governor's ship.

Following instructions, Forbes sends most of the guns to a mysterious woman named "Mrs. Beck," who runs a tavern near the waterfront and will supposedly coordinate the secret shipment to the *Duchess*. The remainder will be ferried aboard by Webb.

The details of how and when Forbes will receive his payment are left open. After he releases the guns, Forbes must simply wait and hope he will be paid as promised—and also hope, of course, that the rebel authorities currently running the city don't somehow discover the illicit transfer of weapons and trace it to him.

Most likely, Gilbert Forbes doesn't sleep so well the night or two after he delivers his rifles—and probably wonders if he'll ever hear back from his accomplices or be paid for the rifles and guns he sent to the ships.

Then, Forbes receives an unusual invitation.

A man wants to meet with him for a confidential conversation.

And this is not just any man—it's a man named David Mathews. That is, the Mayor of New York City, appointed by Governor Tryon himself.

Because Mathews is so closely linked to Tryon, Forbes must suspect that the meeting is connected to the guns he sent aboard the governor's ship.

A few days later, he goes to meet the Mayor. There is no full record of what was discussed at the meeting, but according to Forbes's later account, the Mayor has one key message for Forbes: He will ensure that Forbes is paid for the guns he sold to Governor Tryon.

Mayor Mathews adds that he himself will soon be visiting the *Duchess of Gordon*, at which time he'll retrieve the payment from Governor Tryon personally, and see to it that Forbes receives it.

Suddenly, Forbes is doing business with both the Mayor of the city and the Governor of New York—two of the most important men in the colony.

For Gilbert Forbes—the short, thick gunsmith who wears a white coat and runs a shop on Broadway across from Hull's Tavern—his new friends are about to make life a lot more interesting.

33

———•———

Throughout April and May of 1776, Washington and his officers embark on the massive logistical undertaking of fortifying New York City and preparing their army for the coming British attack.

While trying to accomplish these already momentous tasks, the officers find themselves with another challenge, unrelated and just as difficult: keeping control of their own soldiers in the heart of a major city.

Many of the young men in the Continental army come from poor rural areas and know almost nothing of the world outside the farms, small towns, and country villages of their upbringing.

Even for those from bigger towns or cities, a good number know only the narrow slice of life represented in their home neighborhoods. Most of the common soldiers are uneducated, and more than a few are illiterate. For a large percentage of the soldiers and militiamen who have marched down from Cambridge with the army, and for many recruits now marching in from the farms of Pennsylvania, Connecticut, Maryland, and southern New Jersey, this long journey will be the first time they set foot outside the tiny radius of their homes.

Now, here they are in New York City.

Even back in the 1770s, New York has established a well-earned reputation for one exceptional quality: vice.

As the Continental officer William Tudor puts it in his diary, "Every brutal gratification can be so easily indulged in this place that the army will be debauched here in a month more than in twelve at Cambridge."

To put it another way, this place knows how to party.

It starts with the booze.

By any measure the amount of alcohol consumption in the city is extraordinary. Throughout the early 1770s, New York City issued enough liquor licenses that there was one drink seller for every thirteen adult white men in the city; this was about twice as many drinking establishments per capita as any other large city in the colonies.

This comparison is significant because liquor was popular *everywhere* in the colonies throughout the mid- and late eighteenth century. In 1770, the average annual rum consumption for the colonies as a whole was 4.2 gallons per year per capita, which based on demographics at that time means the typical adult male probably consumed more than five shots of rum per day.

As impressive as this statistic may be, in New York City, the figure is even greater: 6.7 gallons per year per person, or the equivalent of roughly eight shots of rum per day for a typical adult male. And this is only for rum. Other spirits like beer, gin, and the Portuguese wine called Madeira are also popular.

New Yorkers also liked their booze extra boozy. According to a prominent liquor merchant, suppliers in the port of New York demanded higher-proof alcohol than in other ports, because their New York customers wanted stronger stuff.

All this alcohol, and the prevalence of taverns and public houses, made for a hard-hitting drinking culture in the city. Throughout the 1760s, concern had been growing among some civic-minded citizens that excessive drinking was corrupting the moral character of the public.

One newspaper writer complained about the "obscene toasts" heard in taverns that served to "disgust the sensible, to disconcert the modest, and to expose the depravity of taste as well as manners."

Another writer complained that the "drinking houses" were making the lower classes and servants of the city particularly unruly, and that "the suppression of these houses, which subsist only by furnishing the means of drunkenness and debauchery to servants and mean disorderly people, would be highly agreeable to the inhabitants in general."

The taverns' obscene toasts and intoxicated servants were, in fact, the more innocent aspects of the liquor habits in the city. In unlicensed drinking establishments, appropriately known as "disorderly houses," city authorities were constantly arresting people for "quarreling, fighting, gaming" as well as for "drinking, tippling, whoring, and misbehaving themselves to the great damage and common nuisance."

According to city records, almost every category of serious crime occurred within the legal and illegal drinking establishments of the city: attempted rape, assault, rioting, pickpocketing, manslaughter, and murder.

Despite the occasional criticism from the elites, this high level of drinking and debauchery is more or less the regular state of affairs for New York City in the early- to mid-1770s.

Now, in the spring of 1776, suddenly add more than ten thousand young male soldiers to the mix. Most of them are under twenty-five and away from homes and families for the first time.

The results are predictable: young soldiers tearing around the city in groups, running from tavern to tavern, buying bottles of rum from the many sellers eager for business, and generally getting intoxicated at any time of day or night.

Of course, the city offers many other unfamiliar sights and cultural experiences for the young men, but the lure of drink has a way of winning out over the other attractions. One soldier earnestly decides to experience the varied religious services offered in the city, most of them totally foreign to the small town from which he comes. But as the young soldier recounts in his journal, after he sits for two hours in a somber Quaker service, he gets bored and instead goes to a tavern next door for "a bowl or two of grog" before returning to camp.

With so many soldiers in the city, a few bowls of grog during a

Sunday sermon are far from the worst of the army's discipline problems. At night is when the city's taverns come alive, and this is when the wide-eyed soldiers really let loose on the town. On many mornings, the army's officers receive reports of soldiers out all night, intoxicated, disturbing the peace, fighting with residents, fighting with one another, and occasionally ending up in the city's jails.

The army establishes curfews, but they prove almost impossible to enforce.

No one is more dismayed by this behavior than the soldiers' Commander-in-Chief, George Washington. With the impeccable manners of a Virginia gentleman, and his deep convictions of the virtues of modesty and discipline, the Commander is appalled by the drunkenness and debauchery of his troops.

Washington tries to curb the soldiers' drinking with new rules and regulations, both for the soldiers and the liquor sellers in the city. He orders that "the gin shops and other houses where liquors have been heretofore retailed within or near the lines . . . are strictly forbidden to sell any for the future to any soldier in the army."

When Washington's Quartermaster General, Thomas Mifflin, visits the New York Provincial Congress on April 17, he brings the issue before that body as a matter of grave concern:

> General Washington is very solicitous to have the great number of taverns and tippling houses in this city suppressed, because they tend greatly to debauch the soldiers; and requests that this Committee will be pleased to regulate and make out a list of such tavern-keepers and retailers of spirituous liquors as this Committee shall deem necessary.

Washington also creates new rules for the soldiers, in an attempt to restore discipline and curtail the rampant drinking:

> If any soldier shall be found disguised with liquor, as has been too much the practice heretofore, the general is determined to have him punished with the utmost severity, as no other soldier in such situation can be either fit for defense or attack.

The army's general orders are soon peppered with reports of soldiers being disciplined with lashes or fines for excessive drunkenness to set examples for the rest. However, just like the curfews, these rules about drinking are difficult to enforce. If the army were to implement harsher penalties, the result would be self-defeating. The last thing the Continental officers want to do is suspend or expel soldiers when the army so desperately needs to train as many men as possible, as fast as possible.

The need to monitor and discipline unruly soldiers in an unruly city becomes yet another difficult task that befalls George Washington in the spring and summer of 1776, on the eve of the first great battle of the war.

In the weeks ahead, this task will only get harder.

34

---·---

Plots, schemes, and conspiracies.

The enemies of the Continental army—the Loyalists whom the authorities have come to call "the disaffected"—seem to be everywhere around New York City, and contriving secret schemes against Washington's army.

On a weekly and sometimes daily basis, the local Committees of Safety in New Jersey, Long Island, Connecticut, Westchester County, Dutchess County, and all over upstate New York file new reports of clandestine plots and activities engineered by the "enemies of America."

The imminent arrival of British forces for the coming showdown in New York—expected now within the next month or so—has emboldened the enemies of the revolution who reside within the colonies. They'll do everything they can to undermine the war effort, not with an open show of force, but with subterfuge, espionage, and secret schemes.

On May 15, George Washington receives a letter from Fairfield County, in southern Connecticut. The local Committee of Inspection—a colonial body tasked with maintaining public safety—has uncovered a scheme by which Loyalists from the region are being armed and ferried to Long Island, to join forces with fellow Loyalists and plan an uprising.

The Connecticut militia has already apprehended one boatload of men en route to Long Island and returned them to Fairfield County for questioning. Local authorities also arrested several men in the nearby town of Redding. According to the Committee of Inspection's chairman, who pens the letter to Washington: "The circumstances attending this affair are not yet fully known . . . but we think we know enough to convince us that a horrid plot is laid by the Tories to destroy the people of the country, to co-operate with our enemies in every measure to reduce us, and that Long-Island is appointed for headquarters."

Washington quickly replies to the letter, writing that he and his army will provide any assistance to help "root out or secure such abominable pests of society," and that the Fairfield committee's "zeal & activity upon this occasion is truly commendable."

He refers the letter to the New York Provincial Congress for further discovery, urging action. However, none of the committees in either colony is able to uncover more information about the plot. With no names or other details to follow up on, there's little that Washington can do with his army in New York City.

The Connecticut authorities put some of the implicated Loyalists in jail, but the true leaders of the plot are never discovered, and an attempt to locate and arrest one of the alleged organizers on Long Island is not successful. For all anyone knows, more boatloads of Loyalists associated with the scheme could already be en route to Long Island.

The day after Washington receives the report from Fairfield County, he receives an even more distressing letter from the King's County Committee of Correspondence, representing the region around Albany, New York. The letter, written by the chairman of the committee, begins this way: "By the enclosed you will discover the glimmering of such a plot as has seldom appeared in the world, since the fall of Adam by the Grand deceiver & Supplanter of Truth."

That'll get your attention.

The letter goes on to announce a complex Loyalist plot against Washington's army and the American cause: "Believe it the plan is as deep as Hell, many other circumstances and things perfectly agree with this information and we depend on it, that the Tories have a set time . . . to rise against the country."

As ominous as this language may be, the most horrifying part of the message comes in the form of two depositions enclosed with the letter, from witnesses who make an extraordinary claim: One of the masterminds of this Loyalist plot is one of Washington's own generals—Philip Schuyler, stationed in the northern part of New York near Canada.

The depositions claim that General Schuyler is actively recruiting a Loyalist army, including from the ranks of his own Continental troops, with the goal of securing the entire Albany region for the British, thereby cutting off a critical section of the Hudson River.

The accusations are stunning. George Washington's own man—a turncoat.

Washington must have thought about the terrible affair with Dr. Benjamin Church in Cambridge. From that past episode, the Commander-in-Chief learned that even the most outwardly Patriotic friend of the revolution could be secretly consorting with the enemy and committing treason. Anything and everything is possible.

Nonetheless, Washington believes that *this* situation is different.

Philip Schuyler is an aristocrat from a respected family, a man of advanced age with a strong reputation for honesty. More important, Washington had gotten to know him personally at the Second Continental Congress, where Schuyler was one of the delegates representing New York. Unlike Dr. Church in Cambridge, Washington considers Schuyler a personal friend. He can vouch for his character. For George Washington, nothing matters more than character.

Still, he can't be sure. Whatever the truth, time is of the essence to manage this crisis. Once rumors begin to spread among officers and soldiers that one of Washington's top generals is in fact a traitor, the army will be thrown into chaos.

Indeed, the very next day, as Washington determines how to respond, he learns that the King's County committee has already shared the accusation with the Governor of Connecticut, Jonathan Trumbull, as well as with members of the New York Provincial Congress.

With no more time to deliberate, the Commander-in-Chief decides to trust his instincts about one of his top generals.

Washington immediately writes a letter to Schuyler, enclosing copies of the damning accusations. The letter makes it clear that he believes the accusations are false, the work of enemies who are trying to divide the army: "From these you will readily discover the insidious and diabolical arts & schemes carrying on by the Tories and friends to government to raise distrust, dissension & divisions among us."

Washington goes on to assert his faith in Schuyler's honor. "Having the utmost confidence in your integrity and the most incontestible proofs of your great attachment to our common country and its interests, I could not but look upon the charges against you with an eye of disbelief and sentiments of detestation and abhorrence."

Washington further suggests that these accusations serve to highlight how vigilant they must be against these and other Loyalists in the colonies, because "our internal enemies have many projects in contemplation to subvert our Liberties."

Upon receipt of Washington's urgent letter, Schuyler does what Washington hopes. He immediately and forcefully denies the "diabolical tales" and vows to clear his name and bring to justice those who spread them. "It [is] now a duty I owe myself and my country to detect the scoundrels," he writes, "and the only means of doing this is by requesting that an immediate inquiry may be made into the matter." Until there is an investigation, "I cannot sit easy under such an infamous imputation as on this extensive continent numbers of the most respectable characters may not know what your Excellency and Congress do of my principles & exertions in the common cause."

These words are reassuring, as is his demand for an inquiry. Still, Schuyler could be writing all this while *still* masterminding a treasonous plot. Therefore, the inquiry remains critical. Fortunately for Washington, a team of local colonial authorities in western Massachusetts, not far from Albany, where the accusations originated, has already begun conducting an investigation.

On May 26, the leader of this investigation, a lawyer and former militia officer named Mark Hopkins, writes a letter to Washington to share their findings about this "plot being formed for the destruction of these United Colonies." In investigating the plot, they pay particular attention to the scandalous accusations against General Schuyler.

According to the letter, they have reached a clear conclusion: "The said Convention . . . took all those methods they could devise to find out the sentiments of the General. And it is with the greatest pleasure we are now able to acquaint your Excellency that said Convention are satisfied that their suspicions respecting him were wholly groundless."

Washington's instincts were correct. The outrageous claims against General Schuyler are false.

Still, the matter is deeply unsettling. The Massachusetts report also suggests, "That there has been a plan forming among our enemies in the colonies, is beyond doubt."

How far along is this plan? Apparently, the false accusations against Schuyler are in fact part of a larger scheme: "some wicked designing men . . . falsely asserted diverse persons of distinction & merit to be concerned in it, in order to influence the timid, and ignorant, and promote jealousies amongst us."

Secret plots, disinformation, and subterfuge. In an environment where no one can be trusted, and unknown dangers lurk around every corner, these tactics sow fear, confusion, and paranoia. Most of all, they destroy trust.

As with the plot discovered in Fairfield, Connecticut, the scope and nature of the real Albany plot are never fully uncovered. Aside from clearing Schuyler's name, the Massachusetts inquiry fails to offer many other specific details or clues. In the end, most of the participants in the supposed uprising are not identified or apprehended. Presumably, whatever the scheme is, it continues undetected.

Rather than clarify the state of Loyalist activity in New York City in May 1776, these cases and others like them serve only to further confuse Washington and the Patriot authorities. Uncovering these various plots leads not to answers, but to more questions: How many and how strong are the Loyalist ranks in and around the city? Are these different groups connected in any way? How can we separate fact from rumor?

And finally, how much of this activity outside the city can be traced to the former Governor of New York, William Tryon?

Despite these questions, one thing is abundantly clear. Washington's army and the local rebel authorities need a better, more robust system for detecting and investigating the many schemes and conspiracies in and around New York City.

They need a better method of gathering information.

They need to learn whom they can trust, and who is working for the enemy.

They need a system to uncover and prevent the plots against them.

What they need is *counterintelligence*—and they need it fast.

35

——— · ———

Goshen, New York

May 1776

James Mason is a working man. He's a miller by trade.

Unfortunately, for tradesmen like James Mason, finding work is not so easy these days.

Employment is what Mason is looking for when he arrives in the town of Goshen, New York, on or around May 15, 1776. Goshen is in Orange County, about fifty miles north of New York City, to the west of the Hudson River. Goshen is home to one of the largest iron mills in the region, commonly called Ringwood Ironworks. This is where James Mason is hoping to find a wage.

Getting work at the mill apparently isn't easy, though, because Mason gets only a few partial shifts here and there. The mill can't offer him a full-time job.

Soon, he learns of a very different kind of opportunity.

On his days off from the mill, Mason needs a place to board. His search for lodging is what leads him to the home of a man named William Farley, who lives about five miles away and has a room to rent.

Farley, it turns out, is an interesting man—or at least, he has an interesting proposition for the out-of-work James Mason. Within a few days after the two men meet, Farley shares a secret with him: Back in April, he spent four days aboard one of the British ships in New York Harbor.

It was the *Duchess of Gordon*. The ship where the exiled Governor, William Tryon, is headquartered.

That's not all. Farley tells Mason that ever since he went on the ship, he's been working for the Governor. His main job is to recruit men from the colonies to secretly join the British side, all of them ready to take up arms when the British forces arrive.

For any man who is willing to join this treasonous plan, Farley tells Mason: "Governor Tryon would give five guineas bounty and two hundred acres of land for each man, one hundred for his wife, and fifty for each child, upon condition they would enlist in his Majesty's service."

This money will be paid in small weekly installments—about ten shillings a week—and that land is promised in the future, after the British successfully take the city in battle.

Two hundred acres of land for free, plus a salary. It's a pretty good deal, and Mason wants in.

Farley gets something out of it too, for recruiting people to join. He tells Mason that he "was to have a bounty from the Governor for every man he could get . . . that the Governor had desired him to go up and get as many men as he could; that the recruits were to assist the King's troops when they came."

A few days later, Farley and Mason depart Goshen with a plan to travel to the *Duchess of Gordon*, where the new recruits will swear an oath to work for the Governor. Just before they leave, Farley recruits another young man, William Benjamin—a full-time worker at the mill—to join them for the trip and also take part in the Governor's offer.

The path to the *Duchess of Gordon* is dangerous, with sentries from the Continental army now monitoring the roads and waterways. The trio passes through Elizabethtown, New Jersey, where a local contact tells Farley that the routes to the king's ships that used to be easiest—taking a boat directly from Bergen Point, New Jersey, or Staten Island—are now closed off because "there are riflemen staged there," sent by the Continental army to surveil suspicious travelers.

As an alternative, the local contact advises them to catch a ferry to New York City, where they can then secure a boat ride to the *Duchess of Gordon*. The contact gives the name and address of a Manhattan shoemaker near the East River who secretly works for Governor Tryon. The shoemaker will arrange a clandestine ferry from Manhattan to Tryon's ship.

The next day, the three men—William Farley and his recruits, James Mason and William Benjamin—board a boat at Elizabethtown, en route to Manhattan.

If all goes according to plan, James Mason, a miller, and William Benjamin, formerly a laborer at the Ringwood iron mill, soon will swear an oath on behalf of Governor Tryon to join the British and take up arms against their fellow countrymen. In exchange, they'll receive money and the promise of land.

But as they board the boat to Manhattan, there is something that these would-be traitors don't know. They are secretly being followed.

36

New York, New York

May 1776

Soldiers living in filth. Soldiers getting drunk. These are two of the difficulties the Continental army is facing with so many men stationed in close quarters in a crowded urban setting.

Yet, these are nothing compared to another great vice of New York City—perhaps the greatest vice of all.

They call it the "Holy Ground."

It's the city's infamous red-light district, and in the 1770s it is probably the most notorious neighborhood in all the colonies. It's a dimly lit series of blocks toward the southwestern tip of Manhattan, west of City Hall, where brothels, gin shops, gambling clubs, and bawdy taverns line the streets. Every night, drunks, brawlers, sailors, thieves, and other ne'er-do-wells share the streets with the prostitutes and madams looking to lure customers into their houses of ill repute.

How did the Holy Ground get such a perfect name? It's not just because New Yorkers have always been sarcastic—although that may be part of it. In fact, the blocks of the neighborhood are owned by Trinity Parish, the central institution of the Anglican Church in New York City, whose property also includes Trinity Church and St. Paul's Chapel.

Despite the fact that many elite citizens attend these houses of worship, apparently neither the church nor the city authorities do much to curtail the illicit activities that occur on the parish's adjacent property. Perhaps they don't care so long as the brothels and bars are paying their rents. As a disapproving Bostonian visitor once put it: "Look at New York, where even the church makes money from the whores!"

Still, one thing is certain. In the spring of 1776, as thousands of Continental soldiers pour into the city, business in the Holy Ground is booming.

By one tally from the era, there are about five hundred prostitutes operating in the Holy Ground during this period. The city's entire population at the time, including the Continental soldiers, is about 25,000. That means prostitutes comprise roughly 2 percent of the people residing in the city. (Extrapolating to today's Manhattan, that's the equivalent of some 33,000 prostitutes plying their trade, all concentrated in one neighborhood.)

Most of the young soldiers in the Continental army, coming from their small farms and provincial towns, have never seen anything remotely like the Holy Ground. Now, they don't just see it—they see it again, and again, and again.

A young Lieutenant from Massachusetts named Isaac Bangs, one of the relatively few Continental soldiers with a college education, writes in his journal about his first interaction with the ladies of the night: "When I visited [them] at first I thought nothing could exceed them for impudence and immodesty, but I found the more I was acquainted with them the more they excelled in their brutality."

Apparently undeterred, Lieutenant Bangs later makes repeat visits to the neighborhood, without explaining quite why. Another young officer writes a letter home describing the "bitchfoxy jades, jills, hags, strums, prostitutes" he sees at the Holy Ground, and explains that "their unparalleled conduct is a sufficient antidote against any desire that a person can have that has one spark of modesty or virtue left in him."

Whatever they say in their journals, the soldiers and young officers keep coming back, and as long as the army is in town, the prostitutes "continue their employ, which has become quite lucrative."

In fact, the young soldiers' sneering attitude toward the workers in the Holy Ground hides a deeper tragedy. Most of the women are poor, desperate, and vulnerable. The economic depression of the early 1770s has left many people destitute, and the city provides almost nothing in the way of social services. Women of all ages are forced to survive any way they can. Some of the workers in the Holy Ground are single mothers, trying desperately to provide for their children. Every night they contend with intoxicated sailors, soldiers, and criminals. It's a brutal existence, and the risk of violence is constant.

The drunkenness and crime of the Holy Ground can lead to only one thing for Washington's army—trouble. On April 22, a few weeks after the main forces move into the city, authorities make a gruesome find in one of the district's brothels: two soldiers' bloody corpses, one of them "castrated in a barbarous manner."

The authorities can't determine what led to the crime, but soon a gang of soldiers exacts revenge on the brothel by tearing apart the building. Not long after, the body of a prostitute is also found nearby, dumped in an outhouse and left to rot.

Just as with drinking, the army once again institutes various rules and curfews related to this neighborhood of vices. Once again, the rules prove difficult to enforce. The army institutes a special patrol in which on-duty soldiers walk the streets of the Holy Ground to break up fights, put criminals in jail, and keep fellow soldiers out of the brothels.

This is hard work for the patrolmen, because the soldiers who sneak to the brothels don't wear their uniforms, making it difficult to distinguish them from other patrons. Meanwhile, the patrolling soldiers have to contend with the various drunks, brawlers, and prostitutes in the streets.

One young officer assigned to this duty calls it "hell's work" and describes altercations in which he "broke up the knots of men and women fighting, pulling caps, swearing, crying 'murder' and . . . hurried them off to the provost dungeon by half dozens, there let them lay mixed till next day. Then some are punished and some get off clear."

In the end, the greatest danger of the Holy Ground for the soldiers proves not to be drunkenness, brawls, or other violence. The greatest danger is something invisible, but even more deadly: syphilis.

This sexually transmitted disease spreads quickly through the troops as different soldiers frequent the same brothels and same prostitutes.

Indeed, several young soldiers who joined the army die that spring not from battlefield heroics, but from a disease acquired in a brothel. Their final hours are not spent wielding weapons against the enemy, but instead writhing in pain from the gruesome symptoms of a bacterium just as fatal as any musket ball or bayonet.

The men sent to medical facilities for syphilis are not the only soldiers suffering from health problems. The poor sanitary conditions, unclean drinking water, and lack of hygiene in the New York City barracks create a rich environment for digestive disorders and, soon, large numbers of the men are suffering from dysentery and severe diarrhea.

"Our Company are now about one half of them very low with the Camp Disorder, or Bloody Flux, which is very prevalent through out the whole Army," Bangs writes in his journal. While dysentery doesn't claim many lives, the symptoms can be brutal and often incapacitate soldiers for long stretches.

In addition to syphilis and the "bloody flux," the army continues to be ravaged by the most terrifying ailment of all: smallpox. In the previous month or so, with soldiers leaving the service after Boston, thousands making the journey south, and thousands of brand-new recruits and militia units joining for the defense of New York, the logistical nightmare of quarantining afflicted soldiers, diagnosing new cases, and preventing the spread of the disease is even more complex than it was in Cambridge. When positive diagnoses are made, the sick soldiers are ferried to Montresor's Island in the East River (now known as Randalls Island), where army doctors oversee a quarantined-care unit. This removal prevents the disease from spreading too rapidly, but the constant drain on men and resources is a never-ending struggle.

Of the approximately 12,000 Continental troops in New York,

somewhere close to 2,500 are injured, bedridden, incapacitated, quarantined, or otherwise unfit for duty.

For George Washington, the virtuous ideal of a trained, disciplined, orderly army has never seemed further from reality. Instead, his army appears to be spiraling into darkness at the very time when their courage and valor will be needed most.

37

Cold Spring Harbor, Long Island

May 1776

The operation has stalled.

After weeks of effort and high hopes, the work of the counterfeiting collective of Cold Spring Harbor, Long Island, is not moving forward as originally planned.

For a while, the brothers Israel and Isaac Young, along with their collaborator, the engraver and silversmith Henry Dawkins, had seemed to be doing everything right. From Israel's initial planning with Dawkins in the city jail, to the complicated purchase of the rolling press, to the placement of the press in the attic of the Youngs' home to create a private workstation, to the acquisition of sample dollar bills and shilling notes to use as references, to Dawkins's expert early round of platemaking—the team seemed destined for success.

And then the paper. They had everything but the correct paper.

The team had high hopes when they enlisted their acquaintance and neighboring Long Islander Isaac Ketcham to find and purchase the correct stock in Philadelphia. So when Ketcham returned to Long Island in early May, the plotters were unhappy, to say the least, to learn the disappointing outcome of his trip. Not only had Ketcham returned to Cold Spring Harbor empty-handed, but he also informed Israel

Young that "he thought the paper he wanted could not be got" based on his experience trying to procure it.

The Young brothers and Dawkins have no way of knowing whether Ketcham genuinely tried to find the paper or whether he lost his nerve, but for the moment only one thing matters: The counterfeiters are no closer to being able to produce Continental bills than they were more than three weeks ago.

Such is the state of affairs in the Young brothers' Cold Spring Harbor residence on the morning of Sunday, May 12, 1776. Although there aren't any records of how the trio has been proceeding in the week or so since their accomplice Ketcham's failed trip, it stands to reason that they have been planning their next course of action with regard to finding the right stock.

They've now all invested many weeks and significant money to get the operation off the ground, so they aren't about to quit. Surely, they can find some way to track down the correct paper, or find someone else who can do so for them. Or perhaps, by experimenting with different inks or plates, they can figure out some alternative way to mimic the look and weight of Continental currency using some other stock that's easier to obtain.

On this particular Sunday morning, the only people home at the Youngs' house are the younger brother, Isaac Young, and Israel's wife. The two principals of the counterfeiting operation, Israel Young and Henry Dawkins, are both elsewhere in town.

It's a calm, still, and largely cloudless morning as the sun rises over the Sound on the north shore of Long Island, and no one in tiny Cold Spring Harbor has any reason to think anything unusual will happen today.

Then, for Isaac Young, the morning silence is interrupted by a loud banging at the door.

Probably wishing his older brother were there with him, Isaac walks to the door and slowly opens it.

An unfamiliar man stands just outside, wearing a captain's hat and wielding a musket. Other men stand a few steps behind him.

In a split second, the man "immediately enters" the house with no greeting or explanation.

Is this the home of Israel and Isaac Young?

Yes, it is.

The man instructs Young not to raise any alarm or make any noise. He tells him to get dressed—it's time to leave—they're going to nearby Huntington. There, they have some business to take care of.

But first, the man informs Young, he and his men are going to search the house.

In particular, they want to see the attic.

38

---•---

New York Harbor

May 1776

This time, it isn't so easy for the Mayor of New York, David Mathews, to board the Governor's ship.

For several weeks after his initial appointment as Mayor, back in February, Mathews had been able to visit William Tryon on the *Duchess of Gordon* almost at will. Mayor Mathews would send a token request through the Provincial Congress, then get permission from the port master, and book one of the small boats making regular trips back and forth.

Mathews's access was rarely, if ever, denied. Back then, Governor Tryon was still able to hold meetings on the ship with his council—the city authorities still allowed it—and Mathews would often join them.

Mayor Mathews became part of Tryon's inner circle on the *Duchess*. This meant that he was present for some of the special "planning" the Governor oversaw from his quarters on the ship: running spies, ferrying goods and information, and sharing intelligence with onshore sources. Mathews's job was to support these efforts, acting as the Governor's eyes and ears in the city and the surrounding region.

However, once George Washington's top officer, Gen. Charles Lee,

had made it a priority to shut off the governor's communications—
and once Washington himself had arrived with his army—the May-
or's ability to come and go was significantly curtailed.

Now, given the state of the city in April and May of 1776, with
Washington's army in control, Mayor Mathews keeps a much lower
profile. He spends more time at his home in Flatbush, in Kings
County—then part of Long Island, now in the borough of Brooklyn—
and less on the island of Manhattan. Thus far, he has been able to
escape the wrath of the colonial authorities. He'd no doubt like to
keep it that way.

So when the Mayor learns that the Governor wants to meet with
him personally on board the *Duchess of Gordon*, in part to give him
the money to pay back the gunsmith Gilbert Forbes, Mathews needs
to find a legitimate reason to request proper permission from the city
authorities to do so, rather than sneak on and risk getting caught.

The opportunity arises in mid-May. Mathews applies directly to
Gen. Israel Putnam, currently Washington's second-in-command in
New York City, for permission to board the *Duchess of Gordon* in order to "obtain permission from the Governor for Lord Drummond
to go to Bermuda."

This administrative request, involving a matter of diplomatic procedure on behalf of the Scottish official Lord Drummond, is not particularly suspicious or dangerous. General Putnam authorizes the
request.

Once Mayor Mathews is on the *Duchess of Gordon*, no Continental authorities are watching him. He can do or say what he pleases.

Not much is known about what business Mayor Mathews does
or doesn't conduct on this particular visit to the ship—or whether
he ever actually makes the request for Lord Drummond to go to
Bermuda.

However, one part of the visit is known, at least according to
Mathews's later account. At the end of his time on the ship, Mathews
and Tryon have a confidential meeting in the governor's "private
room," away from all other eyes and ears.

According to Mathews, in this meeting the Governor "put a bundle of paper money into my hands," with specific instructions on

how to spend it. The bundle of cash is just short of 120 pounds, or the equivalent of roughly $25,000 in contemporary U.S. currency. The governor's directions to Mathews are clear: "Take out five pounds and give it to the prisoners in the jail, and pay the remainder to Gilbert Forbes."

"Prisoners in the jail" probably refers to various Loyalists connected to Tryon who, for one reason or another, have been thrown into the crowded city jails by the Patriot authorities. Tryon keeps tabs on his allies and spies who land in jail—and could be sending them money in part to keep them on his side.

In fact, the New York City jails have become a significant part of the complex network of Loyalist communications in the city, packed as they are with those who oppose the revolution and are paying the price for doing so. While the exact identity of the prisoners to whom the Governor intends to send money in this payment are not known, the city jails are currently so full of Loyalists, it could be any number of men or women who have schemed with the Governor.

And then there's the rest of the money, meant for Gilbert Forbes. Gilbert Forbes, that short, thickset gunsmith who lives on Broadway across from Hull's Tavern.

Apparently, the nine rifles and eleven smoothbore guns had arrived intact on the *Duchess of Gordon.* So, just as planned, Mayor Mathews will find a way to pay Forbes for them on Governor Tryon's behalf.

After the meeting and the handover of cash, Mayor Mathews leaves the *Duchess* and returns to shore, presumably to his home in Flatbush, across the East River from Manhattan. From this point forward, there is no indication of his being back on Tryon's ship any time in the next few months. Nor is there any evidence of direct written correspondence between Mayor Mathews and anyone aboard the king's ships. Sure, they have other ways to stay in touch, but it must always be invisible to the eyes of the colonial authorities and of the army now controlling the city.

If this really is the last in-person business done between Mayor Mathews and Governor Tryon in the spring and summer of 1776, it is a fairly simple matter. However, on closer inspection centuries later, the math of this particular transaction reveals another layer.

Subtracting the five pounds that were supposed to be given to the prisoners, Gilbert Forbes has almost 115 pounds. The price of the guns he delivered was roughly 65 pounds. This means that the Governor and Mayor are giving Forbes almost twice as much money as he was offered for the sale of the rifles and guns he delivered to the ship. In today's terms, he'll get about ten thousand dollars *more* than what had been agreed upon.

Why? Because Governor Tryon and Mayor Mathews now have something else in mind for Gilbert Forbes.

They're going to ask him to do something far more important than just sell them a few guns.

Gilbert Forbes is about to play a much bigger role in Tryon's grand plan.

39

New York, New York

May 1776

George Washington needs help.

Ever since the Continental forces arrived in New York more than a month ago, Washington and his officers have learned about one Loyalist plot after another, a seemingly endless series of dangerous schemes circulating in and around the city.

Preparing for the British attack is already an awesome undertaking. Responding to the plots of domestic enemies adds yet another layer of fear and uncertainty.

One of Washington's frustrations becomes the lack of a clear and efficient mechanism for assessing these threats. His officers and soldiers don't have the time, resources, authority, or frankly, the skill to embark on complex investigations into civilian activities. The governmental bodies tasked with securing public safety and supporting the war effort are slow moving and sometimes mired in politics. On any issue of concern to the army, Washington has to appeal to the New York Provincial Congress for deliberation, which then often has to take matters to the Continental Congress for approval.

In addition to being slow, the process lacks secrecy. With enemy spies everywhere, Washington and his officers constantly worry about information flowing into the wrong hands.

On May 17, 1776, Washington confers on this matter with Nathaniel Woodhull, the president of the New York Provincial Congress. Washington tells Woodhull he needs a better, faster, and more confidential system for investigating internal plots against the American cause.

Washington's suggestion? He wants a secret committee.

More specifically, he wants a small group focused specifically on these dangers, working with him to uncover, investigate, and try to disable the plots by hostile parties in the region.

The next day, Woodhull presents the request to the rest of the New York Provincial Congress. He explains that in order to curtail the "dangerous machinations" in New York and the neighboring colonies, General Washington wants a small, top-secret team with whom he can strategize: "The General . . . would be obliged by the appointment of a Secret Committee to confer with him on the dangers to which this Colony is exposed from its intestine enemies."

"Intestine enemies" has become one of Washington's chosen terms for the spies, Loyalists, and traitors within the colonies who actively plot against his army or secretly give aid to the British.

That day, the Provincial Congress votes. By a tally of 17 for and 8 against, the congress approves "that [there] be a Secret Committee, on behalf of this Congress, to confer and advise with the Commander-in-Chief," and the resolution is passed.

Initially, the secret committee has five members, appointed from among the congressmen. To allow greater speed and flexibility, any three of them are deemed sufficient to represent the group if all the members are not available on short notice.

The committee will have powers to authorize Washington to take necessary measures against internal enemies without the need for every request to go before the full membership of the Provincial Congress.

Just as important, Washington can share sensitive intelligence with this small committee, and the committee can share intelligence with him—in a confidential manner—without the fear of spies, leaks, or the rumormongering that comes anytime information is shared with a large group.

In a sense, this committee is a small early prototype of an intelligence agency—a team dedicated entirely to gathering information, identifying dangerous parties, and uncovering hostile plots.

At first, the committee is given no particular title, beyond "the Secret Committee," or the "Committee on Intestine Enemies," or, most awkwardly, the "Committee for the Hearing and Trying [of] Disaffected Persons and Those of Equivocal Character."

Clearly, they'll need a better name. For now, the new group will draw up documents to better establish and define the mission of uncovering, investigating, and combating plots against the Continental army and the colonial governing bodies.

Washington hopes this new committee will serve to defeat the Loyalist schemes and conspiracies around New York City, whether arising from Governor Tryon's ship or elsewhere.

In fact, the creation of this secret intelligence team sets the stage for an epic showdown.

Tryon has begun launching a complex plot that, unbeknownst to the Commander-in-Chief, has infiltrated the ranks of the Continental army. This new secret committee has a specific mandate to *prevent* any hostile plots from harming Washington's army or the war effort. Tryon is already on their radar as a known enemy of the colonies and will be an immediate target of investigation.

As George Washington and his new committee try to discover Tryon's scheme, the exiled Governor is working hard to stay one step ahead.

40

In the months since the evacuation of Boston, both England and the colonies have been preparing for all-out military confrontation.

All the while, the two sides have also been fighting a different kind of war—one that's been going nonstop for at least a year.

It's a mail war.

For the two opposing armies and the many political bodies engaged in the conflict, physical mail is *the* means of communication, of relaying information, of passing along instructions, and of sharing reports.

As a result, both sides devise elaborate strategies to steal or intercept the mail of the other. Likewise, both sides work hard to try to keep their own mail lines secured.

The Patriots may have started the worst of it back in 1774 and 1775, when their various local Committees of Correspondence in the New England colonies started aggressively intercepting mail to and from England to gain confidential information about the British Parliament's political machinations. The British and the Loyalists didn't take long to respond in kind, and from the Battles of Lexington and Concord onward, postal espionage in both directions runs rampant.

In Virginia, the Loyalist royal Governor, Lord Dunmore, crafted an especially elaborate scheme of mail interception. At night Dunmore, who had retreated to a ship at the time, sent his sentries to the colony's central mail outpost in Williamsburg to confiscate mail for him. Dunmore and his aides would hold on to any mail with useful intelligence, and secretly return the rest before morning.

In New York, in the spring of 1776, Governor William Tryon has lost all such advantages. Because Washington's Continental army now controls the physical space of New York City, the Patriots have the clear upper hand when it comes to intercepting enemy mail and controlling the postal system.

In fact, one of Tryon's current allies on the *Duchess of Gordon*, the former New Jersey attorney general Cortlandt Skinner, had to take refuge on the ship precisely because one of his personal letters was intercepted by the Patriots. Skinner's letter, written to his brother in December 1775, expressed candid opinions critical of the colonial governments and suggested that his true allegiance was still to England.

When the New Jersey authorities intercepted the letter, they determined that it contained "many sentiments and expressions prejudicial to the peace and welfare of the United Colonies," and ordered Skinner's arrest. Skinner barely escaped New Jersey. Like Tryon, Skinner was forced to take refuge aboard the *Duchess* and now spends his days a fellow exile from the colonies he once served.

The interception of Skinner's letter occurred before Washington's army took over New York City in early April 1776. Now that the Continental forces are garrisoned in the city, the mail lines in the region are even less secure.

Starting in the month of May, Tryon almost entirely ceases sending letters or correspondence, at least within the colonies. Although a British courier boat called the *Swallow* can be used to send letters directly to England, even this is risky, and he limits mail to only the most banal and procedural.

At this stage, everything Tryon does must be kept secret. While he can still send and receive goods, and still send and receive verbal messages by ferrying couriers to his ship, he sends nothing in writing—and certainly nothing that could possibly reveal the scope of his dark ambitions.

For these reasons, Tryon's plans and motives become even more difficult to detect in May and June of 1776. It also happens that at just this time, Tryon's conspiracy against the Continental army is about to take on a shocking new dimension.

41

——— • ———

Life is different now.

Life is different for everyone, really, in the spring of 1776; but life is especially different for Gilbert Forbes, the gunsmith.

For Forbes, the last half of May has been a whirlwind. Ever since he sent the shipment of guns to Governor Tryon on board the *Duchess of Gordon*, his prospects in the world have expanded, almost too fast to keep up with. It starts with money: Forbes made a nice sale with those rifles and smoothbore guns, and he now has the benefit of sitting on a pile of money at a time when many are struggling.

Money is only part of it, though.

After Forbes's secret meeting with Mayor David Mathews, he becomes a known player in the underground web of Loyalist activists and plotters in New York City on the eve of war. Now, he is a familiar presence at taverns like Houlding's and Lowry's, where Loyalists congregate and hold clandestine meetings. The fact that Forbes is a gunsmith with access to weapons probably makes him an especially welcome addition in this circle.

Having made a successful secret sale of arms to the *Duchess of Gordon*, Forbes is also now acquainted with the network of people who regularly run supplies and relay secret messages to and from

Governor Tryon. Among others this includes a Manhattan shoe-maker named Peter McLean, who secretly ferries passengers to the *Duchess of Gordon*, and the woman known only as Mrs. Beck, who had helped deliver the initial batch of Forbes's guns to the Governor's ship.

The exact timeline of Forbes's activities in these few weeks is difficult to trace with certainty, but sometime shortly after his meeting with Mayor Mathews, Forbes meets a man known in Loyalist circles as "Sergeant Graham."

Graham is a former British officer, or at least claims to be, and he now works for Governor Tryon, helping organize Loyalist activity in the region. When Forbes meets him, Sergeant Graham is in the midst of developing a strategy for Tryon to help him deploy Loyalist soldiers on the ground against the Continental army when the British forces arrive.

Through Sergeant Graham, Forbes is now privy to top-secret planning and intelligence. The Governor of New York, the Mayor of New York, and a former British officer are trusting *him*—a gun dealer—to learn their strategy and be part of their trusted circle.

That's not all.

According to what Graham shares with Forbes, a key part of the Loyalist effort, as overseen by Governor Tryon, involves finding and organizing men who will join their cause. Efforts are under way, masterminded from the *Duchess of Gordon*, not just to raise troops from among the Loyalist citizens in the region around the city, but to actively lure Continental soldiers to switch sides.

That's where the extra cash from Mayor David Mathews comes in.

Accounts vary as to exactly how and when the transaction occurs, and as to whether it was a direct handoff or made through an intermediary, but what is known is this: Sometime not long after Mathews visited William Tryon on the *Duchess of Gordon*, the Mayor transfers approximately 115 pounds to Gilbert Forbes.

This money will pay for Forbes's guns, and it will also give him funds for his next, higher-level assignment: bribing rebel soldiers to join the British cause.

Forbes learns that Tryon's operatives have already turned several hundred Continental soldiers on Long Island, in Westchester County, and in New Jersey. Clearly the Continental soldiers are ready to betray their leaders for the right price.

Of course, the soldiers who have already been turned were probably easier prey because they were far removed from the army headquarters in New York City. The soldiers whom Tryon's agents have recruited on Long Island and elsewhere may have been militia members, and not part of Washington's army proper. Or they could have been isolated groups of soldiers stationed far away from their commanding officers—and therefore more open to influence.

Forbes, on the other hand, is asked to operate in the belly of the beast. His shop is in the heart of the commercial district of Manhattan, within blocks of George Washington's headquarters. Barracks of Continental soldiers surround him in every direction. Trying to infiltrate an army so close to its headquarters is risky work for sure. But these soldiers, if they can be persuaded, will be a far greater asset for Tryon.

Graham sweetens the deal by making one additional offer. He promises Forbes, with Tryon's blessing, that if Forbes "exerted himself . . . and raised enough men he should have a company." In other words, if Forbes can enlist enough men to join the Crown's forces, he'll receive an officer's commission and lead his own company when the British fleet arrives.

This once ordinary gunsmith—who wears a white coat and runs a small shop on Broadway—could soon be an officer in the British army, the greatest army the world has ever known.

Life is different now—and for Gilbert Forbes it will never be the same again.

42

---·---

Cold Spring Harbor, Long Island

May 1776

In some ways, Henry Dawkins and the Young brothers, the would-be counterfeiters based in Cold Spring Harbor, Long Island, are just unlucky.

Until the start of 1776, the overwhelmed colonial authorities were not paying much attention to counterfeiting as a crime; they simply had too many other important things to worry about. However, in the early months of 1776, these same authorities suddenly began a concerted effort to crack down on the practice.

Why the change? Once the colonies formed an army and the hostilities began in Boston, the British started using every possible tool to cripple the Continental war effort, including economic warfare. The British soon realized that one of their most effective tools to destabilize the colonial economies was to flood their markets with fake money. An influx of bogus cash devalues the real currency and creates runaway inflation.

In essence, counterfeiting is used as a crude form of economic espionage: all it takes is putting a bunch of fake bills in the hands of a willing colonist, and encouraging him or her to spend it freely at local stores and markets.

The resulting inflation has many brutal consequences for ordinary citizens, whose hard-earned money and savings lose value fast as the currency becomes diminished. On a larger scale, the inflation also cripples the Continental Congress's ability to pay for the massive war effort, because the value of its war chest likewise plummets. As Benjamin Franklin would later explain: "Paper money was in those times our universal currency. But it being the instrument with which we combated our enemies they resolved to deprive us of its use by depreciating it; and the most effectual means they could contrive was to counterfeit it."

Later in the war, British counterfeiting of Continental currency will become so effective that in some regions of the colonies, half the money in circulation is fake. In the early war years, including 1776, the debilitating effects of fake money are just starting to catch the sustained attention of the colonial authorities—and they determine they must crack down on counterfeiting in order to keep the currency as strong as possible during the war.

For all these reasons, the New York Provincial Congress takes the matter very seriously when, in early May 1776, they start hearing rumors of a possible band of counterfeiters based in a small town on Long Island.

The first report comes from a Cold Spring Harbor resident who volunteers to local authorities that he's suspicious of certain activities in the home of two brothers named Israel and Isaac Young. When the matter is brought before the New York Provincial Congress on May 10, the resident has also identified other neighbors as potential witnesses.

Together, these neighbors and townspeople describe accounts and rumors of strange behavior near and within the Youngs' house: unusual tools and supplies brought in and stored in the home, overheard conversations involving the intricacies of inks and currencies, and bragging on the part of one brother or the other about a windfall coming to them soon. Much of the hearsay focuses on someone who's staying at the Youngs'—a boarder named Henry Dawkins—a stranger to town who spends all his time in their attic and only comes down at night to sleep.

After hearing all this sworn testimony, the New York Provincial

Congress decides to act fast. It resolves to send a militia captain to Long Island, where he will hire soldiers and put together a raid. The wording of the resolution is crystal clear:

> *Whereas*, this Congress is informed, on oath, that there is great cause of suspicion that Henry Dawkins, Israel Young, Isaac Young, Isaac Ketcham . . . of Cold Spring, on Nassau-Island, are counterfeiting the Paper currency emitted by the Continental and this Congress:
>
> *Ordered therefore* . . . to dispatch Captain Wool, with a sufficient guard, to Cold-Spring, on Nassau-Island, and that the said guard do take all possible means in their power to apprehend and seize the said Henry Dawkins, Israel Young, Isaac Young, Isaac Ketcham . . . and bring them (together with all suspicious tools and other materials) before this Congress without delay.

The next day, Saturday, May 11, Capt. Jeremiah Wool makes the trip from Manhattan to Nassau County, Long Island. He arrives in the town of Huntington that night, where he's joined by a local militia team. The group spends the night in Huntington, and then, first thing in the morning on Sunday, May 12, a guide leads Captain Wool and his team to the nearby coastal town of Cold Spring Harbor.

Soon, Wool is standing at the front entrance of the Young brothers' residence, with a few of his guards behind him.

This is the very moment when Isaac Young, the only member of the counterfeiting team who happens to be inside at the time, has his quiet Sunday morning rudely interrupted.

Wool, who has already "set guards around the house," knocks loudly on the door; Wool himself will later recount that "Isaac Young came to the door and opened it; that he [Captain Wool] immediately entered; that Isaac Young appeared much surprised."

Isaac Young is even more surprised when the captain tells him to get dressed and be ready for a trip to Huntington with him—and then more surprised still when Captain Wool demands to search the house.

As Wool recounts in his record of the day, his men first search

Israel Young's room without incident; then, their first hint of something out of the ordinary comes when "they proceeded to a room in which they were informed Henry Dawkins usually lodged, and found under the bed in which he was informed Dawkins had lodged, a few Engraver's tools."

Engraver's tools are exactly the sorts of items they would expect to find at the home base of a counterfeiting outfit. Still, there is nothing inherently criminal in owning some tools. What Wool and his men really hope to discover is a printing press, and their initial search through the downstairs does not reveal one.

Perhaps Isaac Young, who is probably sweating profusely at this point, begins to have some hope that the guards won't find anything out of the ordinary—and won't discover the concealed passage to their upstairs workshop.

Then, as Captain Wool later testifies:

> At the head of one of the beds in that room, one of his Sergeants discovered a crack or opening in the wall, which they suspected to be a door; that on removing the bed and other furniture necessary, with a bayonet put into the crevice, they opened a small door, within which was a narrow stairs; that Isaac Young who was present, appeared to be in terror, and trembled.

If Wool has any doubts that the raid will be successful, Isaac Young's visible trembling probably removes them. Wool sends two of his men through the hidden door and up the stairs, and then follows so he can search the secret room for himself.

As Wool later describes it, he "proceeded up the said stairs into a very concealed garret, with one small window, and there found a rolling-press; that the first paper he picked up was a paper . . . appearing to be a copperplated imperfect copy of a Bill of Connecticut money, of forty Shillings."

So there it is. Captain Wool has just found a suspicious printing press and some sample counterfeit money in exactly the place he was *told* to look for a suspicious printing press and some sample counterfeit money.

Over the next couple of hours, the men scour the premises and gather the evidence. First, Captain Wool has "the press, with every utensil thereof, taken down, and brought down stairs." His men search every piece of furniture and "found in a chest in that house, [that] belonged to Henry Dawkins . . . a number of plates." When Wool conducts a second and more thorough search of Israel Young's room, he opens a drawer in a chest and discovers "a copperplate completely engraved for the impressing of two dollar bills, and on the plate a bill appearing to be a two dollar bill of Continental money."

While all this is going on, Captain Wool also does something else. He sends out teams of guards to apprehend the other suspects. First and foremost, they target the other Young brother, Israel, and of course the master engraver, Henry Dawkins.

Another team goes to track down the person whose name had come up in conjunction with the counterfeiting operation: the family man himself, Huntington resident Isaac Ketcham.

Wool's instructions are to bring all these men to an agreed-upon inn in Huntington, where he will process the suspects. That afternoon, one by one, the guards apprehend the members of the team and bring them to the tavern and boarding house called the Huntington Inn. Isaac Young, Israel Young, Henry Dawkins, and Isaac Ketcham are now officially in custody.

There is no record of how the suspects behaved while in Huntington, either to the guards or to one another. Wool's careful account of the day doesn't mention any shouting or altercation. However, it's probably a safe assumption that Isaac Ketcham spent this time cursing the moment he became involved with the other three. Indeed, as soon as he's able, Ketcham makes a statement to Wool that he, Isaac Ketcham, played only a very limited role in the operation, that he was "employed in this business to get paper; that he had not been concerned in making the money."

Wool takes down Ketcham's statement, as well as an initial statement from Dawkins. The next day, they will all travel to New York City, where each of them will be expected to provide full testimony, under oath, before the New York Provincial Congress. Then, after hearing their stories, the Congress will determine their crimes and decide their respective fates.

By all appearances, the Cold Spring Harbor counterfeiting operation of Young, Young, Dawkins, and Ketcham seems to be nearing an end. Yet when it comes to these small-town criminals, the most remarkable part of their story still lies ahead.

43

New York, New York

May 1776

On a warm afternoon in late May 1776, three men—William Farley, James Mason, and William Benjamin—arrive in Manhattan on a boat from Elizabethtown, New Jersey.

The men originally traveled from the town of Goshen, in upstate New York. They are now here in the city for one reason: to commit treason.

Back in Goshen, Farley recruited the other two to betray their country and join the British in exchange for a promise of money and land. The money and land will come from Governor Tryon.

Now that the traitorous trio is in Manhattan, their next destination is the *Duchess of Gordon*, the British ship in the harbor where Tryon is headquartered.

Following directions they were given back in Elizabethtown, the team makes their way to the address of a shoemaker, Peter McLean, who runs a small shop by the waterfront near a market called the Royal Exchange.

When he's not making shoes, McLean operates a lucrative side business. He runs a clandestine ferry service to the *Duchess of Gordon*, delivering goods, spies, recruits, and messages back and forth to Governor Tryon. Tryon pays McLean for the service, and it's up to McLean to avoid the sentries and soldiers from the Continental army.

When the Goshen trio finds McLean at his waterfront shop, Farley does the talking. Unfortunately, the shoemaker has some bad news. As Mason later remembers the conversation, "McLean and Farley whispered together," and then "McLean said there was no opportunity of getting on board in two or three nights."

What are they supposed to do for the two or three nights until they can get on one of the ferries?

McLean recommends they find lodging at nearby Houlding's Tavern, run by a Loyalist named James Houlding. There, they can lie low and be among others sympathetic to their cause. Fittingly enough, the tavern is located very close to one of the main barracks where Continental troops are housed in the city. Even more fittingly, Houlding's is on a small street called Tryon Row, named after the Governor himself.

Farley, Mason, and Benjamin follow the shoemaker's advice and make their way to Houlding's. Sure enough, they are welcomed by the proprietor, James Houlding, after "telling [him that] Mr. McLean had sent and recommended them there as a safe house."

Clearly, there's a secret network in the city who work together on behalf of Governor Tryon—all of them flouting the rules established by the colonial government and the Continental army.

Mason, Farley, and Benjamin will learn more about this network in the coming days, because their stay at Houlding's Tavern lasts longer than expected. Shoemaker McLean continues to have trouble lining up a ferry for them, and after several days, they are still hanging around the tavern.

Despite its proximity to the barracks of the Continental army, Houlding's is a central hub of Loyalist activity in the city. During their time lodging there, the group from Goshen meets an assortment of characters, people of all trades and from all backgrounds, all participating in clandestine operations on behalf of Governor Tryon or other Loyalist operatives. The Goshen men also learn of other taverns, like

Lowry's on Broadway, and Corbie's farther north, where Loyalists meet and confer.

The problem for the Goshen team is that they are running out of money while they await passage. They need to get paid. Until Mason and Benjamin receive their new salaries, and until Farley gets his bounty, they are out of pocket. After complaining of this, they are introduced to someone through Houlding's whom they are told can help.

His name? Gilbert Forbes. The gunsmith.

Forbes, they learn, has recently become something of a ringleader when it comes to recruiting and organizing the men in Governor Tryon's secret army of traitors. Because Mason and Benjamin are having so much trouble gaining passage to the *Duchess*, Forbes says he will swear them in himself, a process called getting "qualified."

Basically, they must participate in a secret initiation in order to join Tryon's scheme.

For this ceremonial swearing-in, Forbes takes Mason and Benjamin to Corbie's, a more isolated tavern than Houlding's, on the northern outskirts of the city. As Mason later describes the initiation, Forbes holds up "the Book"—probably a Bible—and makes him "swear not to divulge anything" to anyone outside their inner circle, and he has to pledge his allegiance to the Crown's forces.

Once Forbes "qualifies" both Mason and Benjamin, he puts their names on a list, which is "to be sent to the Governor." More important for the two newcomers, now that they're qualified, they can start getting paid.

Mason learns that Forbes received a stash of money, rumored to be more than one hundred pounds, from Mayor David Mathews, who himself received it from Governor Tryon. As Mason will later describe it, after his qualification, "Gilbert Forbes promised . . . ten shillings per week subsistence money."

When Mason complained that ten shillings per week was too little, "Forbes said that he could not help it, but he would write to the Governour to try to get it increased to twelve."

After their qualification ritual, Mason and Benjamin continue to wait to go on board the *Duchess of Gordon*, and to receive further instructions from on the ground.

Passage to the ship seems to be forever delayed, so the recruits bide their time on land, mostly hanging around the taverns. There, they continue to hear more about the true scope of the recruiting efforts run by Tryon and carried out by Mayor Mathews and Gilbert Forbes.

For example, Mason meets a fellow new recruit named Clarke, a former schoolmaster also from upstate New York, who says that "he had enlisted about sixty men, of whom he had a list, and who were ready to assist when the troops came." Apparently this list of sixty names "was given to Gilbert Forbes to be sent to the Governour," just as Mason and Benjamin's names had been.

Sixty recruits, from just one region of upstate New York. Those are impressive numbers.

Finally, Mason learns one more remarkable fact about the Governor's recruiting: It's not just millers, laborers, and other ordinary folks. According to what he hears, Governor Tryon—with the help of Mathews and Forbes—has been successfully bribing Continental soldiers to betray their army and join the enemy.

Whatever James Mason may have thought of this scheme when he first learned of it in Goshen, New York, it's clearly bigger and more sprawling than he imagined.

By all appearances, Governor Tryon is planning something truly epic.

No question, James Mason is about to play a major part in Tryon's scheme—but that part will be far from what he expects.

44

—·—

Now that the New York Provincial Congress has formed the secret "Committee on Intestine Enemies," George Washington puts increasing pressure on the congress to take aggressive steps against the plots and conspiracies around New York City.

With Washington's Continental forces already overwhelmed by military preparations, the simultaneous threat of enemies within the colonies is more than the army can withstand. As the Continental army surgeon James Thacher will put it: "Internal secret enemies are always more dangerous than avowed in the field; and so numerous and active are the Tories in the vicinity of our main army, that it has been found necessary to adopt coercive measures."

What should those coercive measures be, exactly? That's what the secret committee must now figure out.

On May 19, the day after the resolution to create the secret committee first passed in the New York Provincial Congress, Washington follows up with another directive: In relation to any activity or measure undertaken by this group, all congressmen with knowledge of it must swear an oath of secrecy.

With these sorts of investigations, the cost of public leaks or information getting into the wrong hands can be ruinous; therefore, secrecy is not just a recommendation, it's mandatory. Any member of the Provincial Congress who violates the oath risks losing their position.

A few days later, on May 21, the congress submits a "Report on Disaffection" to set out some initial findings and help define the mission of the secret committee. First, they acknowledge the problem:

> WHEREAS his Excellency General Washington hath lately exhibited to this Congress sundry informations and evidences, from which it appears that the enemies of American liberty have a general communication with each other through this and part of the neighbouring Colonies;
>
> WHEREAS many ill-disposed persons have lately resorted unto and a great number dwell in Queens County . . . and there are also several ill-disposed persons in the City and County of New York, in Kings County, Richmond County, and in sundry other parts of this Colony, many of whom will most probably take up arms on the part of our foes . . .

Basically, internal enemies are all around. And although the focus of the committee's work is on the colony of New York, and is authorized only by New York's legislative body, the mention of "neighbouring Colonies" makes clear that the committee understands the widespread nature of the Loyalist network. It features interconnected groups operating and communicating across towns, counties, and the entire region. The report also contains the beginning of a mission statement for the new committee:

> WHEREFORE, as well out of regard to the safety of individuals as for the general welfare of America, it is highly and indispensably necessary to take speedy and effectual measures to prevent the hostile intentions of our foes, to stop the channels of intelligence and communication among the disaffected, and to quell the spirit of opposition which hath hitherto prevailed. . . .

In other words, because our enemies are plotting and scheming against us, we need to plot and scheme right back. We need a dedicated team that can uncover the enemies' secret activities, learn their designs, and come up with our own designs to stop them.

First, the committee plans to draw up a list of known persons in every county who are "disaffected." Those persons can now be apprehended.

Second, the committee is authorized to conduct interrogations of any such people suspected of having views "hostile to the United American Colonies."

Third, the committee must operate in complete secrecy to prevent its investigations from leaking to the public or to the enemy.

Fourth, to carry out intelligence missions and to apprehend spies and other dangerous suspects, the committee can request access to Continental soldiers and other resources from the military.

Almost two centuries later, the mission and methods of a group such as this will be given a much fancier name: counterintelligence. The committee's primary goal—to detect enemy espionage activity and take covert action to dismantle it—will be a dedicated field within the realm of intelligence and law enforcement. In the twentieth and twenty-first centuries, advanced counterintelligence teams staffed by highly trained experts will utilize cutting-edge technologies and techniques to uncover even the most sophisticated foreign espionage schemes.

But at this time, in the spring of 1776, the operation is a small group of local elected officials, most with no formal training in spying or military affairs, figuring out a system as they go.

Even so, the committee begins to devise a set of tools and guidelines for how to conduct investigations, how to interrogate suspects, how to maintain secrecy, and how to integrate the role of the military with the role of traditional civilian law enforcement. These same central questions and goals will continue to be the foundation of counterintelligence work even centuries later.

As far as the personnel of this new elite team, the names change several times as the congress figures out the committee's mission and scope. Names are added; names are removed. Within the next few weeks, however, three particular members are added who become critical to the mission of the group.

The first is Philip Livingston, an elder congressman from the legendary Livingston family of New York. The Livingstons have a long tradition of public service and, unlike many other wealthy families in the region who side with the British, the Livingstons have always supported the colonies in their disputes with the Crown. Philip's credentials as a Patriot are impeccable.

The second new key member, Gouverneur Morris,* is a respected lawyer who is also a reliable player in the colony's government. Morris takes one of the harshest lines against Loyalists in New York, showing little mercy for what he believes is their betrayal of the colonies. Interestingly, in private hours, he writes devoted letters to his sister, who is a Loyalist by marriage. Such is the paradoxical nature of the times. Despite this seeming contradiction, Morris is dedicated and exacting in his pursuit of suspected traitors in New York.

Finally, there's John Jay.

Throughout the entire revolutionary era, few men can claim as many titles and will play as many different critical roles as Jay.

In what will be a long and expansive career, Jay somehow always seems to be serving in the most important body, often playing a key role alongside the most important people at almost every critical juncture of the country's founding. Whether as a lawyer, judge, state congressman, delegate to the Continental Congress, future president of Congress, future Governor, future framer of the Constitution, future diplomat, or future first Chief Justice of the U.S. Supreme Court, Jay is always there at the center of things.

However, unlike many of the other Founding Fathers, who adopt public personae and openly seek public influence, John Jay generally prefers to stay behind the scenes. And unlike most of the other Founders, who bicker and feud with one another, Jay mostly stays above the fray and commands almost universal respect.

Of the many areas where Jay will excel in his long and accom-

---

* "Gouverneur" is Morris's actual first name—it's derived from his mother's maiden name—and has nothing to do with the public title "Governor."

John Jay represented New York as a delegate to both the First and Second Continental Congresses. In 1776, he joins a secret committee of the New York Provincial Congress, charged with investigating conspiracies against the Continental army in and around New York City. (*John Jay* by Joseph Wright, 1786; oil on linen, 30 ¼ × 26 inches; negative #6066, New-York Historical society)

plished career, there is one, not always mentioned in history books, in which he shows an early talent as a young man: law enforcement.

He's smart, dedicated, and methodical—with an analytical legal mind and a reputation for integrity. He's the ultimate straight shooter, someone who gets things done and always for the right reasons.

In the spring of 1776, John Jay—thirty years old at the time—is the perfect person to help oversee a first-time American intelligence-gathering and law-enforcement operation in the heart of New York City on the eve of war.

With a mandate from the Commander-in-Chief, a brand-new mission statement, and a talented team at the helm, the newly formed secret committee has an impressive set of tools.

It also starts to use a different name. Instead of the "Committee on Intestine Enemies," it starts to call itself the "Committee on Conspiracies."

Much better.

This elite new top-secret team now has some powerful resources. It will need them all—because in a matter of days, it will embark on a complex, high-stakes investigation that could change the fate of the colonies.

45

———·———

Drinking. Disease. Filth. Prostitutes. Secret plots.

All this, *and* the constant, growing, ominous dread of a coming attack that could annihilate the entire army.

For George Washington, the Commander-in-Chief of the Continental army, his time in New York City must seem like a descent into darkness.

His whole life, Washington has been guided by a sense of honor, and a gentleman's code of virtue. Yet here, in New York City on the verge of war, those values seem to sink into the muck on the streets. His polished Virginia manners and wholesome morals are out of place; they seem woefully inadequate—or at least they do right now. His army seems mired in disorder. They're sick, sullen, and undisciplined.

To survive, Washington can only focus on what he knows.

He knows the fortifications in the city. He knows the redoubts and the barricades, the armaments and the artillery. He knows his officers and his regiments, his arms and his supplies. He can focus on the endless specific concrete tasks that lie before him, and before his men, to prepare for war. He can work, work, work tirelessly, endlessly, and push everyone around him to work as hard or almost as hard as he does.

He knows what he believes: that the "Glorious Cause" is just; that he is fighting for noble ideals; that the people of the colonies have placed their trust in him, and that honor demands he shoulder the extraordinary burden of leadership with every ounce of his will.

Those are all things he knows. But then there are things he doesn't know.

The deception, the disloyalty. The clandestine plots and schemes. The hidden dangers, emanating not from his military foe across the ocean, but from enemies right here, all around him, sometimes in the shadows, sometimes in disguise.

So much of it seems to come from one place—that dark ship, the *Duchess of Gordon*—where Governor Tryon resides. Or at least, so much of it *seems* to come from there, part of a shadowy, unknowable web.

When it comes to all the confusing enemy plots circulating around his army, Washington describes them this way: "The encouragements given by Governor Tryon to the disaffected, which are circulated no one can well tell how; the movements of this kind of people, which are more easy to perceive than describe."

It's these mysterious movements—"more easy to perceive than describe"—that seem to surround the city, that create a constant feeling of uncertainty and menace.

Washington can read the reports, he can study the intelligence. He can review the interrogations, he can intercept correspondence, he can gather facts and confer with his new top-secret committee.

But even so, there are things that George Washington doesn't know—things almost impossible to imagine.

On many nights, Washington and his men travel at sundown from his headquarters at One Broadway, in the heart of the busy southern tip of the city, to his quiet secondary quarters in the woods near the Hudson, almost two miles to the northwest.

Along this route from city into country, Washington probably doesn't even notice that he passes close to a tavern called Corbie's. The tavern isn't far from the manor house where he sleeps. In fact, it's close enough that Washington's staff and personal guards from the residence could walk to Corbie's if they wanted.

Washington doesn't know that one night in late spring, in the last days of May or the first days of June, two men at Corbie's begin a conversation. Their mugs are full. The proprietor of the tavern, Mr. Corbie himself, is probably nearby, serving other customers ale or rum.

The two men speak quietly, in hushed, serious tones.

One of the two is the gunsmith Gilbert Forbes. He has in his possession, either at home or with him that night, a stack of money given to him by the Governor, William Tryon, by way of the Mayor, David Mathews.

The other man is a soldier. Other patrons in the tavern wouldn't know this because tonight he wears civilian clothes.

He's no ordinary soldier, as he has explained to Forbes.

He has special responsibilities and serves George Washington directly. In fact, he is sometimes in close personal proximity to Washington, meant to protect him.

He's a member of the Life Guards.

Gilbert Forbes and the soldier continue to talk in hushed tones, as if everything they say is a closely guarded secret. By the end, they seem to be in agreement, as if they've made a deal.

Then, the two men raise their mugs.

They raise their mugs—and drink to the King.

PART IV

A Most Infernal Plot

46

New York, New York

May 1776

For the men of the counterfeiting operation based in Cold Spring Harbor, Long Island, the month of May 1776 starts badly—and ends worse.

After the surprise raid on the home of the Young brothers on Sunday, May 12, the four men involved in the operation—Henry Dawkins, Isaac Young, Israel Young, and Isaac Ketcham—are arrested and taken to New York City.

They spend the night of Monday, May 13, in New York City's central prison, literally underneath City Hall, awaiting their turn to testify before the New York Provincial Congress the following day.

Just as planned, on the morning of Tuesday, May 14, the suspects are marched upstairs to appear before the congress and tell their stories. The congressmen also summon Capt. Jeremiah Wool, the militia officer who led the raid on the Youngs' home, to provide his first-hand account of the mission.

The first to testify is Captain Wool. Based on the careful records he maintained of the operation, Wool lays out a detailed and precise step-by-step account of his journey to Long Island, his raid, his discovery of the printing press in the attic, and the subsequent apprehension of the other members of the team in Cold Spring Harbor and

Huntington, Long Island. He also presents the physical evidence obtained from the Youngs' house, including the various plates, inks, and forged bills found in dresser drawers and chests.

Together with the original witness testimony from the neighbors who suspected criminal activity and reported it to authorities, the account and evidence provided by Jeremiah Wool make quite a convincing case.

Next, the congress begins to question the suspects themselves.

By any measure, the testimony from the alleged counterfeiters is, at least for the counterfeiters themselves, a total disaster.

The authorities had wisely kept the four suspects—Dawkins, Young, Young, and Ketcham—separated from one another in the days prior to their testimony. They had no chance to get their stories straight or come up with any coherent explanation or alibi for the evidence against them.

Instead they tell wildly contradictory stories of what transpired in the Young brothers' Cold Spring Harbor home during the preceding months, and how it came to be that a printing press surrounded by fake currency ended up in their attic. None of the suspects' accounts matches another, which makes it clear to everyone listening that all of them, in fact, are lying through their teeth.

For the most part, each suspect adopts the strategy of claiming that someone *else* in the group is the criminal mastermind, and that he who is testifying has played only a small, reluctant, or ignorant role in the matter.

According to Henry Dawkins, it is the older brother, Israel Young, who is the clear leader and instigator of the group. The scheme began back in December when Dawkins was imprisoned, and "Israel Young frequently came to visit him." Dawkins testifies that Young took a great interest in his line of work, loaned him some money, and soon encouraged him to board with the Young brothers on Long Island. Dawkins agreed to help Young buy a printing press, but didn't know the purpose.

Then Dawkins says that "after he . . . had been a day or two at Cold Spring, the said Israel Young showed him a large bundle of money, and took out of it a Connecticut bill of forty Shillings, and asked if he . . . could imitate that for him."

So it was Young who instigated the counterfeiting, urged Dawkins into it, and "requested him to do it immediately." Furthermore, "Israel Young told [him] that he would reward him generously, and that he should never want."

As a final note to his testimony, Dawkins says that while he did follow Israel Young's instructions and engraved some plates that could produce fake currency, Dawkins himself never actually ran the press to make any bills. He instructed Young how to use the press, and "showed him how to press the bills and make them; that any others that have been pressed and made were made by Israel Young, or some of the others concerned."

So, in summary, Dawkins was a mostly unwitting accomplice to any counterfeiting, and only engraved a few plates that Israel Young then used for his own purposes.

When Israel Young testifies, he tells a very different story.

The elder brother states flat-out that "he never had any hand in counterfeiting money." He says that he only reluctantly allowed Dawkins to lodge at his home, and that he never loaned him any money.

Young further claims he was unaware what Dawkins was doing with the printing press in the attic, and knows nothing about engraving plates to print fake currency. He adds "that he does not know that Dawkins cut any plates while he was there" and that he, Israel Young, "never applied to any person to cut any plates for him to print or impress money." He did, at one point, suspect that Henry Dawkins might be up to something because he once found a mysterious forty-shilling note in Dawkins's bedchamber, but that "he never asked Dawkins any questions about it."

In other words, according to Israel Young, Henry Dawkins was running a one-man counterfeiting operation in the Youngs' attic, and the brothers were merely oblivious landlords.

Israel's younger brother, Isaac, largely backs up his brother's contention that Dawkins was the sole mastermind of the scheme. He says that "he did not know that Henry Dawkins was engraving plates to print money" and that "he once saw Henry Dawkins rubbing a copperplate, but did not know what it was for." He then makes the somewhat remarkable claim that he personally didn't even know the printing press was in the attic until Captain Wool discovered it during the raid.

Isaac also says that when he started to suspect that maybe Dawkins was printing something that looked like fake money, he spoke to his brother about it, and they agreed that if Dawkins was indeed counterfeiting money, they would "not have any hand in it" because "it was a sin."

Theological considerations aside, the brothers' alibi that they lived in the house for two months with Dawkins and had no idea that he was counterfeiting money in their attic is basically impossible to believe—and fails to account for the fact that Captain Wool and his team found sample fake bills, plates, and ink in almost every drawer and cupboard in the Youngs' home.

When all is said and done, the congressmen come to the only rational conclusion. The team was all in it together, and the idea that anyone in the house didn't participate was ridiculous.

Their guilt firmly established, the team is sent back down to the prison to await their sentence.

There's only one question: What about the fourth conspirator, the neighbor Isaac Ketcham?

Ketcham, it turns out, is the only one of them who tells the full truth in City Hall that day. He admits that he knew that Dawkins and the Youngs were trying to forge currency, and that he had accepted their mission to try to find the right paper stock.

As he puts it, he "had not been concerned in making the money, but that he was taken into the business to provide them with paper." He explains that his one excursion to Philadelphia was a failure, and that he had nothing else to do with any of it.

Truthful as Ketcham's testimony may be, after hearing so much nonsense from the others, the congressmen don't seem eager to parse the truth from the fourth member of the team. Nor are they inclined to consider that his role in the affair was relatively small. To the congress, they all seem like a band of liars and crooks, and so Ketcham is thrown back into jail with the other three.

At this moment, Isaac Ketcham must seriously wonder if he will ever see his children again.

Unbeknownst to Ketcham, however, he is about to receive some help from a most unexpected source.

47

New York, New York

June 1776

The Life Guards.

They're George Washington's elite unit. His trusted bodyguards. The most disciplined men. The best-trained soldiers.

In an army otherwise made up mostly of untrained neophytes, hayseeds, and former criminals, the Life Guards are supposed to be a beacon of excellence and the pride of the service.

Much remains unknown about the Life Guards' personnel and their whereabouts in New York City in the spring and early summer of 1776. And there are surprisingly few records maintained of their daily work. The names of many soldiers who served in the earliest version of this elite squadron have been lost to history, casualties of scattered record keeping or documents later destroyed.

Also, the Life Guards' precise duties were often kept secret or only spoken verbally, given their frequent proximity to the Commander-in-Chief and his innermost circle of advisers. The Life Guards' daily assignments were apparently not meant for the rank and file to know, let alone be put in a written form that could leak to the public or the enemy.

Still, through the haze of secrecy and the passage of time, records remain of at least some of their names and occasional evidence of their whereabouts in the early summer of 1776.

One group of the guards in particular is known to hang around as a sort of posse, both on and off duty. Of the roughly fifty guards total, this little group of a half dozen is often seen together, socializing or walking the streets, getting to know their new city just as the other soldiers and officers do when they're not on the clock.

Who exactly are the members of this group?

There's William Green, a drummer, and supposedly something of a leader among them; James Johnson, a fifer, who is often seen alongside Green; and Michael Lynch, a private of unknown origin. There's a young soldier named John Barnes, originally from Massachusetts. And finally, there's Thomas Hickey, who first joined the guards as a private, but soon became a sergeant. Hickey, originally from Ireland, is described in one record as "five feet six inches high, and well-set," and also "dark-complexioned."

Only two years earlier, Hickey was a soldier in the British army, stationed in Connecticut. As hostilities mounted between the colonies and the British, Hickey deserted the British army and joined the Continental side. This phenomenon was far from unique; in fact, the superior skill and training of former British soldiers made them valuable recruits for colonial militias and the Continental army. Perhaps because of his prior military experience, Hickey is described as "a favorite" of Washington's.

It is hard to know exactly when and how it came to be that in the early summer of 1776, this group of Life Guards—Green, Barnes, Lynch, Johnson, Hickey, and a few others—began to drift away from the course of duty.

Surely the taverns have something to do with it. Both in and out of uniform, these soldiers are seen frequenting some of the less reputable beer halls and public houses in the city, mixing and crossing paths with questionable characters.

In these taverns, there is naturally a lot of drinking. Even more dangerous, there is a lot of talking. Some of the Life Guards, it seems, begin to talk too much. They complain about the Continental army, speak ill of it, sometimes even *curse* it—and do so loudly enough that other patrons notice.

To be sure, low morale is a problem throughout the whole army during this period in New York. The reasons, by this point, are obvious: poor conditions, bad food, shortage of supplies and weapons, and lack of good officers. There is endless frustration about the low pay, and even more so, about not getting paid on time or at all.

The soldiers suffer from dysentery, "camp fever," syphilis, and smallpox. Men who originally signed up to fight instead find themselves doing hard labor, spending hours, days, weeks, and months in the mud or dust, digging ditches and building fortifications. Remarkably, by the end of May 1776, the Continental army under Washington's personal command has been in existence for eleven months and still hasn't fought a proper battle.

Beyond all these complaints, there is also the growing awareness that when these soldiers do fight their first real battle—right here in New York—they may be in for a catastrophic defeat. Even the greenest new recruits soon gain an understanding of the stakes of the war, and it doesn't take much military knowledge to grasp that the small Continental army is badly outmatched trying to protect a skinny island against a coming assault from the world's largest navy.

Some of the soldiers are mostly immune to this fear. These are the men who joined to fight out of pure patriotic zeal, and for the noble ideal of liberty. These are the ones truly intoxicated by the spirit of the "Glorious Cause." For these men, the mix of long hours and long odds are not a deterrent.

For many others, however, concerned with more pedestrian matters like bad pay, bad conditions, and the likelihood of being slaughtered, a forbidden but practical question quickly arises: Is it possible they're fighting for the wrong side?

Of course, the Life Guards, the supposed paragons of duty and discipline in the Continental army, should be the last ones ever to ask this question.

And yet, some do. One or two of them—among those in this

group comprising Green, Barnes, Lynch, Johnson, and Hickey—don't just ask it, but do so publicly, in the taverns.

It seems to begin with the drummer, William Green. One night in the first week of June 1776, Green is at a tavern while off duty. He is drinking—and perhaps talking too loudly.

Another man at the tavern, a stranger, takes an interest in Green, and the two of them start drinking together. Soon, they fall into a "conversation on politicks."

The stranger is short, with a stocky build. He describes himself as a gunsmith who runs a shop on Broadway.

His name, he says, is Gilbert Forbes.

Whatever they discuss regarding the issues of the day, they seem to be in agreement, because after this first conversation, they find one another to talk some more. The conversation always turns to a consistent theme: the inferiority of the Continental army and the likelihood of British victory. As Green later describes it, "I had repeated conversations with Forbes afterwards, and he was always introducing politicks, and hinting at the impossibility of this country standing against the power of Great Britain."

Forbes seems to enjoy their conversations. Then, as Green later remembers, "He invited me to dine with him one day."

That's how Gilbert Forbes would end up at the tavern called Corbie's, seated at a table with one of George Washington's Life Guards, speaking softly.

By the time their dinner is over, the two men have made a deal.

48

---•---

New York, New York

June 1776

William Leary is coming to New York City, and he's on a mission.

He's been sent by his boss—Robert Erskine, who runs the Ringwood Ironworks iron mill in Goshen, New York—to track down some millworkers who have recently fled their work. In particular, he's after a laborer named William Benjamin, who just left the mill a week or so ago and hasn't been seen in Goshen since.

Why go to so much trouble to track down a missing laborer or two?

Erskine, who runs the mill, is a Patriot. So when rumors begin to circulate that some workers at his mill are leaving Goshen to join a treasonous British plot against the Continental army, Erskine isn't about to stand by.

That's why he sends his foreman, William Leary, to personally chase down a few recently departed workers—including Benjamin—and to find out more about this supposed plot. Leary, after asking around and following Benjamin's trail, has traced him to New York City.

Now, at roughly ten in the morning, Monday, June 3, Leary arrives in Manhattan in search of his man.

Under his belt, Leary carries two loaded pistols. Just in case.

Based on leads he acquired along the way, Leary ends up at an address on Broadway, where Benjamin is rumored to be staying. Across the street, on the other side of Broadway, is a sign for Hull's Tavern.

When Leary enters the address, sure enough, there's William Benjamin, the laborer who ran away from Erskine's mill. He must be startled to see his former foreman walk in the door.

What happens next happens fast.

Leary makes a grab for Benjamin—but it turns out that Benjamin isn't alone. A man whose name Leary remembers as "Forbes," who owns the residence where Benjamin is boarding, is also present. As Leary later recounts it, "Forbes ran and got a pistol for Benjamin to defend himself." Benjamin, now wielding a loaded weapon, prepares to do so—but Leary still comes after him. A struggle ensues, and Leary takes "hold of Benjamin and prevent[s] him from using the said pistol."

During the scuffle, Forbes disappears.

Still, Leary has found the man he was originally looking for, and is ready to report him to the authorities. He drags Benjamin out of Forbes's residence, and escorts him by force from Broadway toward the Hudson River. Here, at a dock for ferries bound for New Jersey, he finds a few militia officers to whom he can hand over the prisoner to be detained.

Although Leary has found his main target, his work in Manhattan is not done.

Soon, either from asking around or possibly just by hanging around the taverns near Forbes's place, Leary encounters another familiar face from Goshen: James Mason, a part-time miller who was also briefly employed at Ringwood.

With Mason, Leary takes a different approach. Rather than simply seize Mason, he decides to learn as much as he can about this secret network of apparent traitors with whom his former co-workers have joined forces.

When he approaches James Mason, Leary presents himself as a friend—a friend who is also possibly interested in joining the ranks of exiled traitors. While chatting with him, Leary wonders to Mason if he knows of any other former workers from the mill who are also among the disaffected here in New York City.

Sure enough, Mason knows of three other former mill workers from Goshen who have also taken up with the enemy. Leary asks if he can see them. Mason replies that Leary "might see them if he would take an oath that he did not come to take them up."

Leary carefully declines to take any oath, but claims that he, too, has left the mill and wants to get paid to join the British, as the others supposedly have.

At first, Mason isn't sure whether to trust Leary and tells him that he must "do as he and the rest of them had done," which is to "go and be qualified." When Leary asks him what that means, Mason explains: "Swearing before a gentleman in this town" who is "employed by the Mayor or Governor."

Leary, who is learning more by the second, eventually agrees to be "qualified," and that seems to gain Mason's confidence. Soon Mason brings him to an apartment where three other former mill workers from Goshen are lodging. Like Mason, all have agreed to join the British in exchange for land and money, and all of them have been "qualified" by swearing an oath.

Thus far, Leary's mission to New York City has been quite fruitful. He's rounded up William Benjamin, gained valuable information from James Mason, and just been introduced to three other former workers from the Ringwood mill who have all taken bribes and sworn oaths to betray the colonies and fight on the British side.

But how can he detain these men when it's three against one?

The best plan he can come up with, thinking on his feet, is to chat with them for a while to gain their confidence, then encourage all of them to go for a drink at a tavern. While he walks with them up Broadway, his plan is to lead them casually in the direction of a group of Continental soldiers, "intending to decoy them thither, and have them apprehended."

It's not a bad plan at first. The group walks about "halfway up Broadway," with Leary leading them toward where he knows some soldiers will be on patrol. But then, while the group is walking, one of the men notices that Leary is carrying something unusual under his belt.

Guns.

The three men immediately stop in their tracks. As Leary puts it, "They discovered [my] pistols, and would have fled, thinking . . . that [I] meant to take them up."

Leary tries to explain that the pistols are simply "for his defense" until he can join in their plot, but the men no longer trust him. Moments later, they run off.

William Leary, sent from Goshen, New York on a traitor-hunting mission, may not have been able to apprehend the final trio he encountered. Still, he has successfully tracked down his main target and he learned a lot in a short time about a treasonous scheme—apparently connected to the Governor and the Mayor—to lure men of the colonies to join the British army. He can report all of this to his boss, the patriotic mill owner, Robert Erskine.

This information will be more valuable than William Leary can possibly know.

49

On June 6, 1776, George Washington returns to New York after a two-week trip to confer with the Continental Congress in Philadelphia.

In Philadelphia, John Hancock, John Adams, and several dozen other delegates met with him to discuss every facet of the war plan, trying eagerly to grasp the colonies' prospects for the coming British offensive in New York City.

After this exhausting trip, Washington no doubt feels the familiar pressure: All these politicians, almost none of them with any military experience, are relying on *him* and his ill-equipped army to somehow succeed against the greatest military force in the world. They're relying on *him* to provide hope and inspire confidence despite the staggering odds.

At the time of Washington's return, reports confirm that the British fleet has officially departed from Halifax, Nova Scotia, and is sailing toward them. Many more vessels are en route from England, including the Hessian reinforcements. The latest intelligence suggests that the first arrival of the fleet could be as soon as two weeks.

Now back at his headquarters, Washington throws himself into the many endless tasks and responsibilities associated with the defense of the city. He personally visits and inspects the forts, barricades, and brigades spread all over Manhattan, western Long Island, and eastern New Jersey. A steady stream of messages and instructions flow to and from his headquarters about weapons, gunpowder, provisions, transportation, housing, logistics, training, battle plans, and chain of command.

All the while, Washington remains preoccupied by the continued threat of "intestine enemies" trying to organize against him and subvert his fragile army.

Before he left for Philadelphia, Washington had provided instructions to his top generals—specifically, Nathanael Greene, stationed on Long Island, and Israel Putnam, Washington's second-in-command in New York City—to pursue aggressive action against the Loyalist plotters, particularly those rumored to be organizing on Long Island.

He encouraged them to consult with the new secret committee of the New York Provincial Congress—the Committee on Conspiracies—to round up suspects and help make arrests.

Upon his return, he is disappointed to learn that little has actually been done on this front. The threat persists, no matter how hard he tries to combat it.

On June 10, 1776, four days after his return, Washington writes to John Hancock about this lingering fear:

> I had no doubt when I left this city for Philadelphia but that some measures would have been taken to secure the suspected and dangerous persons of this Government before now, and left orders for the military to give every aid to the civil power; but the subject is delicate, and nothing is done in it; we may therefore have internal as well as external enemies to contend with.

Washington is right to worry. The plots against him are growing deeper and wider. It's not just the Loyalists on Long Island or upstate New York who have fallen in with Governor Tryon's scheme.

Internal enemies.

They're in Manhattan now, much closer to him than he thinks.

His enemies are with him at his downtown headquarters—and even near where he sleeps at night.

In fact, though Washington doesn't know it yet, Tryon's plot has infiltrated his own army, reaching those in whom the general has placed his greatest trust.

50

———·———

The secret committee.

Aka the "Committee on Intestine Enemies"

Aka the "Committee on Conspiracies."

The name has changed a few times, but the mission of this elite new team has crystallized: uncover and investigate plots, conspiracies, and espionage efforts waged against the colonies and/or the Continental army.

Originating with an idea from George Washington, and comprised of carefully selected members of New York's Provincial Congress, this committee is a dedicated intelligence and counterintelligence unit—and one without precedent in the history of the colonies.

Based on the many reports and rumors of Loyalist plots circulating in and around New York City, the focus of the group is on "internal enemies"—that is, spies, traitors, and schemers operating within the colonies, undermining the war effort against Great Britain.

In early June, the congress drafts a series of resolutions establishing the methods and guidelines for the committee.

They have authority to arrest suspected persons, based on their own warrants.

They can detain and interrogate these suspects, as needed.

They have a dedicated budget.

They will share intelligence directly with the Commander-in-Chief.

With George Washington's permission, they have access to Continental soldiers to conduct raids or track down dangerous suspects.

Above all else: They must operate in total secrecy.

On Thursday, June 13, the congress also formally appoints to the committee the thirty-year-old lawyer and former delegate to the Continental Congress, John Jay. Soon, he will take a leadership role, guiding the committee through extraordinary circumstances. For now, he is one of nine members tasked to undertake something none of them has ever done before.

The next day, Friday, June 14, Jay is among the new members to swear a ceremonial oath before the New York Provincial Congress, an oath crafted specially for this unusual committee. One by one, each of them walks to the front of the City Hall chamber and swears on a Bible to "diligently, impartially, without fear, favor, affection, or hope of reward, to execute and discharge the duties imposed on them."

In the previous two weeks, while the first resolutions were being debated and finalized, the committee had already started planning its work. Among the first tasks was to draw up a "List of Suspected Persons" on whom the committee can focus its efforts.

Divided by region, the list includes every person in the colony of New York, from any station of life, who is known or suspected of bearing traitorous designs against the colonies. The committee members have assembled these names—a few hundred of them, and growing—from the past few months of reports, rumors, and information about Loyalist plots in the region. The list will form the basis of where the committee will direct its resources and efforts.

Whose name is first on the list? The most obvious: "William Tryon, on board the Ship of War *Duchess of Gordon*."

The committeemen clearly believe Tryon to be the mastermind of some or all of the plots uncovered thus far, and consider him a profound threat. There is nothing they can do to actually arrest or apprehend Tryon—he is totally unreachable on the *Duchess of Gordon*—but nonetheless the Governor looms large over the committee's mission.

Another name near the top of the list is that of New York City's Mayor, David Mathews. Interestingly, before this point the colonial authorities had so far focused little attention on Mathews, despite his known loyalty to Tryon. Perhaps this is because Mayor Mathews has kept a low profile in the city, spending much of his time at his home in Flatbush, across the East River in Kings County. In any case, by including Mathews's name on the list, the committee now acknowledges him as a potential enemy.

Filled with these and other prominent officials, the list goes on with scores of other names, divided geographically. There are "suspected persons" listed from New York City, Kings County, Queens County, Nassau County, Westchester County, Dutchess County, and other areas of the colony.

The "List of Suspected Persons" will provide a starting point for the secret committee's work. The members can make arrests, conduct raids, interrogate suspects, gather intelligence, and unmask spies and traitors.

Whatever plots are rife around the city, the secret committee will seek to uncover and stop them.

The problem is, it may already be too late.

51

The four Long Island counterfeiters spend the last weeks of May and the first weeks of June primarily in one place: a prison.

For almost four weeks now, they've been held at the underground jail beneath City Hall in lower Manhattan, awaiting resolution to their case. Had the congress deemed them innocent, they would have been released quickly in order to free up space. The fact that they are still in prison suggests a guilty determination is pending, and they are in line to hear their sentence and fate.

With the city on the verge of battle, and with colonial authorities preoccupied by matters of war, the four Long Islanders must surely fear that their case may be forgotten or delayed indefinitely, leaving them in a jail cell alongside hundreds of other forgotten prisoners while war rages above them. What will happen to them if the British take the city while they are still locked up? It's impossible to know.

The group's desperation is such that on at least one occasion in late May, some or all of the foursome try to plan a jailbreak. The specific details aren't known, but on May 28—almost two weeks after their disastrous testimony and subsequent confinement—the Provincial Congress receives a report from the prison that "the persons under guard, charged with counterfeiting Continental and Provincial money, were not properly attended to by some of the guards, and that there is great danger of an escape."

As a result, the Provincial Congress issues the following directive, highly unwelcome to the four prisoners:

> *WHEREAS* it has been represented to this Congress that Israel Young, Isaac Young, Henry Dawkins and Isaac Ketcham, committed to the custody of guards . . . on suspicion of counterfeiting the Continental money . . . are mediating their escape . . . *Ordered*, that the said persons be forthwith put in irons and kept in the place where they now are, and that the guards be directed not to permit any person to have access to them, without license from this Congress.

So now, after whatever escape they attempted or were thought to be attempting, the four counterfeiters are denied any visitors and, even worse, put in painful leg irons within their cells. With chains affixed to the wall, these thick metal shackles on both of a prisoner's legs hinder most movement and often lead to terrible sores, bruises, cramps, and permanent muscle damage.

Although the four suspects were probably initially jailed together, as weeks pass, they are each moved around and reshuffled to different cells in the busy prison, sharing cells with other inmates.

A few other details of the prisoners' confinement are also on the record. On May 30, two days after the foursome is put in irons, the congress receives a petition from Israel Young's wife to visit him in the jail, which it grants on condition that the visit is monitored.

Two days after that, on June 1, authorities apprehend Israel and Isaac's younger brother, Philip Young, and jail him too, on suspicion of also being involved in the counterfeiting operation. After questioning Philip, and after receiving several written petitions arguing for the younger brother's innocence—including one from Dawkins and one from the Youngs' grief-stricken father—the congress releases

Philip, satisfied that he was never involved in the older brothers' criminal scheme.

As the days pass in early June, the prisoners' circumstances appear downright grim. On Friday, June 7, three weeks since the four counterfeiters were first imprisoned, jail guards report to their superiors that Henry Dawkins "is injured by the leg irons, so that his legs swell."

The guards remove Dawkins's irons temporarily. The next day, a sister of Israel and Isaac Young petitions to visit her brothers in jail, expressing fear that she may never see them again. The congress once again allows a brief, monitored visit.

Each of the would-be counterfeiters is no doubt suffering in his own way, but perhaps none of them is as full of regret over their situation as the group's brief accomplice, Isaac Ketcham.

Based on one aborted mission to buy paper stock for the team, he has been seemingly lumped in with the others and is now stuck in irons in the same crowded, filthy prison. From this terrible circumstance, his mind goes again and again to the same place: his children.

Isaac Ketcham has six children back home on Long Island. Their mother is dead. With Ketcham in jail, the children are alone, fending for themselves. Because of Ketcham's one trip to Philadelphia, during which he only halfheartedly pursued the paper that the counterfeiters asked him to find, his children have no one to feed, clothe, or care for them.

Desperate to plead his case, on June 9, Ketcham writes a petition from his cell, proclaiming his profound regret for his minor role in the counterfeiting scheme. He says that he is "deeply impressed with shame and confusion for his past misconduct," and now "most humbly begs to lay his unhappy case before this honourable House."

He also appeals to the congress to take pity, if not on him, then on his little ones. "Your Petitioner further implores the consideration of this House in behalf of six poor children, who are now lamenting the loss of a tender mother and the imprisonment of a father."

He writes that some of his children are "dangerously ill by sore sickness, without any person to attend or comfort them," and asks if he "could be permitted to go to them for a few days, in order to provide some proper persons to attend on them."

Initially, Ketcham's letter doesn't appear to go anywhere. A full week after Ketcham writes it, the congress doesn't seem to have received it, nor is it acknowledged anywhere else. Probably, the jail authorities didn't even consider it worth sending upstairs to the congressmen.

Such are Isaac Ketcham's seemingly hopeless circumstances on the night of Saturday, June 15, when his cell door opens and two new prisoners are escorted in.

These two additions to Ketcham's cell are loud and argumentative. One of them speaks with an Irish accent.

Normally, Ketcham probably wouldn't care who his new jailmates are, or what they have to say. But soon, Ketcham learns that he shares something in common with them: They too have been arrested in relation to counterfeiting. It has nothing to do with the Long Island operation; these two men had obtained some counterfeit bills from some other place, and authorities caught them trying to buy goods with them.

Perhaps because of this commonality, Ketcham and the two prisoners engage in conversation.

Here's where things get interesting.

With the guards out of earshot, the new prisoners start cursing the colonies and swearing their support for Great Britain and the King. This alone is not so surprising—in fact, the New York prisons are full of Loyalists who are jailed specifically for supporting the Crown at a time of war.

It's what Ketcham hears next that makes him really take notice. These prisoners say they are actually soldiers in the Continental army.

If they're Continental soldiers, why are they cursing the rebellion and praising the King?

As the two new prisoners continue talking, Ketcham keeps listening, learning more.

He's stunned by what he hears. He does what he can to keep them talking. To gain their confidence, he tells them that he too is loyal to the King.

Then something dawns on Isaac Ketcham. He's gaining information that could be of great importance. Not so much to him, but to the authorities in New York. Maybe even to the Continental Congress.

By the next morning, once he has a moment to himself, Ketcham starts to write another letter.

Maybe, just maybe, his luck has finally changed.

52

---•---

It's another busy day.

On Monday, June 17, 1776, twenty-six members of the New York Provincial Congress, representing every county in the colony, meet for a regular morning session at City Hall in New York City.

The previous day, June 16, the members had a rare day off, and now the congressmen are prepared for a full docket. These days, *every* day has a full docket. With the city preparing for war, the colony's governing bodies are slammed morning to night, trying to manage the many logistical, legal, military, and criminal matters put before them.

The president of the congress, Nathaniel Woodhull of Ulster County, brings the body to session at 9:00 a.m. sharp, and they get right into it.

The first matter on the day's docket is fairly routine: the swearing in of a new delegate from Cumberland County, recently selected to fill an opening in the congress after a vote in that county.

The second matter is not as routine, but typical of the heated times in which they govern. The body must consider a recently published political handbill, signed by and rumored to have been written by one of its own members, John Morin Scott, who is not present that day.

After the handbill is read aloud, the members must decide whether these political opinions reflect on the "honor and impartiality" of the Congress. The body resolves first to verify whether the author is indeed Congressman Scott, and a messenger is sent to find him and obtain an answer. While they wait, they move on to the next item.

The next matter on the agenda, brought up midway through the morning session, is fairly minor—or at least it seems that way at first.

It's a written petition from a prisoner—a prisoner named Isaac Ketcham—currently being held in the city jail, asking for leniency.

Most of the congressmen probably don't recall the name, and need to be reminded. Ketcham is one of the Long Island counterfeiters, the foursome that they interrogated and put in prison a month ago for trying to forge Continental currency.

For the congress, hearing petitions from prisoners is fairly common business, so there is no reason to think this will be anything out of the ordinary.

The secretary reads aloud two letters written by Ketcham from jail, making appeals to the congress. The first is the letter, written more than a week ago on June 9, in which Ketcham pleads for mercy based on his genuine remorse for his participation in the scheme. Ketcham also pleads on behalf of his six children, some of them sick, who have no mother and who depend on him for care. He asks, at least, if he can go and visit them.

Whether the members of the New York Congress are moved by Ketcham's appeal to his children's welfare is not known. The body never records a response either way. Perhaps, because they receive such petitions all the time from prisoners around the colony, they simply ignore the request or file it away.

However, there is also a second note from Ketcham, shared by the committee secretary right after the first, that is less typical. It's a brief sentence, written by Ketcham from his cell yesterday, June 16, and addressed to the congress.

"I . . . have something to observe to the honourable House if I could be admitted. It is nothing concerning my own affair, but entirely on another subject. From yours to serve, Isaac Ketcham."

Ketcham is requesting a personal audience with the congress, implying that he has important information to share with them, unrelated to his own case.

Upon hearing Ketcham's cryptic request, the congress decides to hear whatever story the prisoner has to tell. The body gives these instructions to the city guards: "*Ordered*, that the officer commanding the guard at the City Hall be requested to bring Isaac Ketcham before this Congress with all convenient speed, and for that purpose that he cause all fetters and irons to be taken off from the said Isaac Ketcham."

This won't take long. The prison where Ketcham is being held is right beneath City Hall where the congress is in session. So, sometime close to eleven that morning, the head of the guard walks down to the crowded jail where Ketcham is shackled and orders his release from the irons and chains. Guards personally escort the prisoner to the chamber in City Hall where the Provincial Congress sits.

For the past month, Isaac Ketcham has been in a dark, miserable jail, awaiting a sentence for a crime in which he barely took part—and for which he believes he has already atoned.

In this climate of coming war, when the very fate of the city and the colony is uncertain, Ketcham knows that this may be his only opportunity to save himself.

He hopes that the story he's about to share can somehow be his ticket out of prison—and allow him to see his children once again.

53

It may be Isaac Ketcham's last chance at freedom.

This fact must weigh heavily on Ketcham's mind as city guards escort him upstairs into City Hall on the morning of Monday, June 17, 1776.

Like everyone who testifies before the New York Provincial Congress, Isaac Ketcham must first swear an oath to speak only the truth.

With Ketcham now sworn and standing before them, the congressmen want to know: What story does the prisoner have to share, that is worth taking the congress's valuable time as the colony prepares for war?

Ketcham answers: It has to do with two new prisoners who just joined his cell in the underground jail right below them. Ketcham overheard them speaking, and then joined in conversation with them.

They were Continental soldiers.

They were talking about a secret plot.

The plot is based on some sort of communication with the British ships anchored in the harbor. This would naturally include the *Duchess of Gordon*, where Governor William Tryon is headquartered.

If the congressmen weren't listening at first, they're listening now.

The plot involves officials on the boats enlisting men from the colonies to betray their country, with some sort of plan to raise arms against the Continental army just as the British military forces arrive in New York. The ringleaders on the ships are offering "free pardon for all those who would come over" and a "considerable encouragement as to land and houses."

What else did Ketcham hear?

He heard the two soldiers say that a blacksmith in the city is a key ringleader in the plot. Ketcham recalls the blacksmith's first name as Gilbert—and the last name sounds something like "Horbush."

Does he recall any more specific details of the plot?

He remembers them talking about a plan for some of the conspirators to destroy King's Bridge, the main bridge out of Manhattan to the mainland, in order to block the Continental army's flow of supplies.

But the most shocking part is simply this: These two jailed Continental soldiers don't just know about this plot—they're *in on it*.

A secret plot. William Tryon. Traitors in the army. The story is shocking. Horrifying, in fact.

Could Ketcham just be making it up?

The congressmen can't know for sure based only on Ketcham's verbal testimony. There is a brief hint in the congressional records that Ketcham also provides some physical evidence that morning—a "piece of paper," the transcripts indicate—to support his story. This piece of paper was not saved and no longer exists, but based on the brief mention it seems to have been a written list of conspirators that the prisoners "showed and gave to" Ketcham in the cell, and which he presented to the Congress. This piece of paper is never listed again, so it is impossible to know what the congressmen thought of it.

Regardless of this piece of paper, there are other reasons for the Congress to take Ketcham's story seriously.

For starters, the congressmen know that at least part of his story checks out. Only the day before, two Continental soldiers had indeed been arrested, and the case had been brought before the Congress. The soldiers were charged with carrying counterfeit bills in the city, unrelated to the Long Island counterfeiting scheme.

Lots of fake money has been floating around the city from a number of sources, and the authorities have been punishing anyone carrying it. When the congress discussed the case, they resolved to send the two soldiers back to the army to receive proper military discipline. In the meantime, the soldiers are indeed held in the prison beneath City Hall, in the same space where Ketcham is detained.

So that part of Ketcham's story is plausible.

But there's something even more troubling. After the prior day's arrest, the congressmen already know the identity of the two imprisoned soldiers. Their names are Michael Lynch and Thomas Hickey.

If these two particular soldiers are part of a secret plot to raise arms against their fellow soldiers, the consequences could be catastrophic.

Why? Because these aren't ordinary soldiers. They're George Washington's Life Guards.

The Life Guards, who spend almost every waking minute physically close to General Washington. They're near him when he works, when he travels, at his headquarters, and at the residence where he sleeps. They are armed at all times, wielding muskets with bayonets.

As Ketcham tells his story, he adds one more terrible detail. According to what he remembers of the conversation, Lynch and Hickey said they weren't the only Life Guards who were part of it. There are other Life Guards in on it too, possibly *several* others.

Those several others are not in a jail cell, but on duty. At this very moment.

George Washington's life is in danger.

Just before noon on Monday, June 17, 1776, twenty-six members of the New York Provincial Congress realize this fact at roughly the same time.

54

The Life Guards are in on a traitorous plot. George Washington's life is in danger.

If the reports are true, it's all happening *right now.*

On top of all that, it's also happening when the British navy is expected to arrive in New York Harbor within a week or two, in the first full-scale battle of the Revolutionary War.

If George Washington is somehow harmed, seized, or—God forbid—killed in the days before or during the British arrival, the consequences will be devastating and, even centuries later, almost impossible to fathom.

Of course, the congressmen don't know if the traitorous plot is real. And if it *is* real, Ketcham has given only a few fragments of information based on conversations in a jail cell.

The members of the New York Provincial Congress have to learn more—and fast. With the stakes so high, they must do everything possible to stop this plot.

At the same time, the congressmen must be incredibly careful with this information. Nothing could possibly be more sensitive than a secret plot implicating Continental soldiers as traitors.

Also, if the people running this plot somehow learn that the authorities are onto them, they can change their plans or take other measures to evade further discovery.

No question, secrecy is absolutely essential. As a result, in the congressional records of that day, immediately after Ketcham's testimony, there is only one entry for the remainder of the morning session: "The charge of secrecy was given from the Chair to the members, relative to the information given by said Ketcham."

In other words, no one can share a word of this with anyone.

By this point, it's pretty obvious who in the congress should be in charge of this explosive situation: the brand new Committee on Conspiracies, its final members having been appointed only three days ago.

So after a short adjournment, the very next item on the day's record is this:

> *Ordered*, That Mr. Ph. Livingston, Mr. Jay and Mr. Morris, be a secret committee to confer with Genl. Washington, relative to certain secret intelligence communicated to this Congress, and take such examinations relative thereto as they shall think proper.

This information is *so* sensitive, only these three members of the committee—Philip Livingston, John Jay, and Gouverneur Morris—will be in charge of it, and they will dedicate themselves entirely to pursuing it.

The language used by the congress here is a little confusing, because the reference to a new "secret committee" of three members is the same wording as had originally been used to describe the formation of the nine-member committee.

In other words, this is a secret subcommittee within the Committee on Conspiracies. Basically, a *doubly* secret committee.

So while the New York Provincial Congress will continue operating as the governing body of the colony in a time of war, and as the nine-member Committee on Conspiracies will continue investigating the "List of Suspected Persons," the new top-secret three-person team consisting of Livingston, Morris, and Jay will focus on this one extremely sensitive and potentially dangerous enemy plot.

From this point forward, there is no mention of the Life Guards' plot in the standard congressional records. Instead, the work of the Committee on Conspiracies—and particularly the work related to investigating this plot—will be kept in separate confidential records. Some of the most critical and sensitive information will not be written down at all.

Amidst the drama of the revelations, one of the first decisions the Committee on Conspiracies has to make right away is a simple one.

What to do about the prisoner Isaac Ketcham?

For the congressmen, there probably isn't much mystery to what Ketcham was hoping for by sharing his information. The combination of his entreaty to see his family, his letter expressing his remorse, and his voluntary offer of intelligence from the jail add up to someone who hopes to secure a reprieve in exchange for his offer of vital information.

For now, however, the committee comes up with a different idea.

Ketcham's testimony contained only a few shards of intelligence on a matter that could have potentially massive consequences. Right now, the two Life Guards in the jail are the only source of knowledge about the plot. The best person to learn more from them without arousing suspicion is, in fact, Isaac Ketcham.

So the new committee gives Ketcham instructions: Go back down to the cell and keep listening. Draw them out. Gain their trust. Try to learn more.

Whatever Ketcham discovers, he'll now report it to the dedicated investigators on the case: Jay, Morris, and Livingston.

Implicit in these instructions is a suggestion. If Ketcham can share more information about this enemy plot, the congress will look quite kindly upon his efforts. Maybe, just maybe, he'll be able to see his family sooner than anyone thought.

For Isaac Ketcham, 1776 has been an extremely eventful year. Since winter he has been many things—family man, counterfeiting accomplice, and prisoner.

Now he's about to start to play another role entirely: spy.

55

---·---

The next two days are full of secrets.

After the surprising testimony from Isaac Ketcham, the members of the Committee on Conspiracies—and in particular the trio of John Jay, Gouverneur Morris, and Philip Livingston—must be trying to figure out what leads to pursue.

What they learned from Ketcham, however provocative, is still vague at best. There are endless questions to answer about this supposed plot. Are the two soldiers just lying or bragging? If they're telling the truth, which other Life Guards or other Continental soldiers might be involved? What exactly are the designs of the plot? How big and wide is the conspiracy's reach?

According to Ketcham's testimony, Hickey and Lynch said the plot involved "Rifle-Men on Staten Island" and "Cape Cod men" in addition to Life Guards and other Continental soldiers. But these terms are vague and hard to follow up on.

They did get one name of a supposed ringleader, a blacksmith in the city with the first name Gilbert and the last name something like "Horbush." That's an interesting lead, but city records don't show a blacksmith by that name.

Is it possible it's all a hoax, just two disgruntled soldiers causing trouble in the city jail? Or a story concocted by Ketcham to get out of prison?

While the conspiracy team is no doubt mulling and debating these pressing questions, their need to maintain secrecy means that little is on the record about the plot during the forty-eight hours following Ketcham's revelations.

On Tuesday, June 18—the day following Ketcham's testimony—the New York Congress meets again at City Hall in the morning, and Jay, Morris, and Livingston are all present. There is no afternoon session, and perhaps the three men converge at that time to strategize in secret. There is no mention of the plot on the congressional record of the day, whether in an official document or personal letter.

The next day, Wednesday, June 19, the congress again meets in the morning at City Hall, and once again Jay, Morris, and Livingston are in attendance.

There is once again no direct mention of the scheme, but another matter involving Loyalist activity does come before the body. The chairman of the Dutchess County Committee of Safety—a law-enforcement body representing that county in the Hudson Valley, north of New York City—gives a report that Dutchess contains so many "disaffected" persons, or Loyalists, that the county officials need to apply for a larger militia to combat them.

As the Dutchess chairman puts it: "The militia in the county have been called out so frequently for the purpose of quieting and apprehending disaffected persons, as to make it necessary, in the opinion of the said committee, to embody, and keep in constant pay, about 150 men."

Coming only two days after Ketcham's revelations from the jail, surely this news of yet more unrest from Loyalists operating upstate must be disquieting.

Still, that day, there are once again no direct references to the plot in any official documents.

Yet behind the scenes, and not on any public record, something very important has taken place.

At some point on one of these two days, John Jay, Gouverneur Morris, and Philip Livingston have lined up a session to examine a witness who may know something related to this plot. The examination will be the next morning, Thursday, June 20, at 10:00 a.m.

The witness is William Leary, a foreman from the Ringwood Ironworks iron mill in Goshen, New York. He says he recently chased down some traitors in New York City. Apparently, he's learned some information that could be relevant to the committee.

That's not all. Leary is going to bring one of the culprits with him—so the committee can actually examine the traitor.

56

When does George Washington first hear about the secret plot?

How does he react when he learns the details?

Based on the available records, there is no precise answer to these questions. Because of Washington's ironclad insistence on discretion and secrecy regarding anything that involves sensitive intelligence, he doesn't openly acknowledge or write about the plot until later, when the revelations become more public.

However, we do know that right after Ketcham's testimony on Monday, June 17, one of the very first instructions for the new secret subcommittee—Jay, Livingston, and Morris—was "to confer with General Washington, relative to certain secret intelligence communicated to this Congress."

Indeed, one of the reasons for creating a secret committee in the first place was to keep Washington personally and confidentially informed on critical matters such as this.

So, given that Ketcham's testimony implicates members of Washington's own Life Guards—and that Washington's safety is now at risk—it is almost certain that the committee members informed the Commander-in-Chief of the plot within hours, if not minutes, of learning of it themselves.

Still, there is no record of exactly what George Washington is told, or how he responds.

In all probability, Washington learns every detail, and begins to confer in depth with Jay, Livingston, and Morris about how they should pursue an investigation.

However, according to the records, there is evidence that in the two-day period following Ketcham's testimony Washington also begins taking his own concrete steps in response.

One of Ketcham's revelations was that the conspiracy may include a plan to destroy the much-traveled King's Bridge, which connects northern Manhattan to what is now the Bronx. At the time one of only two bridges to and from Manhattan, it is regularly used to transport goods to and from the northeastern colonies. As such, the bridge is critically important to Washington's army for the movement of troops and supplies. The destruction of King's Bridge would be disastrous, especially just before or during a major battle.

A day or two after Ketcham's testimony—on either Tuesday, June 18, or Wednesday, June 19—Washington travels up to King's Bridge with a detachment of soldiers to personally inspect the fortifications and defenses surrounding the bridge.

Then, on Thursday, June 20, he reports to John Hancock that "I have been up to view the grounds about King's Bridge," and that "esteeming it a pass of the utmost importance," he has ordered additional troops and fortifications to guard and otherwise bolster the defense of the bridge.

Almost certainly, these efforts are a direct response to the revelation of the plot.

But of course, from the Commander-in-Chief's point of view, the plot is about more than just a military threat. If Ketcham is to be believed, this plot is about the duplicity of his own soldiers. This plot is about betrayal. It's about treason.

After everything George Washington has been through, with the enormous challenges that lie ahead, how does the revelation truly affect him?

True to form, Washington reveals almost nothing of his emotional reaction, now or in the future. Moreover, the need for absolute secrecy means he probably wouldn't talk about it even if he wanted to.

Still, there are some ways to glimpse George Washington's state of mind at this time.

In the two weeks since his return from Philadelphia, every ounce of his energy has been devoted to preparations for the coming British attack on New York—now expected to begin in about a week. Between the state of his army—diminished by sickness, short on arms, short on experienced soldiers—and the inherent difficulty of defending an island city with no navy against such a massive force, the outlook is terrifying. And Washington knows this better than anyone.

The stakes could not be higher. As John Hancock wrote to the New York Provincial Congress the previous week: "Our affairs are hastening to a crisis, and the approaching campaign will in all probability determine forever the fate of America . . . and I trust every man in the Colony of New York is determined to see it gloriously ended, or to perish in the ruins of it."

George Washington, of course, is the one who actually bears the extraordinary responsibility. Rarely does Washington overtly evoke religion in his writing, but he sometimes refers to the semispiritual idea of "Providence"—a sense of fate that lies beyond mortal hands. During this particularly fraught period—facing what could be a cataclysmic defeat and utter failure—he makes repeated references to this notion of Providence, as if he has nothing else left.

He writes to his brother: "It is to be hoped that, if our cause is just, as I do most religiously believe it to be, the same Providence which has in many instances appeared for us, will go on to afford its aid."

And not long before that, to John Adams: "We have nothing, my dear sir, to depend upon, but the protection of a kind Providence and unanimity amongst ourselves."

It's at this moment, already under so much pressure, and with the British fleet only a week away, that he learns about a possible plot against him, from within his own army.

This plot is a violation of every code of honor, every notion of duty, every sense of virtue—basically, a violation of every value on which George Washington has tried to build his army.

These are not just any soldiers, these are his Life Guards.

These are the men in whom he placed his greatest trust, the men who were supposed to *protect* him.

Not only have these Life Guards betrayed their country and their army—they have betrayed him *personally*. And they have done so exactly when he needs to depend on them the most.

At the time, George Washington doesn't write about this betrayal, or share his feelings about it with even his closest confidants.

But let's face it, this had to hurt.

Unfortunately, in the next few days, the pain will only get worse.

57

———— • ————

On the morning of Thursday, June 20, the members of the New York Provincial Congress meet as usual at City Hall.

On this morning, however, two congressmen—John Jay and Gouverneur Morris—do not meet with the rest of the group.

Instead, these two convene in a separate room in the building, for a special private examination of new witnesses possibly connected to the conspiracy.* Only the members of the Committee on Conspiracies will be privy to the testimony, which is to remain top secret and confidential, even from other members of the New York Congress. The only additional person in the room during the examination itself will be a congressional secretary, to transcribe the testimony as the witnesses answer questions.

Jay and Morris will examine two men in succession: William Leary and James Mason, both from Goshen, New York.

How is it that William Leary, the Ringwood iron mill foreman,

———————

* For unknown reasons, Philip Livingston convenes with the main body of the congress on this day, and does not join Jay and Morris in their examination of William Leary and James Mason. In most future examinations connected to the plot, all three members of the secret subcommittee will be present.

and James Mason, the part-time-miller-turned-traitor, ended up tes-tifying at City Hall?

The answer isn't known.

Possibly, Leary approached authorities in Manhattan after his adventure chasing traitors in the city and volunteered that he had information that might be important. Undoubtedly, he would also have named James Mason as a suspect. In this case, it would be pure coincidence that Leary happened to come forward a day or two after Isaac Ketcham shared his intelligence from the jail.

Another possibility, and probably more likely, is that after the Ketcham testimony, the Committee on Conspiracies did some in-vestigating behind the scenes that led them to Leary. For example, if they contacted local officials in counties around the city looking for leads, the officials from Orange County may have suggested they interview Leary, who no doubt reported his story to his bosses at the mill, who then probably shared it with the appropriate local authorities.

In any event, on the morning of Thursday, June 20, William Leary, the foreman of the Ringwood mill, sits in a room in City Hall, di-rectly across from John Jay and Gouverneur Morris.

Promptly at ten o'clock, the examination begins.

First, Leary describes the mission he undertook earlier in the month. He had been sent by his boss—the mill owner, Erskine—to travel down to New York City and track down a missing em-ployee named William Benjamin. Benjamin, rumor had it, had fled the mill to join some sort of traitorous scheme of British sym-pathizers.

Leary describes how, after following the suspect's trail down to New York City, he successfully tracked down Benjamin at the Man-hattan residence of someone by the name of Forbes. He describes how Forbes gave Benjamin a gun to defend himself when Leary entered, and how Leary "took hold of Benjamin and prevented him from us-ing said Pistol."

Leary further describes how, after he apprehended and delivered Benjamin to nearby soldiers, he encountered another former employee at Ringwood, James Mason, who had also fled the mill in Goshen to join the traitorous scheme.

Leary, by pretending that he himself wanted to join the scheme, met Mason's cohorts and learned more about this network of men who planned to betray their country. They had all accepted promises of money to "go on board the Man-o-War"—one of the British ships in the harbor—and take up arms against the colonies.

Leary learned that Mason and his companions had been "sworn" or "qualified" to be members of this secret scheme. When Leary asked Mason who had sworn them in, Mason "replied that it was a gentleman employed by the Mayor or Governor of the town."

As a final note, Leary learned that this group "expected a large body of men to join them from Goshen."

From William Leary's testimony several key facts stand out.

First, there is clearly a widespread effort afoot to bribe local citizens to join the enemy. Although Leary's testimony refers only to recruitment efforts in Goshen, New York, the pattern is consistent with reports they've heard from elsewhere.

Second, apparently many of these recruited traitors travel to Manhattan—right under the nose of the Continental army—where they are sworn in some sort of secret ceremony to join the British side.

Third, there is someone named Forbes in Manhattan who has housed and tried to arm at least one of the new recruits.

Fourth, and perhaps most important, someone "employed by the Mayor or Governor"—that would be David Mathews or William Tryon—is swearing in and apparently paying the new recruits.

Here, in this testimony, some of the most important elements of the plot come into focus. Still, there are many outstanding questions. Is this recruitment effort in Goshen connected to the plot revealed by Isaac Ketcham, and involving the Life Guards? Who is really running this scheme in New York City? And what exactly are all these recruits being paid to do?

A congressional secretary has carefully written down every word Leary has spoken. John Jay and Gouverneur Morris, once they complete the examination, now sign their names to the secretary's written record. This top-secret document is added to the confidential files of the Committee on Conspiracies.

For Jay and Morris, William Leary's testimony has been illuminating. But it's nothing compared to what they're about to hear next.

58

At approximately eleven o'clock, after Leary's paperwork is filed away, Jay and Morris call for the next examinant: former mill worker James Mason.

Unlike Leary, who was a friendly witness, Mason is actually a suspect. Indeed, it was Leary's adventure in Manhattan that led this alleged miller-turned-traitor to be sitting before them in this room.

Once again, Jay and Morris start questioning their witness, while a congressional secretary records the testimony for a secret file.

Mason's story, like Leary's, begins at the Ringwood iron mill in Goshen, New York, about fifty miles northwest of Manhattan. Mason explains that he initially went to Goshen innocently enough, looking for employment as a miller. He got some part-time work there, but not enough to make ends meet—and soon he was lured into an unexpected scheme.

He explains how a local man by the name of William Farley recruited him to betray the colonies and agree to side with the British.

Farley's offer was quite extraordinary. He said that William Tryon, the exiled Governor of New York, was ready to give land and money to any colonist who would secretly "turn" and fight for the King.

More specifically, Farley told him "that Governor Tryon would give five Guineas bounty or two hundred acres of land for each man, one hundred for his wife and fifty for each child upon condition they would enlist in his Majesty's Service." Farley, the recruiter, was also "to have a bounty from the Governor for every man he could get."

Finally, here's the proof: William Tryon is bribing colonists to commit treason. Reports and rumors have long suggested this. But here, in this testimony, is the most blunt and detailed account yet.

The examination continues.

Mason describes his journey down to New York City with the recruiter Farley, also accompanied by another new young recruit named William Benjamin. Mason explains how they took a ferry from Elizabethtown, New Jersey, to Manhattan, where they were sent to meet a shoemaker near the East River named Peter McLean, who "was employed by the Governor" to secretly ferry recruits to the *Duchess of Gordon*.

Instead, McLean sent them to Houlding's Tavern, a Loyalist hangout run by James Houlding. At Houlding's, they met several other Loyalists and traitors closely or loosely connected to the scheme.

For Jay and Morris, these are astonishing details for their investigation. They now have more names of people to apprehend and interrogate, and more places to search, raid, and make arrests.

Mason goes on to describe how, in addition to Houlding's, he and some other recruits were sent to another tavern named Corbie's. This tavern is described to be on the outskirts of the city, close to George Washington's nighttime lodgings to the northwest, near the Hudson River.

Mason describes the process at Corbie's by which he was officially "qualified" into the Governor's plot. Alongside a few other recruits, he says he was sworn by "the Book" not to reveal anything about the plot to anyone. He had to pledge loyalty to the Crown.

Who, exactly, oversaw this process?

According to Mason, the man who "qualified" him is named Gilbert Forbes. A gunsmith. Mason describes him as a "short, thick man who wore a white coat."

Mason further testifies that after being qualified, he was officially on the payroll, and "Gilbert Forbes then promised . . . ten shillings per week subsistence money." When it comes to the overall leadership of the plot, Mason says he "believes Gilbert Forbes is at the head [with] the Mayor & the Governor."

Also of interest, Mason conversed with another recent recruit from Goshen who was "qualified" by Forbes. This man, by the name of Clarke, told Mason that some fifty or sixty persons from Goshen alone had enlisted in the scheme, and were now on the payroll to do the Governor's bidding.

So, as the investigators hear the testimony, they ascertain a pattern that looks like this:

Governor Tryon hires men to find and enlist recruits in the region around New York City and bring them to Manhattan. The recruiters take the newcomers to a shoemaker named McLean, who runs a small shop near the East River. McLean secretly ferries some of them directly to the *Duchess of Gordon*, and sends others to lodge at Loyalist taverns in Manhattan like Houlding's and Corbie's. Those that go to the *Duchess of Gordon* are "qualified" directly by Governor Tryon or his associates on board. Those who stay in Manhattan are "qualified" by the gunsmith, Gilbert Forbes, who then pays their salary from a stash he gets from the Mayor, David Mathews.

Finally, Mason reveals the most troubling details of all—details that confirm Isaac Ketcham's report from the jail. Mason says there are soldiers in Washington's army who wear the Continental uniform, but have secretly joined Tryon's conspiracy.

Not just any soldiers—the Life Guards.

Mason provides even more details than Ketcham did. He explains that after he himself was "qualified" by Forbes, he learned specifically about a number of Life Guards who are involved.

He learned that "Green of the General's Guards, a drummer" is part of it, and adds that he personally saw "Gilbert Forbes in conversation with the said Green" discussing aspects of the plot.

Mason did not provide a first name for Green, but the last name checks out: investigators already know that the drummer of the Life Guards is in fact named William Green.

Mason also says "that one Hickey of the General's Guards he

believes to be concerned, who is now in confinement." This, of course, is Thomas Hickey, one of the two Life Guards now in jail with Isaac Ketcham.

Mason doesn't mention Michael Lynch, the other Life Guard confined with Hickey. But he says he's heard about still other Life Guards who are involved: "one Barnes of the General's Guards and one Johnson a fifer of the Guards . . . are qualified for the same purpose."

According to Mason, Green was something of a leader among the Life Guards when it came to participating in the scheme. He was the one who "administered the oath" to the others, including to Hickey. Green apparently got money from Forbes, and then distributed it to the other Life Guards in the conspiracy. As Mason puts it in the examination, Green "is to have one dollar per man from Forbes for every man he shall inlist."

Mason's testimony, when combined with Ketcham's earlier report, suggests that at least five Life Guards total are in on the scheme: William Green, Thomas Hickey, Michael Lynch, Johnson the fifer, and a private named Barnes.

John Jay and Gouverneur Morris hear all of this before noon on Thursday, June 20. It's a lot to take in. But the evidence is now overwhelming, and the bottom line is this: The plot is real. It's not a hoax or some fake story from Ketcham to get out of jail.

Powerful people are running it, flush with money. Hundreds of men, including soldiers, could be in on it. At least *three* other Life Guards, in addition to the two currently in jail, are implicated.

Whatever terrible plans are in place, they could be in motion at this very minute.

John Jay and Gouverneur Morris now know all of this. The question remains, what can they do about it?

59

It's time to get the Mayor.

For months, George Washington and the New York Provincial Congress had focused their attention on William Tryon as the key "internal enemy" in the colony—and rightly so. But all along they had allowed one of the Governor's closest allies, New York City Mayor David Mathews, to operate in the city without consequence.

Apparently, that was a mistake.

From multiple accounts now, the Mayor is a key player in Tryon's plot, delivering money from the Governor that is then used to bribe colonists and Continental soldiers to join a complex Loyalist conspiracy.

On Friday, June 21, the day after Mason's testimony, the investigating committee decides that when it comes to Mayor Mathews, they need to strike now and strike fast.

However, unlike the other recent arrests, seizing the Mayor might not be as easy.

Mathews is a prominent citizen, with friends in high places. He could have bodyguards or hired soldiers protecting him. Also, as a participant in this plot, Mathews may already have planned a means of escape in case of trouble.

They also know that Mathews's home is not in Manhattan, but in Flatbush, in present-day Brooklyn, which makes his arrest more logistically complicated. In addition, they need to be sure to seize any papers or other key evidence from Mathews's home before he can destroy it.

On top of all that, the investigators have to wonder if it's too late. Despite every effort at total secrecy, there's certainly the chance that word has leaked to the enemy that the plot has been discovered—in which case Mayor Mathews may already have fled. If so, time is more vital than ever.

Determined not to take chances, the investigators don't simply issue a warrant for the local militia to arrest Mathews, as they would a normal criminal suspect. Instead, they utilize one of the new powers of the Committee on Conspiracies: access to the army.

For this, they need to take their request to the top. They go right to George Washington.

At approximately one in the afternoon, roughly twenty-four hours after James Mason's testimony, the team of Livingston, Jay, and Morris, drafts a message to the Commander-in-Chief:

Sir: Whereas David Mathews, Esq. stands charged with dangerous designs and treasonable conspiracies against the rights & liberties of the United States of America—we do. . . . authorize and request you to cause the said David Mathews to be with all his papers forthwith apprehended & secured & that return be made to us of the manner in which this warrant shall be executed.
Given under our hand this 21st day of June, 1776.
PHILIP LIVINGSTON
JOHN JAY
GOUVERNEUR MORRIS

They send the message immediately to Washington's headquarters. Washington, who knows the urgency of the matter, receives the message and formulates a plan to have his army handle the arrest and seizure.

Because Mathews lives across the East River, Washington decides to send the order to his general, Nathanael Greene, who is already stationed on Long Island with a brigade under his command.

According to Washington, Greene shouldn't just send out his men in a mad dash that afternoon to try to find the Mayor. Washington has something more precise in mind. To convey his specific instruction, the Commander sends the warrant from Jay, Morris, and Livingston to Greene, and also includes this handwritten note: "General Greene is desired to have the within warrant executed with precision & exactness by one o'clock the ensuing morning by a careful Officer. Friday afternoon 21th June 1776. G WASHINGTON."

In other words, Washington wants to conduct the arrest in the most tried-and-true method in the history of law enformcement: in the middle of the night. They'll launch a surprise raid on the Mayor's home at 1:00 a.m., hoping to catch him while he's sleeping, and before he can cover his tracks or destroy any evidence.

Out on Long Island, General Greene receives Washington's message that afternoon. He appoints an officer to be in charge of the raid, a colonel named James Varnum. By nightfall, Varnum has gathered an armed detachment of soldiers, all of them ready to conduct a surprise early-morning raid of the Mayor's home.

The Continental army is prepared to arrest one of the ringleaders of the conspiracy. The plan is in place. Now, all they have to do is execute it.

60

Flushing, Long Island

June 1776

It's just after midnight.

On Saturday, June 22, 1776, James Varnum, a colonel under the command of Gen. Nathanael Greene, prepares a detachment of armed soldiers for an overnight raid on Long Island.

Their target is Mayor David Mathews, now a key suspect in a plot against George Washington and the Continental army.

Mathews's home is in the small village of Flatbush, a few miles to the south and due east of the Continental troops' camps. The team—probably between a dozen and twenty soldiers on horseback—sets out in the darkness and races across the largely uninhabited Long Island countryside toward its destination.

Once in Flatbush, they quickly identify Mathews's country home. According to Greene's later account of the raid, Colonel Varnum and his soldiers quietly "surround his house" in the still of night.

This is their moment.

A stroke of luck. The house is inhabited.

Another stroke of luck. Mathews is home.

As the troops storm inside, just as they hoped, their target has no idea what hit him.

After what must have been a profoundly unhappy wakeup for the

Mayor, the soldiers "seized his person precisely at the hour of One." Mathews's wife and children, also home and sleeping at the time, are not harmed.

After the Mayor has been seized and his home searched, there is one disappointment: The soldiers find no papers or other evidence related to the conspiracy. As Greene describes in his report, "Vigilant search was made after his papers but none could be found, notwithstanding that great care was taken that none of the family should have the least opportunity to remove or destroy them."

If the Mayor actually had any documents or other pieces of evidence connecting him to the conspiracy, he was smart enough not to leave them lying around his home.

Still, the authorities have their man. The arrest of Mayor Mathews has gone exactly as planned.

This was no small affair. Imagine what the scene would be today if an armed military unit stormed the home of the Mayor of New York City in the middle of the night, and arrested him on suspicion of conspiring against the United States and working with members of the Secret Service, who are in on the plot.

Exactly. Not a good day.

By the time the sun comes up, Varnum and his soldiers have arrived in Manhattan, delivering their prisoner to the city guard. When the Committee on Conspiracies convenes for a special Saturday-morning session, it learns of the successful arrest.

Exactly five days after first hearing of the secret plot from Isaac Ketcham's unexpected testimony, the Committee of Conspiracies has—with some help from Washington's soldiers—successfully apprehended and detained one of the ringleaders of the plot, who also happens to be the Mayor of New York City.

Not bad, for a few days' work.

Still, there is much more to do—and with the British fleet expected to arrive literally any day, time is getting short.

61

---•---

New York, New York

June 1776

The investigation never stops moving.

On Saturday, June 22, while Jay, Morris, and Livingston prepare for their high-stakes interrogation of David Mathews—planned for the following morning—they also oversee a flurry of additional activity related to the case.

Only forty-eight hours after James Mason's testimony, the committee draws up dozens of arrest warrants for additional suspects and sends emissaries to search relevant locations, and round up witnesses.

That Saturday afternoon the committee also conducts five more examinations related to the case, including the questioning of another Continental soldier who was lured by a recruiter to join the scheme. The day's interrogations contain no huge revelations, but they do corroborate some details from Leary's and Mason's testimony, while also providing new leads for additional arrests.

By the end of the day, they've created a "List of Tories in New York and Orange County" that includes the names of every suspect so far from either the Manhattan or the Goshen end of the plot. Already at almost twenty names, the list will continue to grow on a daily and sometimes hourly basis.

In the wake of the Mayor's dramatic arrest, something else happens: More people learn about the plot. The three main investigators, as well as George Washington himself, have thus far tried to maintain the utmost secrecy. By this point, however, they have no choice but to let a few others know about the conspiracy—especially now that army officers and additional congressional personnel are needed to contribute to the effort. As a result, word starts to spread.

That very day, a twenty-three-year-old officer named Samuel Blachley Webb sits down with his journal and writes one of the very first specific descriptions of the plot from the point of view of someone other than the members of the secret committee.

We don't know exactly how Webb learned about the conspiracy, but only a day earlier he was promoted to be George Washington's aide-de-camp—in other words, one of Washington's top personal aides—after serving the same role for Washington's second-in-command, Gen. Israel Putnam.

Before becoming aide-de-camp, Webb had served as a Lieutenant Colonel when the army was in Boston. Although still a young officer, he has achieved some status—and is now privy to information from both Putnam and Washington himself.

Webb's journal entry, written on Saturday, June 22, is vivid:

> Some days past, the General received information that a most horrid plot was on foot by the vile Tories of this place and the adjacent towns and villages. Having taken the necessary precautions . . . a number of officers & guards went to different places & took up many of their principals; among whom, was David Mathews Esq., Mayor of the city.

Webb continues, describing even more details. And here, in this journal entry, is the first written documentation of the full extent of the plot:

> To our great astonishment we found five or more of the General's Life Guard to be accomplices in this wicked plan; which was, at the proper time, to assassinate the person of his Excellency & the

other General Officers, blow up the magazine, and spike the cannon. It was to be put in execution as soon as the enemy's fleet appeared, if no proper time offered before.

For anyone in the Continental army, "his Excellency" refers to one person only: George Washington himself.

This remarkable journal entry conveys several things. First, Webb is somehow aware that "five or more" of the Life Guards are accomplices. This number is exactly right. The details of the Life Guards' involvement could be known only by someone familiar with the examinations conducted by Jay, Morris, and Livingston. Bound by secrecy, these three probably only shared the information with George Washington or, if they got Washington's permission, maybe with a few top generals.

In other words, Webb is privy to highly confidential information. Perhaps, as a close aide to Washington, he learned it directly from the Commander.

All this makes that second part of his entry even more remarkable: The conspirators' plan is "to assassinate His Excellency & the other General Officers."

Much of the record was kept secret to ensure that no one else found out. But if Webb is correct, we have the most stunning part of the conspiracy. Their plan wasn't just to raise an army or turn soldiers— their plan was to kill George Washington himself.

This goal, by far the gravest and most potentially devastating aspect of the plot, certainly explains the extreme seriousness and speed with which the authorities have responded.

Some might argue that Webb had it wrong—that he was exaggerating in his journal, or maybe heard some faulty information. But that very day, *another* Continental officer also writes a journal entry that backs up Webb's. This officer is considerably more senior: Brig. Gen. William Heath.

A respected officer, Heath is one of the top three or four generals in New York. In the privacy of his diary, on that same afternoon of June 22, Heath writes this:

This day a most horrid plot was discovered, in the city and camp. A plan has been laid to massacre the generals of the army on the first approach of the enemy, to blow up the magazines, [and] spike the cannons. A number both of citizens and soldiers are seized and secured among whom are the Mayor of the city. One Forbes, a gunsmith, who it is said is one of the principals, and several of the Generals' Guard . . . are also in the plot.

So General Heath, too, confirms the very worst fear about the plot—the plan for the Life Guards or others to "massacre the generals," starting, of course, with George Washington.

Interestingly, none of the actual examinations that Jay, Morris, and Livingston have thus far conducted have specifically mentioned a plan to kill George Washington—or at least, there is no mention in the official written transcripts. But in this investigation, not everything is put on the record. Clearly, the authorities are keeping some aspects of the plot secret. For example, at some point in the few days after Mason's testimony, the three suspected Life Guards who were not already in jail—that is, Green, Johnson, and Barnes—were detained and surely must have been questioned or interrogated. Yet, there is no record of when or how these arrests happened, or what was said in any conversations with these men.

In fact, outside the top secret formal examinations, there are no records of any conversations about the plot at all, whether among the investigators and senior officers, or with George Washington himself.

Yet somehow, in the forty-eight hours after James Mason's testimony, two serious and well-regarded officers with inside knowledge of the investigation, and with personal access to Washington, come to believe that the "horrid plot" includes a plan to kill George Washington.

Which raises the question: Where did this bombshell of information come from—and why isn't it in the official investigative records?

One possibility is that clear evidence about a plan to kill Washington did indeed emerge over the forty-eight hours after Mason's testimony—but the Committee on Conspiracies, or perhaps Washington himself, decided that this fact should absolutely not be recorded or shared with anyone, in any public form.

Indeed, there would have been every reason to keep this shocking part of the plot absolutely secret. At that particular moment, with the massive British navy about to arrive in New York for the first full-scale battle of the Revolutionary War, any admission that Washington's life might be in danger from assassination—let alone that his own soldiers were in on it—would likely cause panic both within the army and in the public.

At best, this revelation would betray weakness at a time when the future of the colonies hangs in the balance. At worst, it would create incredible upheaval in the army at a moment when it desperately needs stability. Militarily, the colonies are severely outmatched. All they have is their faith in the "Glorious Cause"—and their belief in the man who has come to symbolize that cause more than any other: the Commander-in-Chief.

The British ships are now expected in less than a week. From everything the investigators have learned, the arrival of the fleet is when the conspiracy will be triggered, and when the traitors will spring into action and raise arms against their fellow colonists.

If Webb and Heath are right, the first victim may be George Washington himself.

The entire future of America could be at stake—and time is running out.

62

During Isaac Ketcham's initial testimony before the New York Provincial Congress on June 17, he made reference to a player in the plot by the name of "Gilbert Horbush," supposedly a blacksmith. According to Ketcham, the two Life Guards who shared his prison cell, Thomas Hickey and Michael Lynch, spoke of this person as a leader or key accomplice in the conspiracy.

After Ketcham's testimony, when authorities try to locate such a person in the city and county records, they draw a blank.

Three days later, when John Jay and Gouverneur Morris conduct a secret examination of William Leary, he specifically recalls that a man named "Forbes" was housing one of the traitors from Goshen, and had even gave the traitor a gun to defend himself when Leary apprehended the man.

"Forbes" sounds a bit like "Horbush," so maybe these two are the same.

Then, when James Mason is examined right after Leary, he independently brings up the name "Gilbert Forbes" as a key person in the plot who swears in new recruits and administers their pay.

That pretty much confirms it: The name that Ketcham heard as "Gilbert Horbush" must really be "Gilbert Forbes," given the similarities in the three examinations. Clearly, this Gilbert Forbes should be next on their list of suspects to arrest.

Mason also gave one additional detail: Gilbert Forbes is not a blacksmith, as Ketcham said, but a gunsmith.

That's the detail investigators need to track him down—but unlike Mayor Mathews, tracking down Gilbert Forbes is easy. Thanks to Mason's testimony, the investigators know precisely where he is. He runs a gun shop "on Broadway, across from Hull's Tavern."

The details of exactly how, when, and where the authorities arrest Forbes are not on the record. Probably, a couple of soldiers or militiamen simply walk into his shop and take him by force. In any case, at some point during the evening of Saturday, June 22—less than twenty-four hours after Mayor Mathews's arrest and only six days after Ketcham's initial revelation—the city guards bring gunsmith Gilbert Forbes into custody in the same prison underneath City Hall where Thomas Hickey, Michael Lynch, Isaac Ketcham, the two Young brothers, Henry Dawkins, Mayor David Mathews, and some others are also detained.

This jail is getting awfully crowded.

Naturally, the three investigators from the Committee on Conspiracies are eager to talk to this man Forbes, who, although totally unknown before, seems to be at the center of the plot. After all, Forbes's name has now come up in connection to Governor Tryon, to Mayor Mathews, to Washington's Life Guards, and to the team of recruits from Goshen.

Obviously, this will be a critical examination. There's only one hitch in the investigators' plan.

Forbes refuses to talk.

The night he's taken into custody, the gunsmith tells his captors he won't answer any questions. He won't agree to talk to anyone. He won't cooperate or give names. Not now, not tomorrow, not ever.

63

———•———

The next morning, Sunday, June 23, the investigators wake up and get back to work.

While the new suspect in custody, Gilbert Forbes, plays tough and refuses to talk, Jay, Morris, and Livingston begin their formal examination of one of their key suspects: the New York City Mayor, David Mathews.

Mathews is by far the highest-profile suspect in custody and, given that Governor Tryon is untouchable—he's still safe aboard the *Duchess of Gordon*, under the protection of the massive British warship *Asia* anchored right next to it—the Mayor is probably the highest-ranking official they will interview.

Some time in the middle or late morning, prison guards make the now familiar trek from the underground prison up to City Hall. From there, they carefully escort the Mayor into one of the building's courtrooms, where he's seated before the three investigators.

Like the other examinations, this one will be top secret, and once again a congressional secretary is present to transcribe the interrogation as it happens.

From the start of the examination, Mathews takes a position of denial. He denies he's a player in any grand scheme; he denies any ill intentions toward George Washington or his army; he denies that he is part of a conspiracy to enlist men or bribe Continental soldiers.

However, right at the outset, the Mayor *does* admit his involvement in an isolated part of the plot.

Mathews tells the story of the one particular time he visited Governor Tryon on board the *Duchess of Gordon*, about a month ago.

Mathews says he initially went aboard the ship to do some administrative work with Tryon. Mathews says he had even obtained official permission from Washington's second-in-command, Gen. Israel Putnam, to make the trip.

He then describes being aboard the ship that day. After he took care of his regular business, and just as he was about to leave the *Duchess*, he says "the Governor took him into a private room, and put a bundle of paper money in his hands."

According to Mathews, Governor Tryon told him to give most of this money—a sum of about 115 pounds—to a man named Gilbert Forbes. It was payment, the Governor said, for some guns he had bought from Forbes that were being delivered to the ship.

Mathews claims that at the time he was "surprised" by the Governor's request—and that his first thought was that "Governor Tryon had put a matter on his shoulders which might bring him into some difficulty."

After revealing this initial incident, Mathews goes on to relate a rather convoluted account of how he carried out Tryon's order. He says that because he didn't know who Forbes was, he had to seek him out through a mutual acquaintance, and then, once he had identified him, he decided not to give him the money right away. It was only after Forbes sought Mathews out and started hounding him that he finally relented and gave Forbes the cash.

Then, the main thrust of the Mayor's story is that once he met Forbes, he actually tried to talk Forbes out of any secret activity with the Governor. He says he told Forbes not to sell the Governor any more guns, and asked him to stop bribing Continental soldiers to join the British side.

He adds that he warned Forbes "he would be hanged if he was found out," and told him that "if he regarded his safety that he would not go on with such schemes." Mayor Mathews says he did every-thing he could to discourage Forbes' involvement—yet Forbes re-fused to listen.

When it comes to the more specific plot details that were revealed by others about the conspiracy, the Mayor likewise claims mostly ignorance. He says that when Forbes began talking about bribing the Life Guards, or gathering men to blow up the Continental army's magazine, or destroying the King's Bridge—and he says Forbes tried to persuade him to join in all these missions—the Mayor "begged of him to desist of such a scheme, for he would certainly be discovered and the gallows would be his lot."

When the investigators press him further regarding Tryon's plan to raise a secret army for the British, Mathews says that he "has no further knowledge . . . relative to any person engaged in the business of en-listing men for the King's service, or in keeping up a communication between the city and the Governor's ship."

Basically, Mathews puts the whole thing on Forbes. If anything, he says he was trying to be a good citizen by dissuading Forbes from pursuing any plot against the Continental army.

After the examination, John Jay, Gouverneur Morris, and Philip Livingston follow the usual procedure and sign the transcript made by the secretary. City guards lead David Mathews back to his cell.

So what to make of the Mayor's testimony?

For the most part, the investigators don't buy Mathews's claims of innocence and ignorance. Their reason is simple: Mathews's testimony contradicts what several other suspects have already said and will say about him.

Most witnesses have independently contended that Mathews is a key leader of the plot—the one responsible for managing the money for bribing soldiers. Naturally, Mathews has a very strong motive to deny culpability—because he fears imprisonment or death by the authorities—whereas the others who name him don't have a particu-lar reason to accuse him falsely.

So, in general, the interrogators are skeptical of Mathews's testi-mony. However, Mathews's examination does move the investigation forward in one critical way. Thanks to his admission about getting money from Tryon's ship, the investigators now have strong, clear evidence that the conspiracy leads all the way up to the Governor.

Of course, they suspected all along that Tryon was pulling the strings—and several other witnesses say they'd *heard* that Tryon was running the scheme—but now, with Mathews's testimony, the Committee on Conspiracies can verify a clear flow of money from Tryon, to Mathews, to Forbes, and then to the Life Guards and other recruits.

This particular flow of money is only part of the bigger picture. There seem to be many other recruiters out there aside from Forbes—and Tryon is pretty clearly paying lots of people to do many different things. But when it comes to the attempt to infiltrate the Life Guards, they now have a clear picture of who is paying whom.

After Mayor Mathews's examination, the investigators keep working. That very afternoon, they interrogate six other suspects and witnesses, including the recruiter William Farley, who originally enlisted James Mason from the Ringwood mill up in Goshen.

All these interviews confirm and enhance their basic understanding of the plot, including the roles played by Mayor Mathews and Gilbert Forbes. They also provide names of yet more people implicated, whom the committee can now arrest and take into custody.

Naturally, there is still more to be done, but the investigators now have a strong sense of the case—and are closing in on a plan to bring the conspirators to justice before the plot has any chance of success.

Then, that same Sunday, June 23, 1776, there's yet another unexpected twist. Perhaps the most shocking so far.

One final coconspirator is about to be revealed, and a close one, too.

Her name is Mary Smith—George Washington's housekeeper.

That's right. Not only are the elite Life Guards in on it. So is the middle-aged woman who runs the household where, on most nights, George Washington sleeps.

She's part of the conspiracy—and the authorities have just seized her.

64

———·———

Of all the surprising developments in the story of the secret plot against George Washington, the involvement of Washington's personal housekeeper, Mary Smith, may be the strangest.

It's also the most mysterious.

Very little is actually known about exactly how and when Mary Smith is removed from Washington's residence, beyond the fact that it occurs on Sunday, June 23.

In fact, the congressional documents, including those of the Committee on Conspiracies, make no mention whatsoever of her arrest, or of her involvement in the plot. Nor is her participation referred to in any military or city records.

The first report of Mary Smith's abrupt removal from George Washington's nighttime estate is seen in a letter written the very next day by an unidentified person in New York who has some sort of inside knowledge of the plot and investigation.

This letter, dated June 24, 1776, is somehow obtained by the *Pennsylvania Journal*, which publishes it on June 26. The newspaper doesn't include the name of the writer or the recipient, it prints only the body of the text. Since the original letter is lost, the identity of the writer remains a mystery.

The letter includes a description of the plot, with many details correct. It ends with this sentence:

I am told the Mayor acknowledges he paid Mr. Forbes, the gunsmith, who is one of the gang now in irons, one hundred and forty pounds, by order of Governor Tryon. Yesterday the General's housekeeper was taken up; it is said she is concerned.

In the usage of the day, "concerned" means "involved." In other words, the letter suggests that the housekeeper is part of the plot.

Although the letter writer is wrong about the exact amount of money that the Mayor paid Gilbert Forbes, the other information is accurate. Whoever the writer is, he or she knows something about the plot. Unfortunately, to this day, no one knows the source of the information about the housekeeper.

Of course, this one anonymous letter would not be sufficient as the only source to verify that Washington's housekeeper was in on the conspiracy—but additional clues also bear it out.

According to Continental army ledgers, Mary Smith's work term for Washington, paid for by the army, indeed comes to an abrupt and mysterious end that weekend. There was no indication beforehand that there was any dissatisfaction with her or plan to fire her. Suddenly, she is removed from the staff, with no explanation.

In addition, a few days later, Washington is desperately looking for a replacement for this demanding position that involves running a household staff and hosting large dinners for politicians and generals. He writes a note to a New York friend that because he had "occasion to part with my Housekeeper," he needs help finding another. Regarding a new woman who had been recommended, he writes, "I beg of you to hasten her to this place . . . as I am entirely destitute, and put to much inconvenience" due to the sudden vacancy.

Mary Smith was clearly removed abruptly, under highly unusual circumstances, during the weekend in which the investigation of the plot was in full swing.

From that point forward, there will be conjecture concerning her precise role, from a rumor that she was a British spy all along, to various infamous theories about how she might be involved in an assassination plot against the General.

Putting aside the rumors, the question remains: If Washington's housekeeper was indeed discovered that weekend to be a part of the conspiracy, why is there no formal record of her arrest—and why didn't the committee examine her on the record like the others?

No one knows for sure, but the answer could fall into the "too embarrassing to reveal" category. Surely, Washington would want to keep this exceedingly sensitive matter as much under wraps as possible. At this critical juncture, right before the first big battle of the Revolutionary War, when the eyes of the colonies and the world are watching, the public revelation that George Washington's own housekeeper is conspiring against him is hardly a display of power and strength.

Mary Smith's potential involvement also suggests something else—that the plot was indeed focused against Washington himself. After all, there are always Life Guards present at Mortier's estate, and as the housekeeper, Mary Smith would have gotten to know them.

There is no particular reason the Life Guards would have brought a middle-aged housekeeper into their plans if their role were to destroy the King's Bridge, or to just spike some cannons. Whereas if they're devising a plan to actually kill George Washington, or capture him for the enemy—well, there are many ways the housekeeper could help with that.

After Mary Smith's sudden departure on that Sunday, June 23, 1776, there is no clear record of what became of her. If she was seized by soldiers as a traitor, they did not take her to jail or otherwise formally detain her. Perhaps they just sent her away from the estate, with a threat to never return.

A rumor would soon arise that she boarded a ship to England, but again, no one knows for sure. To this day, her fate remains an enduring mystery.

65

——·——

When gunsmith Gilbert Forbes was arrested and brought to the city jail the night of Saturday, June 22, he was defiant and stubborn. He refused to cooperate and said he wouldn't answer any questions.

This obstinance from Forbes would last for about fifteen hours.

Then he changed his mind.

What happened?

According to one version of events, the morning after Forbes's arrest, on Sunday, June 23, the authorities sent a young minister named Robert Livingston to visit the stubborn gunsmith in his cell.

At this point, Forbes has just spent a full night in a dark jail, with painful leg irons on. His defiant mood has probably already softened a little.

Livingston, speaking gently to the prisoner, tells Forbes that "he was very sorry to find" that Forbes was involved in this plot. Forbes, hearing this, perhaps thinks that the minister, a man of the cloth, will show some kindness toward him on this day of the Lord.

Instead, Livingston tells Forbes that "his time was very short, not having three days to live," and that therefore, Livingston was there to help him to "prepare himself." Basically, the minister is giving

Forbes his last rites, as if he were a man about to die. After all, Forbes is being accused of treason, and the penalty for such crimes is as serious as it gets.

But as the minister explains, the last rites have a bit of a window. If Forbes will cooperate and answer questions—that is, tell his full story—maybe his fate will change, and he won't need to "prepare himself" after all.

The minister's brief visit seems to have an immediate impact. "This had the desired effect; the prisoner asked to be carried before the Congress again, and he would discover all he knew."

Now, the committee has the man apparently at the very center of the conspiracy—and he's ready to talk.

However, the investigators do things a little differently with Gilbert Forbes. Rather than interrogate him on the record as they did with the Mayor, some combinations of John Jay, Gouverneur Morris, and Philip Livingston speak to him informally, off the record. They want to know what he knows, but they save his formal examination for later.

Why this change of process?

At this point, the investigation is turning a corner. The committee still has more people to arrest and interrogate, but it understands the basic contours of the plot and who's at fault.

And now, there are larger forces at play.

By Monday, June 24, the latest intelligence indicates that the first wave of the British fleet is now only days away.

The Continental army is preparing for an almost unimaginable challenge. Thousands of lives are on the line. George Washington, his officers, and his soldiers need to be in a position of cohesion and strength.

What's more, even if the authorities have mostly stymied the progress of the plot itself, the story of the conspiracy is starting to leak. They've kept it a secret as long as possible, but word is starting to spread.

The story of the plot will cause upheaval in the army and among the public, no matter what. Even if the plot fails, at the center of it is this shocking fact: Some of the most trusted men in the army—the Life Guards—have betrayed their country and their fellow soldiers.

If the worst is to be believed, they were planning to massacre their own leader.

What can Washington and his army do to contain the fallout of these shocking revelations? How can they maintain unity in the army at this critical time?

They need to control the narrative.

They need to make a big public statement.

Gilbert Forbes may be an important player in the criminal plot, but right now, he's only a small part of a greater picture.

Now it's about the integrity of the army on the eve of war.

It's about making sure the guilty parties—especially the traitors in their own army—pay the price for a terrible betrayal.

These men have committed an unspeakable act of treason. All the other soldiers will soon learn this, if they haven't already. The guilty Life Guards must be made an example of, for the entire army to see.

Now, it's time to serve justice.

PART V

Sacricide

66

New York, New York

June 1776

Thomas Hickey.

Along with fellow Life Guard Michael Lynch, Hickey was arrested for the relatively minor offense of carrying counterfeit bills; then, once in jail, he spoke a bit too freely to a cellmate.

This makes Hickey one of five Life Guards named as suspects in the conspiracy. Isaac Ketcham testified regarding Hickey and Lynch, and James Mason's testimony implicated William Green, Thomas Hickey (again), James Johnson, and a private named John Barnes.

Yet by Monday, June 24—a week after Ketcham spoke before the congress, and four days after James Mason gave his blockbuster testimony—the investigators close in on Thomas Hickey as a special focus of their inquiry. Not just in terms of the investigation, but as the one person on whom justice should be served to make a public statement.

This raises the question: If there are multiple Life Guards implicated, why do the authorities turn their focus on just one of them?

The most plausible answer is, they need to make an example of *someone*. The people in charge need to make it clear that if you plot against the Continental army, you're committing a traitorous act—and that anyone who does so must pay the highest possible price.

Basically, the authorities need to set an example . . . and they need to do it swiftly.

For one thing, the story of the plot is starting to leak. Any day now, the general public will learn that there's a conspiracy against the army—and very possibly aimed at the life of the army's Commander, George Washington. As the story spreads, the army wants *already* to have sent a strong, clear message about how such crimes are punished.

Second, the British fleet is now only days away. Based on all the testimony gathered thus far about the conspiracy, the moment of British arrival is when the plot gets triggered. So the Continental authorities desperately need a forceful public resolution to this case before that time—not only to dissuade any remaining plotters from following through on their designs, but to display strength and unity on the eve of a major battle.

At this exact moment in history, speed matters.

So, given the complexity of the conspiracy being investigated—at a time of war, no less—the fastest, simplest way to show the public that the authorities are in control is to pick just *one* culprit and make him the face of the conspiracy; then, prosecute him with an airtight case, and serve justice quickly and forcefully.

Even while the authorities continue to investigate the rest of the complicated case, this one guilty party—Life Guard Thomas Hickey—will face punishment before the rest.

Behind the scenes, probably at some point on Monday, June 24, George Washington and the Committee on Conspiracies agree on a procedure that will further facilitate a swift and clear resolution to the case. The suspects who are soldiers—most critically, the five Life Guards—will be handed over to the military for court-martial, rather than be handled by the civilian judicial system.

A court-martial. Swift and clean.

So with the clock ticking, and with the threat of more potential conspirators still at large, the investigators and generals focus all their attention on one man.

To this day, though, one question remains: Of the five Life Guards who are all considered guilty, why single out Thomas Hickey?

This answer isn't so simple.

For one thing, not much is known about Hickey, as a person or as a soldier, before the events of the conspiracy.

He was originally from Ireland. He served in the British military in the early 1770s, during which time he was sent to serve in the northeastern colonies. At some point around 1774, as hostilities increased between England and the colonies, he deserted the British army and joined one of the colonial militias in Connecticut. Apparently, he lived or was stationed in the town of Wethersfield. From there, he joined the Continental army in the late summer of 1775, along with most of the other new recruits.

When George Washington initially formed the Life Guards in March 1776, Thomas Hickey was among the first group of soldiers selected for this elite unit. The only existing account of Hickey's appearance describes his "dark hair," "dark complexion," and "solid build." He was apparently a good soldier, and was once described as a "favorite" of Washington's. During the army's journey from Boston to New York City, Thomas Hickey may very well have been one of the Life Guards who accompanied Washington.

However, under a bit of scrutiny, Hickey's character seems questionable. His reasons for originally deserting from the British are not known—but given his later reversal, he seems to lack loyalty to *any* cause.

In addition, while the crime of wandering around New York City carrying a few counterfeit bills may not be egregious, it does, at the very least, suggest a cavalier relationship to the law and to army regulations. And of course, above and beyond all that, he willingly chose to take part in a traitorous scheme against the Continental army, potentially signing up to kill the one man whom he'd vowed to protect.

As to why Hickey is singled out from the other Life Guards who are also implicated, there are a few possibilities. From the two key witnesses who were first able to name which Life Guards were in the plot—that is, counterfeiter Isaac Ketcham and mill worker James Mason—Thomas Hickey is the only Life Guard to be named by *both*. For this reason, the legal case against Hickey may have been stronger than against any other single Life Guard.

Another fact that cannot be ignored: Thomas Hickey is an Irishman—originally a native of Great Britain—and a former soldier of the royal army. Hickey's background, and probably his accent, makes him a convenient public face of treason for an army about to fight a massive battle against British forces. Targeting and punishing a kid from Pennsylvania or Massachusetts might have been a less popular choice.

However, there is one reason why the choice of Thomas Hickey as the "fall guy" for the plot does *not* initially make sense. To put it simply, one of the other Life Guards, the drummer William Green, seems more deserving in almost every way.

By multiple accounts, Green was the first Life Guard to get involved in the plot when Gilbert Forbes recruited him. According to testimony, Green was the ringleader among the Life Guards who joined, and was even responsible for doling out the payments to the others. Green also seems to have been the most publicly vocal when it came to insulting the Continental army in taverns around New York City.

As if that weren't enough, Green is *also* a former British soldier, just like Hickey. Green was originally from *England*, so even more ripe as a target of prejudice on the part of the colonial officers and soldiers.

Nonetheless, the authorities begin to single out Thomas Hickey as the stand-in for all the Life Guards.

At some point early in the week of June 24, the Committee on Conspiracies starts sharing documents and information with top military officials, no doubt under George Washington's oversight. Although no records are preserved, a complex coordination must have taken place for John Jay, Gouverneur Morris, and Philip Livingston to provide relevant testimony—as well as the coordination of witnesses and suspects—in order for a court-martial to proceed.

But that's not all.

Also on Monday, June 24, the Continental Congress in Philadelphia sends a resolution to the New York Provincial Congress, establishing legal parameters for how to prosecute "enemies of the Colonies." More specifically, they clarify the necessity for punishing a crime that had never existed before in a colonial context: treason.

Until this moment, words like "treason" had a particular meaning. They meant crimes against England, the mother country.

Now, the Continental Congress insists there's a new kind of treason: treason against America.

67

——— · ———

One Colonel.

One Lieutenant Colonel.

One Major.

Ten Captains.

These are the thirteen officers who are called to serve in the general court-martial of Thomas Hickey, convened on Wednesday, June 26, at the headquarters of the Continental army, at One Broadway in New York City. In this military version of a trial, these thirteen officers will review evidence, hear witnesses, and determine the verdict and the sentence for the accused.

Also present is William Tudor, the army's judge advocate—its lawyer, essentially—who will observe the proceedings and serve as legal counsel for George Washington and the army leadership.

As is customary for such proceedings, George Washington himself is not present, nor are his top generals.

Here today in this room, the army will provide Thomas Hickey a chance to defend himself.

To begin the proceedings, the presiding officer of the court-martial, Col. Samuel Parsons, reads the formal charges brought against the prisoner:

Thomas Hickey, a private sentinel in his Excellency the Commander-in-Chief's Guard. . . . [is] brought prisoner before the Court, accused "of exciting and joining in a mutiny and sedition, and of treacherously corresponding with, enlisting among, and receiving pay from the enemies of the United American Colonies."

Interestingly, there is no mention in the charges of a plan to kill George Washington. Despite the growing belief around the army and top officials that such an act was part of the conspiracy, the topic seems to be completely off-limits for the purposes of the court martial. The officers don't raise it as a question, and none of the suspects or witnesses ever acknowledges the suspicion, whether to confirm or to deny.

Once the charges are read, the proceedings begin immediately. One by one, a total of four witnesses will be called before the military court to testify.

The day starts with a prominent one: William Green, Thomas Hickey's fellow Life Guard.

In his testimony, Green describes his initial interactions with the gunsmith Gilbert Forbes, explaining what led to the Life Guards getting involved in Tryon's scheme. For the most part, Green does not downplay his prominent role in helping several Life Guards join a treasonous conspiracy against the leader they were entrusted to protect.

Green's story starts at the moment he first met Forbes:

[A]bout three weeks ago, I was in company with one Gilbert Forbes, a gunsmith, who lives in Broadway, and we fell into a conversation on politics. I found Forbes's pulse beat high in the Tory scheme. I had repeated conversations with Forbes afterwards, and he was always introducing politics, and hinting at the impossibility of this country standing against the power of Great Britain. He invited me to dine with him one day; and a day or two after asked me if I would not inlist into the King's service.

It was simple, really. Forbes sensed that Green was a corruptible target and recruited him to be a traitor.

Forbes's promise? Money, of course. He offered it to any Continental soldier who would join the conspiracy.

Green tells the court that he was curious about the source of Forbes's promised payments. As Green describes it, "I asked him where the money was to come from to pay me for the service; Forbes replied the Mayor would furnish money."

Once again, there's the Mayor, David Mathews, implicated as the paymaster in the scheme.

As Green's testimony continues, he again establishes that among the Life Guards, he was the unofficial leader, in charge of recruiting the others. He states, "Forbes left it with me to inlist and swear the men."

Green adds that he specifically lured fellow Life Guard Thomas Hickey into the plot. "Hickey agreed to the scheme, but did not receive any money, except two shillings which I gave him." Hickey was just one of several soldiers and Life Guards whom Green says he successfully recruited. "I enlisted ten or a dozen, and told them all my plan. The prisoner [Hickey] wrote his name upon a piece of paper with five others, which I gave to Forbes."

Green's testimony seems strongly incriminating, not just of Hickey, but also of himself. Green does make a feeble attempt to argue that his true motives for joining the treasonous plot were actually patriotic. He says that what he really wanted to do was rip off the people who were running the conspiracy. "I was pleased with the notion of getting some money from the Tories, and agreed to the scheme, with a view to cheat the Tories, and detect their scheme."

He says he shared this patriotic motive with Hickey. "I mentioned the matter . . . to Hickey. I told him the principle I went upon, and that we had a good opportunity of duping the Tories." Green even says that he and Hickey were planning to tell George Washington about the secret plot and were just waiting for the right moment. "I proposed to [Hickey] to reveal the plot to the General, but Hickey said we had better let it alone till we had made further discoveries."

Taken as a whole, Green's testimony tells the story of how the Life Guards first became involved in the plot, and the relative roles of Green and Hickey among them.

Now the court is ready to hear from someone even deeper in the conspiracy—one of the key players—to see if the stories match.

Gilbert Forbes, the gunsmith.

At this court-martial, Forbes will testify only to the specific issue of Hickey and the Life Guards; in a few days, he'll be interrogated again more broadly about the plot as a whole.

There is no record of Forbes's demeanor, tone, or attitude when he is called to testify during the court-martial. Based on the letter of the testimony, he seems mostly cooperative—unlike his earlier belligerence upon arrest.

In any case, the gunsmith begins by describing his initial interactions with the Life Guards, and his recruitments of William Green. According to Forbes, it all began shortly after George Washington first arrived in New York City, when Green happened to enter the same drinking establishment as Forbes:

> A night or two after General Washington arrived in New York from Boston, Green fell into company where I was. We were drinking, and Green toasted the King's health, and I did so too. A day or two afterwards Green called upon me, and said, that as I had drank his Majesty's health, he supposed I was his friend, and immediately proposed to enlist some men into the King's service, and told me he could procure considerable numbers to join him.

Clearly Forbes is trying to paint a different picture from Green's testimony. The way Forbes tells it, Green was the instigator of the whole thing, and the one aggressively offering to turn his fellow soldiers to the British side. Forbes says that at first, he tried to back away: "I put him off, and declined having any hand in the business." He says Green kept asking and eventually wore him down. "But in repeated applications from him, I at last fell into the scheme."

So according to Forbes, *he* was a reluctant participant, and William Green, the Life Guard, was the mastermind. The problem with

Forbes's version of events is, among other things, it contradicts what almost every other witness and suspect has told investigators. By everyone else's account, Forbes acted as a key recruiter, was at the center of the plotting, and was a liaison between various parties.

Though when it comes down to it, the difference between Forbes's and Green's account is not particularly significant. The end result is still the same: Forbes begins paying Green to be in the scheme, and also to enlist other Continental soldiers, in particular other Life Guards, to join as well.

Naturally, the officers also ask Forbes about Thomas Hickey's specific role.

According to Forbes, Hickey is one of the first fellow Life Guards whom Green recruited to join them. "In a day or two Green gave me a list of men who had engaged, among whom was the prisoner, Hickey. Soon after which, Hickey asked me to give him half a dollar, which I did."

Other than this one payment to Hickey, Forbes says that he mostly gave lump sums to Green and let Green funnel the payments to the other Life Guards. "Green received eighteen dollars, and was to pay the men who inlisted one dollar apiece, and we were to allow them ten shillings per week subsistence money."

So where does Forbes say he got the money to pay Green to pay the others? Once again, it's the Mayor—David Mathews. "I received upwards of a hundred pounds from Mr. Mathews, the Mayor, to pay those who should enlist into the King's service." After the initial pay of a half dollar or a dollar for each Life Guard, payment would continue at ten shillings a week so long as the recruits swore that they would "play their proper parts when the King' s forces arrived."

Certainly, Green's and Forbes's testimony is damning for Hickey, because they both clearly name him as a paid member of the cabal.

However, their testimony must also be taken with a certain suspicion. Both of them are a part of the conspiracy, so have a motive to make Hickey look worse in order to take the focus off themselves.

Fortunately, the officers of the court-martial have another witness to call forward who is not himself in the conspiracy, and whose testimony they can therefore trust.

Isaac Ketcham.

Accused counterfeiter, father of six—and jailhouse spy.

68

For the last nine days, ever since he first informed the congress of his alarming conversations with fellow cellmates Thomas Hickey and Michael Lynch, Isaac Ketcham has remained exactly where he was before that momentous day—locked in a cell in the city prison beneath City Hall.

In every other way, however, Ketcham's circumstances have dramatically changed.

Instead of being a prisoner with little hope of reprieve, Isaac Ketcham is now serving as an informant for the very congress that holds the power to release him—while also gathering top-secret information from Hickey and Lynch in an investigation that could affect the future of the colonies.

Unfortunately, there are no records of the communications between Ketcham and the investigators as he fed them information during those nine days. Since his first testimony, the details of how and when he shared his discoveries with the Committee of Conspiracies are not known.

However, one aspect of his role as secret jailhouse spy is obvious: Ketcham was groomed by both the congress and the military to be a key witness in the court-martial of Life Guard Thomas Hickey.

On June 26, 1776, after William Green and Gilbert Forbes testify, the officers of the court-martial call Isaac Ketcham before them
to tell his story.

Ketcham describes how he got Thomas Hickey to reveal information to him. He says that by pretending to Hickey and Lynch that he
was also on the side of the British and the Loyalists, Ketcham won
his cellmates' trust. After this, Ketcham says, Hickey expressed his
antipathy toward his own army and its leaders. "In different conversations he informed me that the Army was damnably corrupt."

Then Ketcham jumps to the heart of it. He says that in the jail,
Hickey told him "that the fleet was soon expected; and that he and a
number of others were in a band to turn against the American Army
when the King's troops should arrive." As Ketcham recounts it, Hickey
even "asked me to be one of them."

There, in a nutshell, is yet more damning testimony against Hickey,
this time from someone who is not himself implicated in the plot.

Ketcham continues to reveal more of what he learned, including
one startling detail: He says that Hickey told him "eight of the General's Guard were concerned, but mentioned only Green by name."

If Hickey was right, *eight* Life Guards were in on it. It's a remarkable number—more than the investigators knew. In addition, the
mention of "Green" suggests once again that William Green was a
leader of the cabal, given that his was the only name Hickey thought
to bring up when describing the plot.

Ketcham's testimony, brief but strong, seems to lock the case
against Thomas Hickey as a traitor to his army.

Still, the officers call another witness. He's a man named William
Welch, an English immigrant now living in New York, who describes
a conversation he recently had with Thomas Hickey.

According to Welch, Hickey pulled him aside one day and complained about the Continental army's failings. He told Welch about
the plot he had joined, and tried to convince Welch to join too. As
Welch describes it, Hickey told him that:

[T]he enemy would soon arrive, and that it was best for us Old
Countrymen to make our peace before they came, or they would

kill us all. That we Old Countrymen should join together, and we would be known by a particular mark, and if I would agree to be one among them, he would carry me to a man who would let me have a dollar by way of encouragement.

The conversation didn't go any further because "I did not relish the project, and we parted." His testimony ends there.

Welch's story doesn't add much to what is already known. Perhaps the most significant aspect of Welch's role at the court-martial is that he is there at all—because his name has never been mentioned in the Committee of Conspiracies' investigation, nor is there any record of him being summoned or examined in any prior setting.

This suggests that for the investigating committee and the military officers preparing for the court-martial, there was more behind-the-scenes activity—additional arrests, conversations, examinations, and lines of inquiry—than what appears in the official records.

After hearing from the four witnesses brought before the court—William Green, Gilbert Forbes, Isaac Ketcham, and William Welch—the officers have one more critical person to hear from as they decide Thomas Hickey's fate.

In fact, he may be the most important witness of all: Thomas Hickey.

For the first time, the Life Guard will have a chance to tell his side of the story.

69

This is it. Thomas Hickey, the Continental soldier and Life Guard accused of "mutiny and sedition" and "treasonable correspondence" with the enemy, is about to speak in his own defense.

If Hickey understands the seriousness of the allegations being made against him, the dark-haired, Irish-born Life Guard doesn't show it in court.

There is no record of his demeanor or behavior, so we don't know if he was angry, defiant, or resigned about the accusations made against him.

His testimony, transcribed by a secretary, suggests he had barely considered his own line of defense. Although he had officially pled not guilty to the charges, he fails to bring any evidence or witnesses, and doesn't have much of an answer for the allegations against him.

Indeed, after a full day of incriminating testimony about him from the other witnesses, Hickey makes a statement before the court of barely a sentence. The court-martial records show only this:

> The prisoner being here called upon to make his defense, produces
> no evidence; but says, "he engaged in the scheme at first for the
> sake of cheating the Tories, and getting some money from them,

and afterwards consented to have his name sent on board the man-of-war, in order that if the enemy should arrive and defeat the army here, and he should be taken prisoner, he might be safe."

Basically, Hickey admits outright that he joined the treasonous scheme. His first excuse is that his true motive for doing so was just to "cheat" the plotters by taking their money. His second excuse is that because he secretly thinks the British forces will prevail in the coming battle, he wants to save his own skin by putting his name on the list of colonists willing to betray the Continental army and join the British.

Either way, it's not much of a defense. Greed is hardly a legitimate reason to betray your own army and join an enemy plot; neither, of course, is cowardice. These aren't arguments likely to win over senior military officers in a court-martial.

Hickey is led away from the court just as quickly as he was brought before it.

After Hickey's brief testimony, the court-martial recesses, giving the officers time to consider the evidence. They can't have deliberated for long. That same afternoon, in the same room, they formally announce their verdict and sentence.

Thomas Hickey, a member of George Washington's Life Guards, is guilty as charged.

70

—— · ——

The verdict, read by Col. Samuel Parsons on the late afternoon of June 26, 1776, is as brutal as it is brief:

> The Court being cleared, after mature consideration, are unanimously of the opinion that the prisoner is guilty of the charge against him, and of a breach of the fifth and of the thirtieth articles of the Rules and Regulations for the government of the Continental Forces; and the court unanimously sentence and adjudge that the prisoner, Thomas Hickey, suffer death for said crimes by being hanged by the neck till he is dead.

Thomas Hickey's fate is sealed.

Maybe Thomas Hickey wasn't the only Continental soldier involved in the traitorous scheme.

Maybe Thomas Hickey wasn't even the one who played the greatest role in bringing the Life Guards into the plot.

Maybe other suspects were more deserving of being singled out and punished for joining or enlisting others to join the treasonous crime.

Maybe so. But Thomas Hickey was clearly guilty of being involved in the conspiracy, and the evidence against him is overwhelming. As a result, in late June 1776—in the days before some of the most memorable moments in American history—the Irish-born soldier is about to become the public symbol of the deadly plot against George Washington and the Continental army.

From the moment officers of the court-martial read their verdict and sentence, a chain of events races forward with inexorable speed.

The officers no doubt transmit their verdict immediately to George Washington, probably that evening.

Washington, according to protocol for making important decisions, convenes a council of war for the next morning, to discuss the court-martial's verdict and sign off on a course of action.

First thing the next morning, Thursday, June 27, Washington meets at his Broadway headquarters with six senior officers, including his generals Nathanael Greene, Joseph Spencer, Lord Stirling, Thomas Mifflin, John Morin Scott, and William Heath.

Washington informs his officers of the preceding day's court-martial. They are then encouraged to deliberate and advise him as they see fit. As the council's brief written log shows, the officers reach a relatively clear and hasty consensus:

> The General communicated to the Council the proceedings of the Court Martial on Thomas Hickey—[the council] unanimously advised to confirm the sentence & that it be put in execution tomorrow at 11 o' Clock, for which purpose the General is to issue his warrant.

This warrant is a warrant for execution. The council has determined that Hickey should receive the ultimate punishment.

According to the Continental army's regulations, only the Commander-in-Chief himself, George Washington, can issue a warrant of such magnitude. Then the warrant must go to the Provost Marshal, a special officer in charge of enforcing lawfulness within the ranks.

George Washington doesn't hesitate. And within a few hours, Washington and his officers finalize an even bigger plan. Hickey's execution will not be only a show of justice—it will be a public *statement*—a statement for the citizens, for the army, and for the enemy.

Also, this justice will be *swift*. Hickey will die tomorrow morning.

By that afternoon, Washington reveals his plan in the day's general orders—for every officer and every soldier to hear. These orders provide an answer to the questions that are by now spreading through the ranks of the soldiers, filled with stories of a rumored plot and traitors among them. The orders spell it out:

> Thomas Hickey belonging to the General's Guard having been convicted by a General Court Martial . . . of the crimes of "Sedition and Mutiny, and also of holding a treacherous correspondence with the enemy, for the most horrid and detestable purposes," is sentenced to suffer death. The General approves the sentence, and orders that he be hanged tomorrow at Eleven o' Clock.

The language is crystal clear. As an interesting embellishment—or perhaps as an expression of anger—Washington or his aides added the language "for the most horrid and detestable purposes" just for the general orders, because it did not appear in the original court-martial charges.

The orders go on to stipulate another key aspect of Hickey's punishment. The execution will take place in the open, and the entire army will see it. Washington is clear: Everyone has to watch.

The orders further command that "all the officers and men off duty" from all four brigades stationed in New York—those stationed farther away on Long Island are excluded—should "be under arms, on their respective parades" to march to a designated rural field in Manhattan, just north of the city line, in order to "attend the execution of the above sentence."

The army sends the general orders by midafternoon, and as always, they are quickly distributed to every officer to share with the troops.

Before the end of the afternoon, word spreads from soldiers to residents of the grim event planned for the next morning, including the planned location. There is no indication that the Continental army disapproved of this; more likely, officers encouraged their soldiers to share the news.

Within hours everyone knows what's coming. This isn't just a hanging; it's a public execution.

The decision is made; the stage is set—but as with everything else in the story of the first conspiracy, yet more surprises lie ahead.

71

———— • ————

Friday, June 28, 1776.

This day is rarely highlighted in the history books. Yet, there aren't many twenty-four-hour periods in America's history that contain as many dramatic and remarkable events, all transpiring basically at once.

For George Washington, the day starts with a letter. More specifically, a letter composed by Washington and his aides to John Hancock, the president of the Continental Congress. Washington's letters to Hancock are frequent, often containing lengthy updates, requests, and plans concerning every aspect of the war effort.

This particular morning, Washington updates Hancock and offers opinions on several logistical matters of the army—the pay of chaplains, for example, which he argues should be higher; also, a complicated discussion of the relative merits of appointing two commissary generals rather than one to manage the flow of army provisions—a bureaucratic question but one of urgent importance as the army continues to struggle desperately for want of supplies on the eve of battle.

Fairly typical matters, so far. But today, Washington also has to inform Hancock about something else—something more sensitive.

He needs to tell Hancock about Thomas Hickey, and the state of the plot that has quickly become the biggest rumor in the army.

This letter is the first time Washington or any other Continental army officer has communicated anything about the plot directly to the Continental Congress, probably because Washington insisted on maintaining absolute secrecy up to this point.

In fact, this note to Hancock represents the first time Washington himself describes the plot in writing to *anyone*, despite the fact that news of it has now been spreading and generating rumors for more than a week.

In the letter, Washington's language is careful, striking a calm, measured tone—no doubt hoping to convey to Congress that the matter is now under control. Interestingly, he begins by acknowledging that news of the secret plot has already spread around the colonies. And then:

> Congress I doubt not will have heard of the plot that was forming among many disaffected persons in this city and government, for aiding the King's troops upon their arrival . . . several persons have been enlisted and sworn to join them—The matter I hope by a timely discovery will be suppressed and put a stop to. Many citizens & others, among whom is the Mayor, are now in confinement— the matter has been traced up to Governor Tryon & the Mayor appears to have been a principal agent or go between him and the persons concerned in it.

Although Washington carefully includes the names of his key enemies in the conspiracy—namely, Governor Tryon and Mayor Mathews—he declines to provide any details about the goals of the plot, and certainly avoids mention of the unspeakable detail that has begun to reach the public: that the plot may have included a plan to assassinate Washington himself.

He does, however, share with Hancock the most scandalous aspect of the plot, namely the fact that some in his own ranks were party to it. This admission, of course, leads to the breaking news about the fate of his Life Guard, Thomas Hickey:

The plot had been communicated to some of the army, and part of my Guard engaged in it—Thomas Hickey one of them, has been tried and by the unanimous opinion of a Court Martial is sentenced to die, having enlisted himself and engaged others—the sentence by the advice of the whole Council of General Officers will be put in execution today at Eleven O'Clock.

Regarding the other conspirators currently in custody, Washington says only that "the others are not tried."

Finally, he ends on a resolute note, explaining his swift administration of justice: "I am hopeful this example will produce many salutary consequences and deter others from entering into the like traitorous practices."

The letter is written. Now comes the event itself.

By early morning, Generals Heath, Stirling, Spencer, and Scott had called their brigades of soldiers to attention, at their respective encampments in Manhattan. At exactly ten o'clock, each general begins marching his brigade of soldiers northward, through the city streets, alleys, parks, and pathways, toward the agreed-upon location: an open field north of the city limits at the time, near present-day Grand and Chrystie Streets, east of the Bowery.

By roughly half past ten, the four brigades have reached the field and assembled under the morning's overcast sky, a total of close to ten thousand soldiers, standing at attention, armed and in uniform. Not very often since the first formation of the Continental army one year ago have so many officers, soldiers, and army aides all gathered in one place.

But it's not just soldiers who have gathered for this event.

Starting the previous afternoon, once the time and place was set, word quickly spread about the unusual fate of one of George Washington's soldiers. Whether from posted handbills or from the mouths of troops and officers, news of the scandal traveled through the entire region—and by morning every resident and citizen seemed to have learned about it.

Now, almost all of them are gathered, standing in a crowd of many thousands, apart from the army but almost as great in size.

In total close to twenty thousand people assemble in this field—almost the entire population of New York City at the time, including the army stationed there. No question, some of the onlookers also traveled across the East River from Long Island, or across the Hudson River from New Jersey, or from the north, across the King's Bridge from Westchester County into Manhattan.

The fledgling country has never seen a spectacle quite as big as this.

At the center of the vast crowd, next to a large tree in the field, is a hastily built wooden structure.

It's a gallows.

Above the raised platform hangs a single noose, silhouetted against the gray sky.

All these gathered people, citizens and soldiers alike, are here to witness one thing: justice served to the traitor, Thomas Hickey.

At approximately a quarter to eleven, a separate group of soldiers, not standing in line with the rest of the brigades, begins to march from behind the formations, moving toward the gallows.

Following instructions given in the general orders of the previous day, the majors in charge had provided "twenty men, from each Brigade, with good arms and bayonets, as a guard on the prisoner to and at the place of execution."

Certainly, eighty soldiers are not necessary to guard one man; this flourish is for show rather than for safety. The purpose? A procession, so everyone watching can see the lone criminal flanked formally by several dozen armed soldiers, marching solemnly toward the gallows. It's a final message to the crowd.

Thomas Hickey, Irishman, formerly of Wethersfield, Connecticut, with dark hair, dark complexion, and sturdy build, walks to the foot of the gallows, at which point he's led up to the low platform.

Joining him, there are two people: a chaplain and the Provost Marshal, who today is tasked with administering the most serious form of punishment there is.

Most of the written records of the event by eyewitnesses describe the vast crowd size and the impressive array of soldiers. Only a very few onlookers are close enough to observe the human drama of what transpires in the final minutes. One of those who is close enough and later describes it in writing is the young army surgeon, William Eustis, who stands and watches in formation among his fellow enlisted men.

As Eustis relates it, Thomas Hickey maintains an air of defiance; at least, he does until the very end. Eustis writes:

> He appeared unaffected and obstinate to the last, except that when the Chaplain took him by the hand under the Gallows and bade him adieu, a torrent of tears flowed over his face; but with an indignant scornful air he wiped 'em with his hand from his face, and assumed the confident look.

The tears are gone. But Hickey's confident look will be short lived.

There is no record of whether any final sentence or formal proclamation is read aloud by the Provost Marshal, but Eustis adds one more surprising detail to his description: some final words from Hickey.

Words that, at first anyway, are puzzling.

Eustis writes of Hickey's last moment. "With his last breath the fellow told the spectators, that unless General Greene was very cautious, the Design would as yet be executed on him."

Eustis assumes, in his written recollection of the day, that Hickey refers to Gen. Nathanael Greene—one of Washington's favorite generals, currently stationed in Long Island.

Word would later spread of this anecdote, and for many years the accepted wisdom was that Hickey must have borne some personal grudge against General Greene, or somehow blamed Greene for his own terrible circumstances.

The problem, however, is that none of it makes sense. General Greene's only particular role in uncovering the plot was his oversight of the midnight arrest of Mayor David Mathews. There's no other way in which Greene played a part in the arrest of the Life Guards or the investigation of the case. He had nothing to do with the court-martial. In fact, because General Greene has been almost entirely stationed on Long Island since the army traveled from Boston, Thomas Hickey was probably rarely, if ever, anywhere near him.

So why would Thomas Hickey feel such hatred for Nathanael Greene that he would single him out in the final moment before his own death? And if he *was* referring to the general stationed on Long Island, it's hard to fathom what Hickey meant by saying that the "the Design would as yet be executed on him."

A much more likely explanation is that Hickey's final words weren't referring to *General* Greene at all. Rather, he must have actually been speaking about his fellow Life Guard and coconspirator, the drummer William Green.

Eustis, the army surgeon, probably had never heard of William Green, and simply assumed that when Hickey uttered the word "Green," he was referring to the best-known Greene in the army. So when Eustis later wrote his account of the day, he used the words "General Greene" as part of that assumption.

Thus, it seems more likely that Hickey was really expressing his rage toward William Green. If so, that fact may help explain, indirectly, how it was that Hickey ended up being singled out for punishment among the Life Guards to begin with.

Very possibly, the conspiring Life Guards all agreed never to inform on one another; indeed, when they were "qualified" to be in the scheme they each had to take a vow of secrecy regarding the plot.

Perhaps William Green, once authorities interrogated him, realized the gravity of his situation and chose to offer testimony against his fellow conspirator Thomas Hickey. This would provide the authorities something they really wanted: a clear guilty party, with strong testimony to support the case. Hickey, at least as far as the records show, never mentioned Green's name to authorities before or during his court-martial; nor did he try to make the case that it was Green, and not himself, who was the leader among them.

In other words, if the Life Guards all had vowed not to inform on one another, Hickey may have kept the vow and Green did not. In this scenario, perhaps Hickey realized only after receiving his death sentence that Green had betrayed him. This would explain Hickey's otherwise cryptic statement just moments before his execution.

In any case, Hickey's final words don't linger in the air for long. At exactly eleven o'clock, the Provost Marshal secures the noose around

Thomas Hickey's neck—and the vast crowd of onlookers watches as the platform drops and the soldier's life ends.

Thomas Hickey, of George Washington's Life Guards, is the first soldier to be executed for treason in the Revolutionary War. With almost twenty thousand spectators—soldiers and citizens alike—Hickey's hanging is also, at that time, the largest public execution ever to take place in North America.

72

In the wake of Hickey's hanging, the first army document to allude to the execution is a rather grim one. It's the formally executed warrant for the soldier's punishment, now signed by the Provost Marshal, and with the following language:

> By virtue of, and in obedience to, the foregoing warrant, I have this day, at the time and place therein ordered and directed, caused Thomas Hickey, the prisoner within mentioned, to suffer death in the way and manner therein prescribed, and accordingly return this warrant fully executed.

This official notice at least brings the grisly event to a formal close.

Of course, after George Washington returns from the dark spectacle, he must also make some statement about the dramatic event to his army and officers, to reinforce the terrible gravity of what they've all witnessed—and to make sure the harsh public display sends the message he intends. Within hours after the hanging, he sends a general order about the matter, for every officer and soldier to see. Here's how he characterizes the scene they've all just witnessed:

The unhappy fate of Thomas Hickey, executed this day for Mutiny, Sedition and Treachery; the General hopes will be a warning to every soldier, in the army, to avoid those crimes, and all others, so disgraceful to the character of a soldier, and pernicious to his country.

Brief, solemn, and to the point. But then, in the same paragraph, Washington adds one more line that takes his statement in an unexpected direction:

And in order to avoid those crimes the most certain method is to keep out of the temptation of them, and particularly to avoid lewd women, who, by the dying confession of this poor criminal, first led him into practices which ended in an untimely and ignominious death.

Wait. "Lewd women"?

Of all the mysteries left in the wake of the plot against George Washington, this final line in his June 28 general order may be the most baffling. To whom, exactly, is the Commander referring?

In the entire records of the Committee on Conspiracies' investigation of the plot, including several dozen arrests and examinations, there is not a single mention of any woman, let alone a "lewd woman"—in the language of the day usually meaning a prostitute—who played a role leading Hickey into the scheme. Nor is there any mention of any such woman in the records of the New York Provincial Congress, or of the army's court-martial.

Could Washington be obliquely referring to his mysterious former housekeeper, Mary Smith, who was so suddenly removed on suspicion of being involved in the plot? After all, one scenario is that she was secretly conspiring with the handful of Life Guards posted at Mortier's estate, where Washington usually sleeps and dines.

While not totally impossible, this seems highly unlikely. Washington has maintained absolute silence and discretion so far regarding his fired housekeeper, so it would be very strange if he were suddenly to allude to her in a general order for the entire Continental army to read or hear.

What's more, this housekeeper, whatever her politics or schemes, was a middle-aged woman who had been hired based on recommendations from aristocratic families who had employed her in the past. It seems inconceivable that Washington would refer to her as a "lewd woman."

Is it possible that Hickey made some sort of "dying confession" that Washington was privy to, either before or at the time of his execution, that referred to a woman who lured him into the scheme? Perhaps.

If so, though, it remains strange that there is no other reference anywhere to such a woman or such a confession, nor is there even a clear place in the known narrative of the plot in which "lewd women" could play a role.

One other explanation—and probably the most likely—is that George Washington is simply using the opportunity of the moment to do what he often does: urge and scold the soldiers to stay out of trouble, to follow laws and regulations, and to conduct themselves safely and honorably.

Few aspects of the soldiers' behavior in New York City have appalled Washington so much as their frequent and repeated trips to visit the red-light district of the so-called Holy Ground. Maybe Hickey was known to be a customer there, and Washington saw a good opportunity to link the debauchery and crime of the neighborhood with Thomas Hickey's terrible fate.

73

⸺ • ⸺

Even today, it's hard to know how the soldiers and officers received Washington's message about their fellow soldier's swift punishment.

However, early signs indicate that the event of the hanging itself—coming so soon after rumors about the plot were flying—met with a kind of steadfast approval by the witnesses and the public in general.

One newspaper writer who attended the event quickly filed a report for a local broadsheet called the *Constitutional Gazette*, using some arcane rhetoric against the British to augment his depiction of what happened.

> This forenoon, was executed in a field . . . in the presence of near twenty thousand spectators, a soldier belonging to his Excellency General Washington's guards, for mutiny and conspiracy; being one of those who formed, and was soon to have put in execution, that horrid plot of assassinating the staff officers, blowing up the magazines . . . on the arrival of the hungry ministerial myrmidons.

Like most other reports and discussions of the plot now emerging, this writer includes specific reference to an assassination plot, in this case against all the staff officers. Others who write about it specify Washington as the primary or sole target of assassination. For example, one civilian describes it this way:

> A hellish plot has been lately discovered at New York to murder General Washington and some other officers of the first rank, blow up the magazine, and spike the cannon. . . . It was to have been put in execution on the first arrival of the [British] Army. . . . One of General Washington's guards has been put to death for being concerned in it. The Mayor of the city, and some others, are confined. . . . It is said the matter has been traced up to Governour Tryon.

Clearly, by the day of Hickey's death the narrative and accepted wisdom about the plot—believed by officers, soldiers, and citizens alike—is that the plot included a plan to kill George Washington, on the brink of battle.

It's on that same afternoon of Hickey's execution—probably within a few hours of it—that William Eustis goes back to his headquarters and writes a detailed letter describing the event, sharing everything he knows or has heard about the plot that led to it. It's in this letter that the young army surgeon will invent that truly memorable word:

> Their design was upon the first engagement which took place, to have murdered (with trembling I say it) the best man on earth: General Washington was to have been the subject of their unheard of SACRICIDE.

Sacricide. Derived from the Latin, it means "slaughter of the sacred," or "slaughter of the good."

Eustis goes on to write: "In order to execute their design upon our General, they had enlisted into their service one or two from his Excellency's Life Guard, who were to have assassinated him." Then he captures what was probably a widespread feeling in the army that day when he expresses horror that "any set of men could be so lost to every virtuous principle, and so dead to the feelings of humanity as to conspire against the person of so great and good a man as General Washington."

Another eyewitness to Hickey's hanging that day was a young artillery captain from New York by the name of Alexander Hamilton. He had joined the New York militia in early 1776 while still finishing his term at King's College, and now, aged only twenty-one, leads a unit in the Continental army. He has already gained some notice as a young officer of intelligence and dedication.

Like most witnesses to Hickey's death, Hamilton takes satisfaction in the harsh justice administered by the army in response to the plot. Regarding the other suspects, including the other Life Guards who are now confined, he writes: "It is hoped the remainder of those miscreants now in our possession will meet with a punishment adequate to their crimes."

While Hamilton and others may derive strength from the army's swift response to the plot, an interesting question remains.

What about George Washington himself?

Washington never writes and apparently never talks about his actual feelings concerning the execution, beyond the carefully crafted general orders.

Nevertheless, the revelations of the plot must have taken a toll on the Commander-in-Chief.

On the day of Hickey's hanging, it has been almost exactly a year since George Washington first arrived in Boston to take command of the Continental army. Although himself an inexperienced general, he took his command full of lofty notions of what an army is supposed to be. He truly believes in the codes of honor and character associated with serving, whether as a soldier or an officer.

Since then, he has so often seen reality fall short of his noble ideals. Over and over, he finds that his own army is dirtier, drunker, has worse morale, and is more plagued by desertions, infighting, and bad behavior, than he had hoped.

Now, a year later, at a time of genuine peril, he's had to administer the most severe punishment against his own soldier for the ultimate military sacrilege: treason.

Of course, it's not just Thomas Hickey. The fact that so many colonists, perhaps hundreds in the region, have been lured to join Tryon's secret army must be deeply frustrating, and distressing, at a time when the army needs as much public support as possible. Likewise, Washington and his officers' inability to prevent nefarious plots from forming within their own army—let alone be ready to face another in battle—can hardly be reassuring.

More than anything, this act of *betrayal* on the part of his own soldiers must weigh on Washington's soul. Literally nothing could be further from the ideal of honor that he has tried to impart to his men. Whether or not Washington ever feared for his own life is immaterial. The sheer level of betrayal is profound and deep.

These were the *Life Guards*. These are the men that he chose to defend him, men he trusted to protect his life, and now, in front of the whole army, they have shamed themselves and their unit with conduct that is not just disrespectful, but deplorable.

So, in the hours after watching one of his favorite Life Guards dangle from the gallows, it's hard to imagine that George Washington isn't walking under a black cloud on this day, June 28, 1776.

Yet, amidst all this darkness, what Washington doesn't realize is that there will soon be a ray of extraordinary light.

The Commander doesn't know it yet, but even as he grapples with the ugly spectacle of one of his own soldiers being put to death, something else of great magnitude is also under way at this very moment.

Unlike the death of Thomas Hickey—an event inspired by acts of treachery and treason—this other event is inspired by the most enlightened ideals.

It's not happening in New York City, where Washington's fragile army braces for battle. It's happening somewhere else.

About two hundred miles away—in Philadelphia.

74

———— . ————

Philadelphia, Pennsylvania

June 1776

It started—or it started for *real*, anyway—sometime back in April.

At that point, the Continental Congress had been managing a budding war for more than nine months, supporting George Washington and his new army through the long siege of Boston, approving and authorizing payment and provisions and supplies, devising rules and regulations from scratch, and coordinating the various colonies to work together to support the war effort.

Throughout this period, the delegates were also doing something else: grappling with the most profound political questions, debating the nature of government, and trying to determine the truest course for the future of the North American colonies in relation to their mother country, England.

It's remarkable in hindsight that in early 1776, more than half a year since the convening of the Second Continental Congress and the formation of the Continental army, the prevailing wisdom of the majority of delegates—and indeed the majority of colonists—was that the goal for raising arms was to change specific *terms* of the existing subservient relationship to the mother country.

The delegates all agreed that the colonists needed a greater degree of self-governance and greater forms of representation for their citizens—and were generally united in making bitter complaints against Great Britain regarding repressive tax and trade policies.

Yet, apart from a feisty minority in the Continental Congress known as the radicals, the delegates had mostly envisioned a future of greater rights and self-governance within the colonial framework— meaning that the North American colonies would always be answerable, ultimately, to Parliament and to the King.

In other words, the primary goal was *reconciliation*—and restoration of once-friendly relations—only with more favorable terms.

But by the spring months, this goal increasingly began to seem both unrealistic and profoundly disappointing.

The reasons for this shift are vast and there are too many to describe easily. But England's belligerence in the wake of the Boston evacuation— including the continuation of punitive trade embargoes, the burning of some colonial coastal cities, and Parliament's refusal to accept the legitimacy of the Continental Congress—certainly contributed to it.

Also critical was the publication, back in January, of Thomas Paine's landmark essay *Common Sense*. Paine's full-throated argument for a complete break with Great Britain had a clarity and force that made the treatise a sensation. In many ways, Paine was ahead of the politicians when it came to grasping public sentiment; *Common Sense* sold an unprecedented 100,000 copies in three months.

More and more, the radicals' vision for the future is gaining momentum: they should now forego any attempt to compromise, and seek to free themselves from the mother country.

As John Adams, one of the most outspoken and influential radicals among all the delegates at the Continental Congress, puts it in May 1776: "Great Britain has at last driven America, to the last step, a complete separation from her, a total absolute Independence, not only of her Parliament but of her Crown."

What's more, the long-term ambiguity of Congress's political position has consistently hampered the war effort. When the political leaders' posture is so tentative, the army's morale is lowered; soldiers, maybe more than any others, crave clarity of purpose.

The political leaders at Congress must ask: Are these young soldiers really going to sacrifice their lives in order to negotiate a slightly better tax policy? Or are they going to sacrifice their lives in pursuit of something bigger?

The Continental army needs something to fight *for*, not just something to fight against.

And of course, these fierce debates touch upon the deeper ideals at stake in the conflict—the ideals about liberty, freedom, and justice. Once these hopes had been roused in the hearts of colonists, the notion of a return to a modified form of subservience to Great Britain became increasingly hard to accept.

Having come this far, the colonists want self-government, not monarchy. The colonists want to rule themselves, not be ruled by another. The colonists want rights derived from a just government, based on liberty and enshrined in law—rights they believe are currently denied them by the all-powerful Parliament and King.

For all these reasons and more, the radicals began to gain ground in the early months of 1776, despite the continued resistance of both the conservative delegates and some of the colonies' local governments, whose will the Continental Congress could not legally ignore.

After a complicated series of legislative gambits throughout the spring, by June 1776, the pro-independence faction within Congress gains support to at least form a committee to draft a sample document, based on some previous resolutions already seen, that outlines their position. Later, this document—a so-called Declaration—can be put to a vote.

The formation of this drafting committee in early June, on its face a mundane bureaucratic development, nonetheless opens the door to a new energy and hope. Even the *contemplation* of independence begins to reshape the sense of possibility, changing the entire notion of what the war is about.

Everything these delegates have been working toward takes on a heightened meaning and significance. With independence as the goal, the war can be considered a genuine *revolution*. If successful, all the grandiose principles and ideals can soon be put into practice—a chance to reshape human society with a brand-new political system. As Adams writes:

Objects of the most stupendous magnitude, and measures in which the lives and liberties of millions yet unborn are intimately interested, are now before us. We are in the midst of a revolution, the most complete, unexpected and remarkable, of any in the history of nations.

For help in crafting a draft document in committee, Adams selected an unexpected candidate—a relatively little-known delegate named Thomas Jefferson. Jefferson, a thirty-three-year-old Virginian, was only in the Continental Congress as a sort of understudy— he had been rushed up to Philadelphia as a quick replacement to fill a slot after Patrick Henry, the eldest of the Virginia delegates, fell ill in late summer of 1775 and could no longer serve.

Since that time, Jefferson, a skinny redhead, had not exactly become a powerhouse in the convention hall. Indeed, he was usually shy and quiet. However, the Virginian had one very notable quality: He was good with his pen. Adams and the others in the drafting committee had noticed the quality of Jefferson's prose, and decided to take a chance and let the young delegate write the first draft.

For two weeks, starting on June 14, Jefferson went to work. Toward the end of that time, Adams and some of the other committee members weighed in and suggested revisions. For the most part, they left Jefferson's original prose—written with the inspiration born of a tight deadline—largely intact.

Then, on the morning of Friday, June 28, 1776—at almost the same hour that Thomas Hickey is approaching the gallows—Adams presents Jefferson's legendary first draft of this document to the Continental Congress.

Throughout the day, the various members of the Continental Congress, representing all thirteen colonies, read the now-famous passages in this new "Declaration of Independence" for the very first time.

They read them, they think about them, and they start to debate them feverishly.

In a few days, Congress will vote whether to ratify this document— and potentially change the war . . . and the world . . . forever.

75

New York, New York

June 1776

In New York City on the afternoon of June 28, 1776, the vast majority of soldiers, citizens, and even most officers have no idea that anything of interest is happening in Philadelphia. The efforts of a special committee to write a draft document for the delegates of the Continental Congress are probably the last thing on their minds.

So after the massive public spectacle of a public hanging just north of New York City, soldiers and citizens return to their stations or go back to their normal workdays.

But this is 1776—and normalcy can never last very long.

In fact, it won't even last a full afternoon.

That day, out at sea, the captain of a colonial sloop sailing along the New Jersey coastline south of New York City spies an unusual ship passing by in the distance.

After circling back and communicating with another captain who saw something similar, the captain takes another look.

It's a ship called the *Greyhound*.

That's a British vessel, and not just any. It's Gen. William Howe's ship—the Commander of British forces in North America.

If Gen. Howe's ship is here, that means something else. The main British fleet isn't far behind.

According to the officers on the sloop, the *Greyhound* was last spotted heading toward Sandy Hook, south of Long Island and not far from the entry into New York Harbor.

In the late afternoon of June 28, 1776, George Washington receives a message originally sent from the sloop's captain, informing the army of what he's seen.

As soon as Washington reads the note, he quickly sends messages of his own to the surrounding colonies with a simple order: Send all the extra militia troops you have, and send them fast.

New York will need all the reinforcements it can get.

Only a matter of hours after Thomas Hickey swung from the gallows, the British aren't just coming. The British are *here*.

76

——— · ———

Just after dawn the next morning, Saturday, June 29, a young Continental rifleman named Daniel McCurtin is standing sentry on a small hill with an elevated view of New York's Lower Bay.

He takes a break to use an outhouse that happens to provide a view toward the water.

The young rifleman recounts what happens next: "[I] was upstairs in an out-house and spied as I peeped out the bay something resembling a wood of pine trees trimmed . . . I could not believe my eyes."

What McCurtin actually sees are vertical masts, basically a forest of them, spread wide across the harbor.

As he describes further, "In about ten minutes the whole bay was full of ship[s] as ever it could be. I declare that I thought all London was afloat."

This first wave of General Howe's fleet is between forty and fifty ships, sailing just above Sandy Hook, and east of Staten Island. Soon, everyone in the area can see them.

In New York City, everyone promptly begins to panic.

Residents start running to the streets away from shore, soldiers run to stand guard at their positions, and the paths leading out of the city become choked with people ready to flee.

Later that afternoon a second wave of ships sails in; now it's over one hundred ships instead of forty or fifty. The ships make no sign of attack, but their sheer number is awesome to behold. Still, there is little that the Continental army can do but wait.

By the next day, Washington and his officers can discern the British strategy. They're disembarking and setting up encampments on Staten Island, about three miles due south of Manhattan by water. Based on observation and intelligence reports, the British plan becomes clear. They'll take control of the harbor and waterways, encamp thousands of troops on Staten Island, continue to wait for reinforcements, and take their time preparing an offensive.

On Sunday, June 30, the New York Provincial Congress—including the Committee on Conspiracies—vacates New York City for fear of the impending invasion. They make hasty plans to reconvene in White Plains, away from battle.

In this situation, there's not much Washington and the Continental army can do but watch helplessly. With no navy to speak of—not a single genuine fighting vessel—there is no real way to challenge or threaten the British warships, frigates, and transports now anchoring or docking all along the Staten Island shores.

A few more tense days pass, and more ships continue to pour into the harbor. Washington sends messages to the Continental Congress with regular updates: 110 ships, now 150, now over 200.

Meanwhile, Washington tries to put his army on a footing for the impending battle. On July 2, he writes a general order to be read to all troops. It's about as rousing a call to arms as could be put into words:

The time is now near at hand, which must probably determine whether Americans are to be . . . consigned to a state of wretchedness, from which no human efforts will probably deliver them. The fate of unborn millions will now depend, under God, on the courage and conduct of this army. Our cruel and unrelenting enemy leaves us no choice, but a brave resistance or the most abject sub-

mission. This is all that we can expect. We have, therefore, to resolve to conquer or die.

Interestingly, Washington uses the phrase "Conquer or Die,"
which is the Life Guards' motto. Perhaps he's signaling that whatever
some of the Life Guards did or didn't do in the past, they all have to
forget about that and move forward to confront the challenge at hand.

From this point on, the soldiers shift to a constant state of being
on guard, filling every post, monitoring every lookout, ready for battle
every single day.

More days pass. The British take their time, setting up a full headquarters and base of operations on Staten Island.

General Howe, among other things, is still waiting for his brother's
naval fleet to arrive, a fleet that will be accompanied by thousands of
Hessian reinforcements.

Meanwhile, General Howe also sends a message: He requests a
diplomatic meeting with the American leadership. England still hopes
to reconcile with the colonies without further hostilities.

Without a doubt, this standoff will take longer than everyone expected. Washington and his army look as if they'll have to wait helplessly, on the verge of war, possibly for weeks, with no realistic way to
attack the enemy.

Yet whatever diplomatic attempt the British have planned, they're
in for a surprise—because the Americans have something very different in mind.

77

Philadelphia, Pennsylvania

July 1776

After receiving Thomas Jefferson's first draft of the new Declaration on June 28, the Continental Congress orders that it "lie on the table" for a few days, a process by which the document can be edited and amended.

Meanwhile, as some revisions are made, the delegates engage in the furious politics of determining who will vote for it, who won't, and how to get the governing body of every single colony on board.

Remarkably, during this three- or four-day period, the delegates also learn of the arrival of the British fleet in New York Harbor, signaling the pending start of the largest battle of the war.

The stakes couldn't feel higher, and the sense of epochal world events unfolding in real time must be palpable for every delegate there.

On July 2, after furious debates, machinations and no small amount of editing, the Declaration is finally put to a vote.

The ayes have it.

The Declaration has passed the Continental Congress.

The colonies are no longer part of the British Empire, or at least they're ready to fight to make it so.

After another round of revisions, the wording of the Declaration is finalized for good on July 4, 1776. Contrary to popular belief, there is no signing ceremony on this day; that won't happen for another few weeks. But the delegates' signatures aren't what matters. As of July 4, the colonies' Declaration is final—and now there's no turning back.

That night, the Congress sends a handwritten version of the Declaration to a printer named John Dunlop, who runs a press near the Pennsylvania State House. Dunlop prints two hundred copies overnight, now ready to be mailed or delivered.

The next day, the delegates send copies to each colony's governing body, as well as to key officials in different cities.

John Hancock, who has served as the president of the Continental Congress since the day it voted to form an army just over a year ago, personally sends a copy to New York City.

This copy has George Washington's name on it.

78

———— • ————

New York, New York

July 1776

It's about time.

There are few people in the colonies who have been waiting for this document, the Declaration of Independence, more than George Washington, the Commander-in-Chief of the Continental army.

For months, Washington has been frustrated by the ambiguity of the Continental Congress's position with regard to the war. Up to this point, he's been tasked to lead an army without a clear vision of what they're fighting for.

Since the early part of the year, Washington had given up on the idea of a diplomatic solution to the war. In fact, he had once gently mocked the Continental Congress for dining on the "dainty food of reconciliation" while the harsh reality of full-scale war lay right before them.

Now, with this Declaration, the war has clarity and moral purpose.

Now, the great threats that Washington and his soldiers face are no longer part of some ambiguous, long-drawn-out, confusing diplomatic plan.

Now, his army is fighting a War of Independence.

Now, it's a revolution—an *American* Revolution.

Washington first receives his printed copy of the Declaration at his New York City headquarters the morning of Tuesday, July 9, 1776.

There is no record of how George Washington reacted when he read the words of the Declaration for the first time, but his actions speak louder than any words he can say or write.

Right away, he has his aides send out a general order with a special request.

Even with hundreds of British warships sitting in New York Harbor at that very moment, he orders each brigade of soldiers to be ready to stand at attention at six o'clock that evening. Those stationed in lower Manhattan are to converge in the Commons, New York City's town green, centrally located near Broadway.

For the second time in eleven days the Continental army—officers and soldiers—will gather for a special ceremonial event.

This occasion, however, could not be more different from the one eleven days ago, on June 28. The execution of Thomas Hickey was an event of solemnity and death, the harsh outcome of treasonous acts.

Tonight's gathering is about something very different.

At the designated time the troops converge on the Commons, with the uniformed soldiers standing divided by company.

According to George Washington's orders, one of his officers—which one exactly is not known—stands on an elevated platform and holds the special document the Commander-in-Chief has given him to read.

With thousands of troops and other onlookers listening, with George Washington himself standing nearby—and with the British warships not far away in the harbor—the officer begins to read.

Of course, today we've all heard the phrases countless times—but on this night in 1776, the vast majority of these officers and soldiers hear the words for the very first time:

We hold these truths to be self-evident, that all men are created equal, that they are endowed by their Creator with certain unalienable Rights, that among these are Life, Liberty and the pursuit of Happiness. . . .

These are the words.

These words are why they are fighting.

These words are worth not just fighting for, but dying for.

The reading continues, even as the light begins to fade. Soon the officer gets to the final sentence: "And for the support of this Declaration, with a firm reliance on the protection of divine Providence, we mutually pledge to each other our Lives, our Fortunes and our sacred Honor."

By every account from witnesses and participants in this extraordinary gathering, when those final words are spoken the entire crowd of more than ten thousand soldiers lets out a massive cheer.

George Washington, looking at this throng of joyful soldiers in front of him, must feel he's looking at a different army from the one he looked at eleven days ago.

At this point, after this reading, the soldiers are so full of energy and excitement that letting out a cheer isn't enough.

From the Commons, the excited soldiers parade down Broadway through the center of the city, cheering and yelling as they go. Soon the crowd finds a new destination at the Bowling Green, near the southern tip of the island, and in front of the army's main headquarters. The soldiers have a target.

The statue.

Yes, *that* statue: the pompous equestrian statue of George III, His Majesty the King of England, riding high on horseback above the citizens of New York City, dressed in Roman robes like an emperor from the ancient world.

George Washington doesn't even try to stop them. In an hour of barely controlled chaos, soldiers find some ropes and tools, and with them tear down the massive lead statue, breaking it into pieces as they go. Some keep fragments of it as souvenirs. After the statue is down, the soldiers continue to parade and cheer and race around the city streets. One report has it that the troops push around King George's head in a wheelbarrow, before affixing it to a pike that they plant in the ground.

The revelry will continue late into the night.

As for General Washington, after the reading of the Declaration, he turns around and gets ready to head back to his headquarters.

In just the past few weeks, so much has happened.

The plot against him has been stopped.

The Declaration has been read.

But for George Washington, there is no time to celebrate.

The Revolutionary War is only just beginning, and he has so much work to do.

PART VI

Aftermath

79

——— · ———

After everything the Continental army endured in the previous several months, and after all that George Washington *personally* endured—including a conspiracy against him that involved his own soldiers—there's a version of the battle for New York City in the late summer of 1776 that would be gratifying to hear.

It would go something like this: Against all odds, the small but scrappy Continental army, buoyed by the ideals of the brand-new Declaration of Independence, bravely stands up to its much more powerful foe. Through sheer determination, Washington's little army repels the larger enemy force and nobly defends the great city of New York from British control.

It's a classic David versus Goliath story.

But that's not how it happens.

The *real* battle for New York—or Battle of Long Island, as the main clash in the campaign is known—could not be more different.

In fact, the theater of war in and around New York City in 1776 is, in almost every way, a catastrophe for the Continental army.

The British, after the initial dramatic arrival of their fleet, wait through a series of delays due in part to logistics and in part to time spent on a failed diplomatic mission. Meanwhile, as the British army bides time, a seemingly endless series of reinforcements arrive. The Continental army can do little but watch passively throughout July and into early August as wave after wave of ships sail through the Narrows and into New York Harbor, transporting massive amounts of supplies and a mix of British soldiers and German auxiliaries.

By early August, over four hundred British ships patrol the harbor and surrounding waterways. A total of roughly 34,000 enemy troops are either encamped on Staten Island or stationed on the ships.

The British have arrayed what was then probably the largest and most powerful expeditionary force in world history—and now, they're primed to attack.

On August 22, 1776, the British send a first wave of troops from Staten Island to Long Island, preparing for the offensive. Washington had expected them to move on Manhattan first, so the Continental army has too few troops stationed on Long Island for the defense.

Once the British troops land ashore, the superior numbers and skill of their forces quickly overwhelm and confuse the Continental forces in middle and southern Long Island. Over the course of the next few days, the American soldiers retreat westward toward Kings County—present-day Brooklyn—where they attempt to stage a defense.

In the so-called Battle of Brooklyn, on August 27, the British outflank and almost surround the American troops. Accompanied by Hessian mercenaries, the British forces begin a brutal onslaught. In a series of skirmishes and retreats, several American regiments are badly decimated, and some are almost completely destroyed.

One regiment of Marylanders, originally comprising around 250 soldiers, has all but a few dozen men either captured or killed. In one grisly episode, American troops try to retreat through the waterways of the swampy Gowanus region, but many injured or exhausted soldiers get trapped in the mud and water—where Hessian soldiers proceed to slaughter them with bayonets.

By August 28, the depleted Continental forces in Brooklyn—about nine thousand, including their Commander-in-Chief, George Washington—are bottled up on the bluffs of present-day Brooklyn Heights, along the East River, with the water on one side and the massive British forces closing in from the other.

In Manhattan, the rest of the Continental army can only send another twelve hundred reinforcements without leaving the city totally exposed. This puts the British, with their larger numbers, in a position to steadily move in and squeeze the Americans in Brooklyn from several directions; their plan is to force a surrender of the army and capture its senior officers.

If they can accomplish this, the British can then easily cross the water to take New York City, while maintaining control of Long Island and capturing most of the American troops.

George Washington's Continental army is now on the brink of either total surrender or total annihilation.

Washington himself made several mistakes to get to this point. He incorrectly judged the first British move to Long Island to be a feint, so kept far too many troops in Manhattan, waiting around uselessly. There were mishaps and communication gaffes throughout the battles, a result of poor planning. He and his generals failed to post defensive troops at a key pass in Brooklyn that proved to be of great use to the enemy.

In many ways, Washington's inexperience in large-scale warfare was exposed. He was, quite simply, out-generaled by the more seasoned British commanders. Almost across the board, the Continental officers and soldiers were outmatched and overwhelmed.

However, there is one thing that George Washington does exactly right in this battle: He realizes at just the moment when he's been beaten.

Stationed with his soldiers in Brooklyn Heights the day before the final assault is expected from the British, he sees with clarity how futile their defense will be. Whereas many generals would have fought on regardless, and others would simply have surrendered rather than fight, Washington comes up with a third option: a daring escape.

That night, during a massive downpour, Washington and his officers devise a secret plan. Sending covert messages across the river, they arrange for all watercraft docked along Manhattan's eastern shore to be commandeered and brought across the East River, to the ferry landing beneath the bluffs on the shores of Brooklyn Heights.

Meanwhile, one regiment at a time, the soldiers and officers on the Heights begin to sneak down under cover of rain and darkness to the landing below. There, they board the boats, one after another.

This long, drawn-out overnight escape is extraordinarily tense. If the British should detect the movement, they would instantly move in and rout the soldiers in midescape, while British ships could quickly capture or destroy the small transports on the river.

Somehow, the unlikely plan works, and every soldier miraculously makes it onto a boat across the East River to Manhattan by morning.

During this all-night rain-soaked evacuation, the troops witness something else. George Washington, their leader, makes sure that every soldier is evacuated *before* he himself will get on a boat—despite the fact that every passing hour could mean capture or death for him, if the evacuation is discovered.

In other words, the soldiers see Washington risk his own life to save the lives of his men.

The next morning, when British troops move in on what they thought was Washington's position on the bluffs of Brooklyn Heights, they are stunned to find that no one is there. Washington's army has moved on.

Once in Manhattan, Washington and his exhausted army at first begin to prepare a defense of New York City.

However, it soon becomes clear that with Howe's massive forces controlling both Brooklyn and Staten Island, and with British warships able to encircle southern Manhattan by water, Washington's forces don't stand a chance.

With no other choices, Washington and his army retreat north to the high ground in upper Manhattan. Soon, he'll be forced to retreat even farther, over the river to White Plains.

During Washington's northward retreat, General Howe sends additional forces from Staten Island toward lower Manhattan Island. These British troops land at Kips Bay on the East River and, with Washington's army now on the run, easily occupy southern Manhattan.

Just like that, the British troops have captured New York City.

George Washington unequivocally lost his first major battle—and ceded the second-largest city in the colonies to the enemy.

From that day forward, the British army will occupy and control New York City for seven long years, using it as their central base of operations throughout the war.

It's a devastating loss.

For the colonies, there's only one consolation: George Washington and his army somehow escaped capture, and live to fight another day.

80

The British army's capture and occupation of Manhattan in September 1776 has many enormous consequences. Consequences for the city, for the colony, and for the entire war.

The occupation also has very specific consequences for one man in particular: the exiled Governor William Tryon.

Finally, no more *Duchess of Gordon*. After so long in exile, the Governor is free to live and work again, out in the open, on land, under the comfort of British control.

That's not all. Tryon also gets his previous job back.

By the end of November 1776, after General Howe's forces have occupied all of Manhattan and put New York City under martial law, William Tryon resumes his position as Governor of the colony.

By any measure, it's been an extraordinary year for Tryon. In almost exactly twelve months' time, he had been forced into exile from his Governor's mansion and onto a ship, had run a spy network up and down the east coast, and had masterminded a complicated plot against George Washington and the Continental army.

Now, he is Governor once again.

Still, Tryon is not content to settle back into his previous role. For one thing, the British have occupied just the New York City region, so claiming mastery over the entire colony works only on paper. His true governorship is now of limited scope. Even in New York City, with General Howe's army controlling the city under martial law, Tryon's role as governor is somewhat ill defined.

Plus, like everyone else, Tryon knows that the most critical matter in the colonies is the war effort. Nothing else really matters.

Before he was a politician, Tryon was a military officer. He had served during the Seven Years' War in the 1750s. He understands warfare and knows how to lead men. With a war now raging, Tryon is ready to play his part.

In early 1777, William Tryon gains an officer's commission to lead a company of "provincial troops"—in other words, Loyalists from the colonies rather than British regulars from England. He achieves a rank of provincial major general and leads a regiment of soldiers active in New York and Connecticut.

Tryon is an effective officer, and a year later, in 1778, he gains a more prestigious commission leading regular British soldiers now as a full major general in the English army.

True to form, Tryon soon finds controversy as a military officer, just as he did as a politician.

In July 1779, he leads a series of diversionary raids along the Connecticut coast in which he instructs his men to target civilian property. His goal is to draw out American troops stationed nearby along the Hudson. The operation may be just a decoy, but the raids are brutal, with Tryon's soldiers allegedly slaughtering unarmed townspeople, and burning down homes, churches, and farms.

After these raids, Patriot leaders accuse Tryon of waging war against "women and children," and even some British officers criticize his conduct.

The royal authorities pardon Tryon for his alleged misdeeds, but the controversy is enough to end his time as an officer in the colonies. Soon after, he returns to England, where he serves out his days helping run the war effort from the motherland. William Tryon dies in England in 1788, five years after the war ends.

Today, Tryon's name still appears in various places in North Carolina, and the Tryon Palace—his opulent former Governor's mansion in New Bern—remains a historic site and museum. Throughout the state, other streets, parks, and even a small town also bear his name.

In New York, Tryon's name also appears more than one might think, given the justifiable antipathy that American officials held toward him after the war. Fort Tryon Park, a large historic site near the northern tip of Manhattan, just above 190th Street, is the most prominent example. There's also a street in the Bronx named after him, and in New York State's capital city, Albany, a few streets and buildings also bear his name.

Tryon's career in the colonies in the Revolutionary War era was full of intrigue and controversy. From the point of view of the Americans, he can only be viewed as a villain. Nonetheless, he was a man of influence and power, who was often at the center of seismic events. Most important, if his plot had been successful, American history—and perhaps America itself—might not exist as we know it today.

However one views Tryon's career as a whole during the Revolutionary War, one question remains: What are we to make of the audacious conspiracy he masterminded in the spring and summer of 1776?

81

———•———

Whatever grand designs William Tryon had for his scheme, when the British fleet finally arrived at New York City at the end of June 1776, much of what Tryon tried to plan was successfully thwarted before it could come to fruition.

Thanks to the round-the-clock efforts on the part of the Committee on Conspiracies, the local and colonial authorities had already disabled much of the conspiracy—and just in time. In total, they made almost forty arrests and took the handful of guilty Life Guards out of the picture.

Also, Hickey's public hanging probably discouraged other plotters who were still out there from following through on their plans.

In the end, the conspirators never destroyed the King's Bridge, they never blew up the powder magazine in New York City, and no Life Guard ever actually made an attempt on George Washington's life.

Yet there is no question that Tryon successfully recruited many colonists and some Continental soldiers to join the British side that summer. When the British arrived, Governor Tryon's many Loyalist recruits became part of their war effort. Before and during the Battle of Brooklyn, these Loyalists also served as valuable local scouts—with intimate knowledge of the territory, they could guide the British troops through the complicated terrain and waterways of the New York region. Very likely, when Tryon commanded provincial forces in 1777, many of his soldiers originally came from his secret recruitment scheme the previous summer.

On the American side, the stories and rumors about the conspiracy almost immediately take on a life of their own. The treasonous nature of the plot and the drama of Thomas Hickey's hanging, as well as the many aspects of the scheme that still remain mysterious, all combine to give the entire episode the quality of a legend or myth.

In its immediate wake, rumors and tall tales begin to emerge about what "really happened" in the scandalous Hickey plot.

George Washington's cryptic comment about "lewd women" alone generates a small cottage industry of stories about prostitutes, mistresses, adulteresses, and other femmes fatales who may have played a role behind the scenes.

One noteworthy example comes from the writer Washington Irving, whose 1850s multivolume biography of George Washington includes a letter that mentions a mysterious woman, possibly a mistress of George Washington. According to the letter, this woman is the one who first warns the Commander of the assassination plot against him.

However, the most famous tall tale about the entire episode is undoubtedly the legend of the poisoned peas. There are many variations of the story, but the common thread is that Thomas Hickey, perhaps with the help of the housekeeper Mary Smith, attempted to assassinate George Washington by poisoning his dinner peas.

In many versions of the story, Washington actually sits down at his dinner table with the plate of lethal peas in front of him. Then, at the last minute, a female servant on his staff dramatically races to the table, grabs the plate, and throws the peas out the window. Minutes later some chickens outside the window eat the peas off the ground—and promptly drop dead.

It's a pretty good story, and allows for many variants. In one version, the young servant is the daughter of Samuel Fraunces, a friend of Washington's who ran the legendary Fraunces Tavern in Manhattan where Washington sometimes dined while stationed in New York that summer.

In another variant, the young servant is Thomas Hickey's mistress, who was originally in on the wicked scheme, but has a last-minute change of heart and saves the General.

Although no part of the poisoned-peas story has been verified—and most versions of it are easy to debunk—the story rose to prominence in the nineteenth century and has been told and retold enough over time that it's still sometimes repeated and shared today.

Another set of legends regarding the conspiracy is born not in America, but in England. In these, George Washington and the Continental authorities are generally painted as the villains, and the entire plot was a sham cooked up by the authorities to imprison good Tories and loyal English subjects under false pretenses. In many of these accounts, to further besmirch his character, George Washington is also portrayed as having a secret mistress.

Essentially, these versions are postwar British propaganda, used to discredit the Americans and the Continental army. The most striking example comes in 1786 when a London writer publishes an elaborate text soon to be called *Minutes of a Conspiracy Against the Liberties of America* that purports to be the full story of the plot and the investigation based on original documents. In fact, the text cleverly intermixes real information with fake names and events. Two fictional women make an appearance, one named Mary Gibbons and the other a mysterious "Judith," with the former in the role of Washington's supposed mistress. Despite these sensational elements, the overall presentation of the text is convincing enough that to this day researchers and writers sometimes mistake it for a legitimate historical source.

Yet, in the end, all these legends raise a basic question about the conspiracy that the authorities never quite answered at the time: What exactly were the conspirators planning to do to George Washington? Was it really an assassination plot or was it something else?

We may never know for sure. But one compelling answer comes from an unexpected source: the former Mayor of New York City, David Mathews.

82

Since the day Mayor Mathews offered testimony to the investigators on the Committee on Conspiracies—back on June 24, 1776, four days before Thomas Hickey was hanged—he had very few open lines of communication with anyone from his former social circle. For the most part, his only company were fellow inmates, most of them common criminals, in the city jail where he was held.

Not a very nice way to spend time, especially for a man used to mingling with politicians and aristocrats—and also known for his expensive clothing and tastes.

As a result, during his imprisonment, the Mayor suffers. A lot.

Of all the suspects and prisoners who were enmeshed in the elaborate conspiracy plot, Mathews is also the one who most loudly continues to proclaim his innocence.

Almost immediately after his imprisonment, Mathews writes numerous letters to friends and city officials, disparaging the charges against him and insisting he has been unjustly accused.

He claims to be appalled, in particular, by the idea that he was involved in any plan to kill George Washington, which, in the wake of Hickey's execution, became the accepted belief as to what the conspirators were plotting.

In July, the New York authorities, now confronted with the arrival of the British fleet, transfer Mayor Mathews and the other prisoners associated with the conspiracy to a jail in Litchfield, Connecticut. There, the Mayor is to await trial indefinitely for his role in the plot.

On August 20, after a month in Connecticut, Mathews writes a letter from jail to a former friend who is now a colonial official and who Mathews hopes can help gain his release. Mathews asks him to provide a written certificate that will vouch for his innocence:

> [Your certificate will] enable me to contradict a most hellish report that has been propagated, and is verily believed throughout this colony, that I was concerned in a plot to assassinate General Washington, and to blow up the magazine in New York. The Convention well know that such a report prevails; they also know that it is as false as hell is false.

The New York colonial authorities, when they learn of this letter, send a letter back to Mathews directly, rejecting his claim of innocence:

> You well know the cause of that treatment which you deem so cruel. You well know that you stand charged with being concerned in a deep conspiracy against the rights and liberties of America; and . . . it is the duty of the Convention that you be secured for trial: that you were privy to it, in a great measure, your own examination evinces.

Mathews continues writing more letters, appealing for any chance to exonerate himself. Today, after reading Mathew's pleas of innocence—a few of them genuinely despairing—some might argue that he may, in fact, have been unjustly accused and unfairly treated.

After all, back when the Committee on Conspiracies first examined Mathews in June, he claimed that his only involvement was brief and tangential, limited to that one occasion on the ship when Governor Tryon asked him to deliver money to Gilbert Forbes, whom

Mathews said he didn't even know. Furthermore, Mathews said he did so only very reluctantly, and even tried to dissuade Forbes from engaging in the plot. If this is true, his role in the plot was less significant, and his imprisonment perhaps unduly harsh.

However, David Mathews himself will soon show that his elaborate proclamations of innocence are, in fact, "false as hell is false."

In early September 1776—just after the British occupy New York City—Mathews manages to escape from his jail cell in Connecticut. He sneaks back down to Manhattan, where he reconnects with William Tryon. When Tryon becomes Governor again, he likewise grants Mathews the Mayorship of the city. Mathews remains mayor until 1783, when the British ultimately lose the war and relinquish the city.

But the real twist comes after the war, when Mathews is appointed to a very different part of the British Empire—Cape Breton Island, off Nova Scotia. There he holds a few managerial positions and eventually becomes attorney general.

Soon, it will be former Mayor David Mathews, of all the conspirators, who will finally reveal one of the most compelling details about the plot.

He doesn't do it to correct the record. Or even to brag. He does it for money.

In 1784, the year after the war is over, David Mathews travels from Cape Breton to visit London, England. He makes the trip in order to appeal before a parliamentary board called the Royal Commission on the Losses and Services of American Loyalists. It's an agency set up to reimburse British colonial subjects who made unusual sacrifices or suffered financial setbacks as a direct result of the war.

Mathews, when making a case for how he should be recompensed for his wartime efforts, tells the commissioner about his work as a public official and his loss of personal property in the conflict. But in his application Mathews also states, under oath, that in 1776 he "formed a plan for the taking of Mr. Washington & his Guard prisoners but which was not effected."

There it is—revealed by the man at its very center—the plot against George Washington.

Talking to British authorities, despite all his earlier denials, the

Mayor now says that not only was he part of the plan—he *formed* the plan.

More important, and of greater historical significance, Mathews reveals that the goal of the plot was the "taking of Mr. Washington & his Guard prisoners." In other words, if Mathews is telling the truth, the real goal of Tryon's plot was not necessarily to assassinate George Washington, but rather to seize or kidnap him for the British.

The question now is: Which was the truth? At the time, former Mayor Mathews no longer had any need to lie. In fact, if his goal was to receive even more compensation, he actually had a bigger incentive to exaggerate and say that assassination was the goal.

While there is no definitive way to verify David Mathews's statement, his admission of a kidnapping plot makes sense. Kidnapping generals and leaders was a tried-and-true tactic during the revolutionary era. In fact, delivering George Washington still alive to British authorities would have been the greatest possible outcome for the Crown and the British army. They could gain intelligence from him, possibly torture him, and use his capture to humiliate the colonies on the world stage. So, while many Americans at the time believed that the goal of the plot was to kill Washington, a plan to kidnap him may have been more likely.

A century later, a similar debate would surround the death of another American President: Abraham Lincoln. To this day, we know that John Wilkes Booth murdered Lincoln—but at the time, many of his coconspirators insisted, until their own deaths, that the goal was to kidnap Lincoln, not kill him.

Either way—whether the plan was to "seize" George Washington or assassinate him—the Commander's life was most definitely at risk. Indeed, the final result of a kidnapping would probably have been exactly the same: If the British officials captured Washington, they would likely execute him—eventually—to make an example. After all, at the start of the war, Washington was a "traitor" to the British for his role leading the colonies' insurrection—and as history shows, the punishment for treason is usually death, sometimes in public. So during the Revolution, those at the highest levels of American leadership expected that if they were captured, they would be hanged as traitors.

Only at lower levels were captured officers like Charles Lee, Washington's second-in-command, exchanged for a British general.

In any case, Mathews's statement under oath during an application for funds before the relatively obscure Royal Commission board—a statement made in 1784, a full eight years after the plot itself was discovered—may be the most convincing evidence of what really lay at the heart of the conspiracy.

As for Mathews himself, he lived out his days with his family in Cape Breton, and died in 1800.

Was he proud of his role in the plot against Washington? Mathews later named one of his sons William Tryon Mathews, after his mentor and coconspirator. So that tells us something.

Today, unlike Tryon, David Mathews doesn't have his name attached to many streets or public spaces in New York or Long Island, despite his years of public life in the region.

There is, as far as we know, only one exception. Deep in the Bronx is a small public park and playground called *Matthews Muliner Playground*. This modest park has a few trees, a couple of handball courts, two jungle gyms, and covers about a third of a block otherwise comprising large concrete buildings.

The two names have nothing to do with each other—"Muliner" is Thomas Muliner, a seventeenth-century English settler—but the "Matthews" part is indeed named after the former Mayor, David Mathews, albeit with an alternate spelling.

This playground boasts a plaque whose inscription gives a bit of the history of the two men. The inscription ends with these sentences:

"Matthews was installed as the Loyalist mayor. Matthews was known as a thief, an embezzler, and a spendthrift."

There, in a park in the Bronx, amid laughing children and handball players, lies the hallowed memory of Mayor David Mathews.

83

The greatest legacy of the first conspiracy has little to do with the plotters who planned and participated in it—rather, it's the people who uncovered and investigated it.

Throughout the history of intelligence gathering and law enforcement, this elaborate plot—and the successful thwarting of it—provides an early model of how to detect and subvert clandestine hostile operations, in particular those launched by "internal enemies" rather than by foreign governments.

George Washington, for one, took a clear lesson from all the plotting and scheming against him in the spring and summer of 1776. By the end of that summer, after his first year as Commander-in-Chief, he came to see the absolutely critical role played by espionage and intelligence in what would be a long and complicated war.

In September 1776, less than three months after Thomas Hickey's death, Washington sends his first famous spy, a young officer named Nathan Hale, into British-occupied Long Island to pose as a Loyalist and learn about enemy troop movements.

Tragically, Hale is discovered, imprisoned, and soon hanged in New York City by the British. According to legend, the young American martyr speaks these words on the gallows: "I only regret that

I have but one life to lose for my country." The legend is probably not true—that line was probably crafted by a playwright—but Hale's bravery and sacrifice are undeniable.

After this tragedy, Washington both expands and improves his army's espionage activity, devising increasingly complex ways to protect and communicate with undercover agents behind enemy lines.

By 1778—now into the third year of the war—Washington is something of a spymaster, personally overseeing a top secret network of spies and double agents known as the "Culper Ring." All involved have code names—Washington's own code name is "711"—and they ferry intelligence throughout the New York and New Jersey region using complicated signals, letters written in invisible ink, and even coded messages published in newspapers. The leader of the group is Benjamin Tallmadge, a young officer whom Washington gives the title "director of military intelligence."

To this day, the methods of the Culper Ring (and a version of their invisible ink) are still used by the modern CIA. In fact, Americans didn't even know there *was* a Culper Ring until the 1930s. That's how good its members were at keeping secrets.

For George Washington and his officers, this spycraft takes the Continental army's operations to a new level, adding more sophistication and nuance to their war planning.

However, perhaps the even more vital lesson learned from the Hickey plot, or "Tryon's plot" as it is also called, is that *counter*espionage is just as important as espionage—and that *counter*intelligence is just as important as spying.

Here, in fact, is where the first conspiracy may have had the longest-term impact. The key to this impact is not George Washington, but rather John Jay, who by the end of the summer was the official chairman of the Committee on Conspiracies.

In many ways, the Committee on Conspiracies—created to uncover and subvert Tryon's clandestine operations against the Continental army, and tasked specifically with investigating the Hickey plot—serves as an early example of what we now might call an "intelligence agency."

The committee was a top-secret team of expert civilians—not

military officers—with a dedicated mission to not just gather intelligence about the enemy, but to detect and thwart the enemy's intelligence operations against America. Along the way, Committee members used the tools of law enforcement to unmask enemy spies and traitors, and also to uncover and disable enemy plots and schemes.

The most influential aspect of their work will not come during Tryon's plot, but shortly after it, and as a direct result.

In the late fall of 1776, after the British occupy New York City, the Continental army escapes west into New Jersey, and the members of the New York Provincial Congress flee the city and regroup farther upstate.

Immediately, the members of this Congress, in communication with both Washington and the Continental Congress, recognize the urgent need for an even more sophisticated counterintelligence organization now that the British army has a base of operations in New York City.

Led by John Jay, and using his experience investigating the Hickey plot as a model, the New York officials create a new, more elaborate intelligence committee with a slightly expanded and now formalized name.

The Committee for Detecting and Defeating Conspiracies.

This new organization, helmed by Jay but otherwise with an entirely new set of members, takes the counterintelligence methods first utilized during the Hickey plot and enhances them.

According to its own mission statement, the Committee is formed for "inquiring into, detecting and defeating all conspiracies which may be formed . . . against the liberties of America." Just like the original group, the members are all sworn to secrecy and keep confidential records under seal, separate from standard government records. Also, like the original committee, very few people even know of its existence.

First convened on October 17, 1776, in Fishkill, New York, the Committee on Defeating and Detecting Conspiracies operates almost nonstop in various forms for well over a year, improving its methods as it goes. The members make arrests, conduct interrogations, utilize moles and spies, and coordinate intelligence from all over the New

York region regarding Loyalist plots and British espionage operations. They even have a dedicated thirty-person militia team at their disposal to conduct raids and hunt down suspects.

Although technically a body of New York State—thanks to the Declaration of Independence, New York is now a state and not a colony—Jay's new committee is inextricably linked to the efforts of the Continental army, and the committee regularly feeds intelligence to George Washington and his generals.

As a result of John Jay's efforts—both during the Hickey plot and in the running of this new committee—he becomes a genuine pioneer in the fields of intelligence and law enforcement.

Today, the Central Intelligence Agency acknowledges the Committee on Detecting and Defeating Conspiracies as the first dedicated intelligence agency, and credits John Jay as "America's first counterintelligence chief" for his work creating the discipline almost from scratch during the early years of the Revolutionary War. The CIA headquarters in Langley, Virginia, even has a conference room named after Jay.

Long after the war, John Jay has an illustrious career, spanning both law and politics. He serves as a congressman and Governor, and becomes a key framer of the Constitution of the United States; later he'll author some of the legendary *Federalist Papers* to defend it.

Over the years, George Washington develops such respect for John Jay that, when Washington becomes the first President of the United States in 1789, he gives Jay first choice of any position on his cabinet or in his administration. Jay, always ready to do the most serious work without public acclaim, chooses to be the first Chief Justice of the U.S. Supreme Court.

Of course, when it came to John Jay's high place in the hierarchy of President Washington's favorites, it probably didn't hurt that Jay may earlier have saved Washington's life—by thwarting the conspiracy against him in the summer of 1776.

84

———•———

Back on that historic day in Philadelphia—June 16, 1775—when George Washington first accepted the command of the Continental army, no one there could possibly have known what the future would hold.

A few days after accepting the command, while preparing to leave for Boston, Washington wrote a letter to his wife, Martha, back in Virginia. In the letter he predicted that he would most likely be home in Mount Vernon later that fall, when the hostilities are over.

In fact, from the day that George Washington left Philadelphia for Boston to meet his new army, he didn't see his home in Virginia again for six years, and then for another two years after that. That's how long the Revolutionary War lasted—eight years—and Washington was on the road with his army for all of it.

That summer of 1776 in New York City, as he was forced to prepare for the first major British attack, Washington would, in many ways, be given his first epic tests of the war.

In those trying months, he was working to get his ill-equipped new army into fighting shape. He had to contend with the deadly plot against him, including from his own men. And he experienced a near-cataclysmic defeat in the first full-scale battle of the war.

On that rainy night in Brooklyn Heights—August 29, 1776—Washington's daring overnight evacuation and escape came to symbolize the essence of the war—and the essence of the man himself.

His army was beaten, battered, outfought, outgeneraled, and stuck on a rainy bluff with the enemy closing in. Almost everything had gone wrong. Yet somehow, some way, George Washington led his troops to escape and survive. More important, he showed his army that he was willing to give his life for his men—and for their cause.

A few weeks later, Washington's troops similarly had to flee New York City and retreat. After fighting a battle in northern Manhattan, they fled even farther. After fighting and being forced to retreat from White Plains, they escaped to New Jersey. The entire fall of 1776 was basically a long campaign of losses.

But the American army somehow stuck in there.

Washington's enduring reputation as a great military leader is not based on his technical skill as a tactician. He would win a few impressive battles, but overall he lost more than he won. What made him great—at least in the particular circumstances of the Revolutionary War—was his sheer staying power, his total devotion to his army, his relentless sense of duty, and a stubborn refusal to ever give up.

That summer and fall of 1776 alone, the war could have ended at least three different times had the British successfully crushed or captured Washington's army. But General Howe couldn't quite finish them off. Despite the overwhelming British victories during this campaign of the war, where they totally dominated most battles and claimed control of New York City and the surrounding region, the British slowly learned a painful truth:

As long as Washington and his army were out there somewhere, the British could never really win the war.

As a leader, George Washington's personal identification with the army became so complete that he himself became almost synonymous with them. They all suffered extraordinary setbacks together, again and again. They never had enough funds, enough provisions, enough supplies, enough officers, enough men.

Washington was with them in the snow, in the mud, in the rain, in the sleet, in the ice. He dealt with the endless politics, the staffing, the funding, the organizational challenges. He slogged through count-less problems with logistics, recruiting, weapons, food, sickness, and transportation.

It never got easy, and he never gave up.

This is why, looking back at the strange events of America's first conspiracy—all taking place in the first year of a long, drawn-out war—the most momentous question is: What if the conspirators *had* actually killed or captured George Washington?

The question itself is a speculative game, but it's also so difficult to answer, because, when it comes to the Revolutionary War and the seismic events surrounding it, it all seems so totally unthinkable with-out George Washington at the center. And this is before we even get to Washington becoming the nation's first President.

Somehow, this rural kid from Virginia became totally interwoven with the founding of the country. The fact is, if Washington had been killed or captured in the summer of 1776, America's history would be different in ways that are impossible to guess or even imagine.

As the old joke goes, we might all still be sipping tea.

Still, in the end, one more detail deserves a mention from the battle of New York.

In the late fall of 1776, as the Continental army flees from New York City to northern Manhattan, fighting various skirmishes along the way, George Washington takes notice of a young artillery cap-tain from New York who conducts himself bravely. Washington re-members his name: Alexander Hamilton.

That winter, when the freezing army is encamped in New Jersey, Washington gets to know Hamilton better. The young man is proud, stubborn, and dedicated. The General sees a bit of himself. Washington learns something else. Hamilton was an orphan from a poor back-ground, and never knew his father.

Soon, Washington takes Hamilton under his wing. He mentors him and becomes his role model. With Hamilton serving as a close aide, Washington will strategize some of the great victories that turn the tide of the war.

Earlier, the greatest losses in Washington's boyhood were the deaths of his father and his half brother. Years later, with people like

Alexander Hamilton, Henry Knox, John Jay, and Benjamin Tall-madge; with his team of officers, as well as the countless local officials and citizens who aided the war effort; and, most important, with the thousands of dedicated soldiers and volunteers—men and women—who would give their lives for this cause, Washington forged more than a new brotherhood. He forged a nation—and proved, over and over again, the one truth at the core of both the Revolution and America itself:

That in our lowest moments, we can find our greatest strengths.

Acknowledgments

From Brad:

As I mentioned in the Author's Note, this book started as a detective story. So first and foremost, I need to thank my fellow detective, Josh Mensch. Five years ago, on the TV show *Lost History*, we met on a quest to find the missing 9/11 flag that the firefighters raised at Ground Zero. From the start, Josh was determined. It was the same in these pages. So let me just say it: There aren't many people like Josh. He is a meticulous researcher and a wise analyst, dedicated to finding that most elusive reward—the truth. In addition, he's a true story-teller with a natural knack for knowing which historical nuggets to polish and display. Josh, thank you for being a kind and thoughtful collaborator, as well as a dear friend. This book wouldn't exist without you.

I also owe thank-yous to the following: My first lady, Cori, who I fight for every day. Jonas, Lila, and Theo are my life. This is a book about character and, through them, I've learned so much more about my own. Jill Kneerim, my friend and agent, believed from Chapter 1. Friend and agent Jennifer Rudolph Walsh at WME made this entire dream a reality. I mean it; she built it. Special thanks to Hope Denekamp, Lucy Cleland, Ike Williams, and all our friends at the Kneerim & Williams Agency.

I want to also thank my sister, Bari, who is proof of the power of a shared history. Also to Bobby, Ami, Adam, Gilda, and Will, for always supporting us.

My Committee on Conspiracies is rightfully small: Noah Kuttler,

Ethan Kline, Dale Flam, Matt Kuttler, Chris Weiss, and Judd Winick help shape every page by never letting me get away with anything. Additional love goes to Chris Eliopoulos, Katy Greene, Marie Grunbeck, Nick Marell, Staci Schecter, Jason Sherry, Jim Day, Denise Jaeger, Katriela Knight, Eling Tsai, and Maria Venusio.

When it came to research, we could've never managed the minutiae of Revolutionary history—as well as all the George Washington details—without our expert in arms, Barnet Schecter. His knowledge and expertise is interwoven throughout. Thank you, Barnet, for answering every question.

Special thanks to Joseph J. Ellis, for encouraging me from the start; to Archivist of the United States David Ferriero and James Swanson, for being guiding lights as I had questions; our family on *Lost History*, and at HISTORY and Left/Right, including Nancy Dubuc, Paul Cabana, Mike Stiller, Ken Druckerman, Mike Mezaros, Mary Robertson and Lee White; and to Rob Weisbach, for being the very first.

I also want to thank everyone at Flatiron and Macmillan: Fearless leader and friend Don Weisberg, Cristina Gilbert, Marlena Bittner, Aileen Boyle, Steven Boriack, Nancy Trypuc, Amy Einhorn, the production team of Rafal Gibek, Lena Shekhter, Emily Walters, Donna Noetzel, and Keith Hayes, as well as Astra Berzinskas, Jeff Capshew, Malati Chavali, Hank Cochrane, Cristina Cushing, Patricia Doherty, Leigh George, Jenn Gonzalez, Ken Holland, Jonathan Hollingsworth, Matt Johnson, Don O'Connor, Laura Pennock, Brad Wood, Jeanette Zwart, and the entire sales force who do all the heavy lifting. I've said it before, and I'll never stop saying it: They're the true reason this book is in your hands.

I want to add a special thank-you to our incredible editor, Jasmine Faustino, who helped at every level and put out every fire. She is unflappable and unstoppable. Finally, I need to thank our true Commander-in-Chief Bob Miller. He is a steadfast friend, and it's his vision that opened up this chapter of my life. I owe him forever for that. Thank you, Bob, for your faith.

From Josh:

First and foremost, I'd like to thank Brad Meltzer for providing me the opportunity to embark on this journey through history. It's been a privilege, and one for which I'll always be grateful. Brad and I have now told stories in multiple mediums about many eras of America's past, with hopefully more to come. It's rare to find a creative partner who is both a great collaborator as well as a great person, and Brad is both. For this reason, special gratitude also to Ken Druckerman, and Mike Mezaros Left/Right, and everyone else from the *Lost History* team who made the collaboration possible. Also, thank you to Brad's wife, Cori, for her input and her hospitality.

On this project, I owe a huge debt of gratitude to Barnet Schecter, our historical consultant. Barnet's knowledge and impeccable scholarship were an inspiration, and I relied upon his feedback in ways too numerous to list. Barnet's book *The Battle of New York* is one of the most thoroughly researched texts about New York City during the Revolutionary War, and essential reading for anyone studying the era.

I'd like to thank Bob Miller at Flatiron for making this project possible. His enthusiasm and support kept the wind at our backs. I'd also like to extend the sincerest gratitude to our editor, Jasmine Faustino, who guided us patiently through the challenges of this undertaking. Her expertise, organization, and input made our story so much better.

No book of history is possible without the libraries and historical societies on which our research depends. In our case, the resources and personnel of the New-York Historical Society, the Brooklyn Historical Society, the Massachusetts Historical Society, the New York Public Library, and the Clements Library at the University of Michigan were invaluable. Special mention also to the superbly organized digital resource *Founders Online*, a joint project of the National Archives and Records Administration with the University of Virginia Press, on which I frequently relied.

Every manuscript needs great readers, and three of the greatest are in my family. My mother, Elizabeth Mensch, my father, Steven Mensch, and my stepmother, Pamela Mensch, all provided excellent feedback at critical times. Beyond the specific input, their engagement provided inspiration and challenged me to work harder. This engagement applies not just to this book, but also to my life.

When it comes to family and friends, there are so many others to whom I owe gratitude. Thanks again to my mom and dad, for their constant support. Thanks to my brothers, Jon, Jake, and Joe Mensch, and James and Jeremy Freeman; to Greg Patnaude; to Mariana Barzun and my wonderful nieces Libby and Claire; to Mary Ellen Smith; to John, Anna, London, Mila, and August Acunto; and to Lynn James, who makes every day possible. Thanks to my close friends from every phase of life, and to the many great colleagues I've been lucky to collaborate with on television and documentary projects over the years.

Finally, my deepest gratitude of all goes to my wife, Mary, and our son, Malcolm. I simply can't imagine life without you. With every challenge we grow stronger. I'm the luckiest man alive.

Cast of Characters

(in order of appearance)

GEN. GEORGE WASHINGTON—Commander-in-Chief of the Continental army.

GOV. WILLIAM TRYON—Governor of the colony of New York.

GEN. NATHANAEL GREENE—Oversees Long Island operations while the Continental army is stationed in New York City in the spring and summer of 1776.

HENRY DAWKINS—Engraver, silversmith, and member of counterfeiting operation based in Cold Spring Harbor, Long Island.

ISRAEL YOUNG—Ringleader of a counterfeiting operation based in his home in Cold Spring Harbor, Long Island.

ISAAC YOUNG—Brother of Israel Young, and fellow member of a counterfeiting operation based in Cold Spring Harbor, Long Island.

COL. HENRY KNOX—Continental artillery specialist instrumental in the siege of Boston in early 1776.

ISAAC KETCHAM—Accomplice to a counterfeiting operation based in Cold Spring Harbor, Long Island.

MAJ. GEN. CHARLES LEE—George Washington's second-in-command in the Continental army, sent to fortify New York City in February 1776.

GEN. WILLIAM ALEXANDER, AKA "LORD STIRLING"—Continental officer sent to fortify New York City in March 1776, after Gen. Charles Lee's departure.

DAVID MATHEWS—Mayor of New York City, appointed by Gov. William Tryon in February 1776.

GILBERT FORBES—Gunsmith based in Manhattan.

JAMES MASON—Part-time mill worker at the Ringwood Ironworks iron mill in Goshen, New York.

WILLIAM FARLEY—Recruiter for Gov. William Tryon based in Goshen, New York. [As indicated in our note on page 380, Farley's actual name was William Forbes, but we've changed it to "Farley" within the text to avoid confusion with the gunsmith, Gilbert Forbes.]

WILLIAM BENJAMIN—Laborer at the Ringwood Ironworks iron mill in Goshen, New York.

PHILIP LIVINGSTON—New York congressman appointed to a secret committee in June 1776 to investigate plots against George Washington and the Continental army.

GOUVERNOUR MORRIS—New York congressman appointed to a secret committee in June 1776 to investigate plots against George Washington and the Continental army.

JOHN JAY—New York congressman appointed to a secret committee in June 1776 to investigate plots against George Washington and the Continental army.

PVT. WILLIAM GREEN—Soldier in the Commander-in-Chief's Guard, aka the Life Guards.

PVT. JAMES JOHNSON—Soldier in the Commander-in-Chief's Guard, aka the Life Guards.

PVT. MICHAEL LYNCH—Soldier in the Commander-in-Chief's Guard, aka the Life Guards.

PVT. JOHN BARNES—Soldier in the Commander-in-Chief's Guard, aka the Life Guards.

SGT. THOMAS HICKEY—Soldier in the Commander-in-Chief's Guard, aka the Life Guards.

WILLIAM LEARY—Foreman at the Ringwood Ironworks iron mill in Goshen, New York.

Notes

ABBREVIATIONS

AA: Peter Force, ed., *American Archives: Consisting of a Collection of Authentick Records, State Papers, Debates, and Letters and Other Notices of Publick Affairs.* 4th Series. 6 Vols. (Washington, DC: M. St. Clair Clarke & Peter Force, 1837–1853)

CHM: *Calendar of Historical Manuscripts, Relating to the War of the Revolution, in the Office of the Secretary of State.* 2 Vols. (Albany: Weed, Parsons, and Company, 1868)

GW: George Washington

JPC: *Journals of the Provincial Congress, Provincial Convention, Committee of Safety and Council of Safety of the State of New-York, 1775–1777.* 2 Vols. (Albany: Thurlow Weed, 1842)

PGWR: *The Papers of George Washington*, Revolutionary War Series. Vols. 1–8. Edited by W. W. Abbot, Philander D. Chase, and Dorothy Twohig. (Charlottesville: Univ. Press of Virginia, 1985–1998)

PROLOGUE

1   *wooden manor house*: The house is on a property owned at the time by Abraham Mortier, situated on what is now the corner of Charlton and Varick Streets in Manhattan. *Abstract of Wills on File in the Surrogate's Office, City of New York* (New York: New-York Historical Society, 1900), 8: 285. Mortier's estate was also known as "Richmond Hill," a name that would remain attached to it for many decades.

1   *For the last ten months*: The night described is on or near April 19, 1776. As the story will soon cover, George Washington was first appointed Commander-in-Chief of the Continental army on June 16, 1775 (as formalized in GW's address to Continental Congress, 16 June 1775, *PGWR*, 1: 1–3).

2   *about two miles north*: In the 1770s, New York City comprised only the southern-most tip of Manhattan, extending north to approximately present-day Chambers Street. Most of Manhattan Island above the city was woods, farms, and some wealthy estates. The geography of the region at the time is described in more detail in Chapter 6 of this book.

2   *next few weeks or months*: The first ships of the British fleet arrived on June 29, 1776, approximately eleven weeks from the night described. At the time, GW and his officers expected the arrival to be sooner.

2 *elite group of specially trained soldiers*: The origin and initial formation of George Washington's Life Guards is described in detail in Chapter 19 of this book.

2 *three miles away due south*: This distance is approximate, and the precise location of the Governor's ship in the waters around Manhattan will sometimes vary.

3 *one of the city's underground jails*: The jail referred to is under New York City's first City Hall, located on the corner of Wall and Broad Streets in lower Manhattan where Federal Hall now stands. Barnet Schecter, *Battle of New York: The City at the Heart of the American Revolution* (New York: Walker, 2002), 12.

3 *the largest public execution*: In this context "largest" refers to the number of spectators, rather than the number of persons executed.

PART I: The Commander

7 *King George . . . Fredericksburg*: George Washington was born in Westmoreland County, and as a young child his family moved twice before settling in King George County. For more details on his earliest years see Ron Chernow, *Washington: A Life* (New York: Penguin Press, 2010), 6–8, or Rupert Hughes, *George Washington* (New York: William Morrow and Co., 1926), 1:17–21.

7 *financial turmoil*: As one key example, after Augustine Washington's death the family could no longer afford college educations for the younger children, including George. Chernow, *Washington*, 10.

8 *different mother*: Lawrence was the oldest surviving child borne by Augustine Washington's first wife, Jane Butler. After Jane's death in 1729, Augustine married his second wife, Mary Ball, and together they had six more children, of whom George Washington was the oldest. Ibid., 5–7.

8 *"his loving brother George Washington"*: Release from Lawrence Washington, 17 June 1752. *The Papers of George Washington*, Colonial Series, ed. W. W. Abbott (Charlottesville: Univ. Press of Virginia, 1983), 1: 51–52.

9 *"trust reposed in me"*: GW to Robert Dinwiddie, 10 June 1752, ibid., 50–51.

12 *"rebellion"*: Joint Address by both Houses to the King, 9 February 1775, *Parliamentary Papers, Consisting of a Complete Collection of King's Speeches, Messages to Parliament, Addresses and Representations of Both Houses to the Throne* (London: J. Debrett, 1797), 2: 233.

12 *the British and the colonists suffered heavy casualties*: The colonists suffered around 90 dead or wounded total, and the British close to 250. Richard R. Beeman, *Our Lives, Our Fortunes, and our Sacred Honor: The Forging of American Independence* (New York: Basic Books, 2013), 193.

12 *". . . to us or to our fathers"*: Dr. Matthew Thornton, "Address to the Inhabitants of the Colony of New-Hampshire," June 2 1775. *Collections, Topographical, Historical and Biographical, Relating Principally to New Hampshire*, ed. J. Farmer and J. B. Moore (Concord, NH: Hill & Moore, 1822), 1: 88.

13 *sixty-five delegates:* Total number of delegates is from Beeman, *Our Lives, Our Fortunes*, 197.

13 *Only one colony, Georgia*: Georgia sends one delegate, representing only part of the colony, on May 13, 1775. It will be two more months before Georgia sends a full delegation to join the Congress. Ibid; 198.

14 *"men are in Arms"*: Joseph Hewes to Samuel Johnston, 11 May 1775, *The Colonial Records of North Carolina*, ed. William Saunders (Raleigh, NC: Edwards & Broughton, 1886), 9: 1247.

14 *"begin the World over again"* Thomas Paine, *The Writings of Thomas Paine*, ed. Moncure Daniel Conway (New York: G. P. Putnam's Sons, 1894), 1:118.

15 *between Fifth and Sixth Streets*: The building, now known as Independence Hall, still stands on the same block in Philadelphia. The street names haven't changed. As a historic site and museum open to the public, Independence Hall attracts millions of visitors a year.

16 *"much service to us"*: John Adams to Abigail Adams, 29 May 1775, *The Adams Papers*, Adams Family Correspondence, ed. Lyman H. Butterfield (Cambridge: Harvard Univ. Press, 1963), 1: 207–208.

16 *"among ten thousand people"*: Benjamin Rush to Thomas Ruston, 29 October 1775, *The Letters of Benjamin Rush*, ed. Lyman H. Butterfield (Princeton: Princeton Univ. Press 1951), 1: 92.

16 *"gift of silence"*: John Adams to Benjamin Rush, 11 Nov 1807, quoted from John A. Schutz and Douglass Adair, eds., *Spur of Fame: Dialogues of John Adams and Benjamin Rush, 1805–1813* (Carmel, CA: Liberty Fund, 1966), 97–98.

16 *didn't give a single speech*: From Joseph Ellis, *His Excellency: George Washington* (New York: Alfred A. Knopf, 2004), 69.

17 *multiple committees . . . military affairs:* Ibid.

19 *"character of an honest man"*: GW to Alexander Hamilton, 28 August 1788, *The Papers of Alexander Hamilton*, ed. Harold C. Syrett (New York: Columbia Univ. Press, 1962), 5: 206–208.

19 *"as far as I can consistently"*: GW to Joseph Reed, 14 January 1776, *PGWR*, 3: 87–92.

20 Rules of Civility & Decent Behavior: The version of the text exactly as transcribed by GW is compiled in *Washington's Rules of Civility & Decent Behavior in Company and Conversation*, ed. J. M. Toner (Washington, DC: W. H. Morrison, 1888).

20 *Rule 5 . . . Rule 7*: Ibid., 11–12.

20 *"to those that are present"*: Ibid., 11.

20 *"aggravate his misery"*: Ibid., 21.

20 *"he evades them rather than seeks them"*: Charles-Louis-Victor, Prince de Broglie, *Narrative by the Prince de Broglie of a visit to America, 1782,* ed. Thomas Balch, trans. E. W. Balch (Philadelphia: 1877), 14.

21 *to secure the dying officer's body*: For more details of GW's rescue of Braddock's body, see Barnet Schecter, *George Washington's America: A Biography Through His Maps* (New York: Walker, 2010), 56–57, and Chernow, *Washington*, 59–60.

21 *flee the room*: This is how John Adams later described GW's sudden exit from the proceedings: "Mr. Washington, who happened to sit near the door, as soon as he heard me allude to him, from his usual modesty darted into the Library Room." John Adams, *Diary and Autobiography of*

John Adams, ed. Lyman H. Butterfield et al. (Cambridge, Mass.: 1961), 3: 322–323.

22 *give him a salute...* "*General*": Anecdote is from Chernow, *Washington,* 187.

23 "*with their lives and fortunes*": *Journals of the American Congress: From 1774 to 1788* (Washington, DC: Way and Gideon, 1823), 1: 85.

23 "*the command I am honored with*": GW address to Continental Congress, 16 June 1775, *PGWR,* 1: 1–3.

24 "*sober, steady, & calm*": Eliphalet Dyer to Joseph Trumbull, 17 June 1775, Paul H. Smith et al., eds., *Letters of Delegates to Congress, 1774–1789* (Washington, DC: Lib. of Congress, 1976–2000), 1: 500.

24 "*a trust too great for my capacity*": GW to Martha Washington, 18 June 1775, *PGWR,* 1: 3–6.

24 "*the cause will suffer*": GW to Burwell Bassett, 19 June 1775. Ibid., 12–14.

24 "*the ruin of my reputation*": Patrick Henry originally recounted this incident to Benjamin Rush, who later shared Henry's recollection in his own autobiography as written. Benjamin Rush, *The Autobiography of Benjamin Rush,* ed. George W. Corner (Princeton, 1948), 113.

24 "*I hope the people*": John Adams to Abigail Adams, 11 June 1775. *The Adams Papers,* Adams Family Correspondence, 1: 215–217.

25 *some twenty thousand people are here*: Crowd size as reported contemporaneously by the *Constitutional Gazette,* New York City, 29 June 1776.

26 "*You will doubtless have heard*": Dr. William Eustis to Dr. David Townsend, 28 June 1776, *New England Historical and Genealogical Register* 23, no. 1 (1869): 206–209.

26 "*and to ruin us*": Ibid.

28 *draw up his will*: The actual will has been lost, but in a June 18 letter to his wife, GW revealed that he has just sent instructions to draw up his will to family friend and legal adviser Edmund Pendleton. GW to Martha Washington, 18 June 1775, *PGWR,* 1: 3–6.

28 "*bible of the British army*": Humphrey Bland's treatise is referred to as such in many places, for example Kevin J. Hayes, *George Washington: A Life in Books* (New York: Oxford Univ. Press, 2017), 176.

29 *spontaneous applause*: Beeman, *Our Lives, Our Fortunes,* 237.

30 *carriage known as a phaeton*: Ibid.

30 *population of about 25,000*: Exact estimates vary, but 25,000 is a common number for the city's population in early to mid-1775, at the onset of the Revolutionary War. See for example Ira Rosenwaike, *Population History of New York City* (Syracuse: Syracuse Univ. Press, 1972), 14.

31 *Among the onlookers... Hamilton*: Ron Chernow, *Alexander Hamilton* (New York: Penguin Press, 2004), 66.

32 "*ready to receive either*": *JPC,* 1: 54.

32 *Tryon has remained a strong supporter*: Most of the governors in the colonies were like Tryon, and remained loyal to England in the period leading to the war. One notable exception was Governor Jonathan Trumbull of Connecticut, who became an ardent patriot and remained so throughout the revolutionary era.

33 "*appeared grave... and said little*": William Smith, *Historical Memoirs of William Smith, Historian of the Province of New York,* ed. W. H. W. Sabine (New York: Sabine, 1956), 1: 228.

33 *"much shouting in the procession"*: Ibid.

34 *Raised in an aristocratic family*: Tryon's birthplace, date of birth, and other early details are from Paul David Nelson, *William Tryon and the Course of Empire: A Life in British Imperial Service* (Chapel Hill: Univ. of North Carolina Press, 1990), Chapter 1.

36 *"your King, your country, and your laws"*: William Tryon message to Great Alamance Camp, 16 May 1771. *Historical Sketches of North Carolina: from 1584 to 1851. Compiled from Original Record, Official Documents, and Traditional Statements* (Philadelphia: Lippincott, Grambo and Co., 1851), 1:16.

36 *charged the encampment*: There are varying first- and secondhand accounts of exactly how the standoff between Tryon and the Regulators escalated into bloodshed. One colorful depiction of events, citing eyewitness accounts, is found in William Edward Fitch, *Some Neglected History of North Carolina, Being an Account of the Revolution of the Regulators and of the Battle of Alamance* (New York: Fitch, 1914), 215–218.

36 *"may the Lord have mercy on your soul"*: Chief Justice Martin Howard of Hillsborough, NC, 19 June 1771, *Colonial Records of North Carolina*, ed. William L. Saunders (Raleigh, NC: Josephus Daniels, 1886), 8: 643.

37 *"no difficulty in ordering of it"*: GW to Philip Schuyler, 25 June 1775, *PGWR*, 1: 36–40.

37 *"unexceptional"*: Philip Schuyler to GW, 1 July 1775, ibid., 47–49.

PART II: Spies in Boston

43 *"the most wretchedly clothed"*: Benjamin Thompson, "Observations of Benjamin Thompson," 4 November 1775, quoted from *Report on the Manuscripts of Mrs. Stopford-Sackville, of Drayton House, Northhamptonshire* (Hereford, UK: Hereford Times Co., 1910), 2: 14.

43 *"excrement about the fields"*: Quoted from David McCullough, *1776* (New York: Simon & Schuster, 2001), 31.

43 *"Some are made of boards"*: Rev. William Emerson, quoted from George E. Ellis, *Celebration of the Centennial Anniversary of the Evacuation of Boston by the British Army* (Boston: Boston City Council, 1876), 146.

43 *"a numerous army of provincials"*: GW to Samuel Washington, 20 July 1775, *The Writings of George Washington from the Original Manuscript Sources, 1745–1799*, ed. John C. Fitzpatrick (Washington, DC: U.S. Government Printing Office, 1931–1944), 37: 512.

44 *"licentiousness and every kind of disorder"*: GW to John Hancock, 25 September 1776, *PGWR*, 6: 393–401.

44 *"Their officers are generally speaking"*: GW to Lund Washington, 20 August 1775, ibid., 1: 334–340.

45 *"such a dirty, mercenary spirit"*: GW to Joseph Reed, 28 November 1775, ibid., 2: 448–451.

45 *"did not utter a word for half an hour"*: Gen. John Sullivan to New Hampshire Committee of Safety, 5 Aug 1775, *Provincial Papers: Documents and Records Relating to the Province of New Hampshire, from 1764 to 1776*, ed. Nathaniel Bouton (Nashua: Legislature of New Hampshire, 1873), 7: 572.

46 *New York is a city of Loyalists*: See for example Paul David Nelson, *William Tryon and the Course of Empire: A Life in British Imperial Service* (Chapel Hill: Univ. of North Carolina Press, 1990), 136.

47 *"I receive with satisfaction"*: William Tryon's Answer to the Address of the Mayor, Alderman, and Commonality of the City of New York, 7 July 1775, *AA*, 2: 1534–1535.

47 *"I confess my disappointment"*: Ibid.

48 *"I am authorized to say"*: Ibid.

48 *a mob of revolutionaries . . . night*: For more on the raid on King's College, including the role played by Alexander Hamilton trying to prevent violence against Myles Cooper, see Chernow, *Hamilton*, 63–64.

49 *Committee of Correspondence, etc*: The complicated evolution of New York's governing bodies during this period is summarized succinctly in Edwin G. Burrows and Mike Wallace, *Gotham: A History of New York City to 1898* (New York: Oxford Univ. Press, 1999), 215–225.

50 *"It would not do to treat the New Yorkers"*: Extract of a Letter from Boston, 20 August 1774, *AA*, 1: 724.

51 *"ribband to distinguish myself"*: GW expense memorandum, 10 July 1775, *The Writings of George Washington from the Original Manuscript Sources, 1745–1799*, ed. John C. Fitzpatrick (Washington, DC: U.S. Government Printing Office, 1931–1944), 3: 339n83.

51 *this simple ribbon*: The light blue ribbon GW purchased and wore during these months is still intact and on display in the Museum of the American Revolution in Philadelphia, Pennsylvania.

52 *"His Excellency was on horseback"*: James Thacher, 20 July 1775, *A Military Journal During the American Revolutionary War, From 1775 to 1783* (Boston: Cotton & Barnard, 1827), 33.

52 *"sour and unwholesome"*: GW, General Orders, 7 July 1775, *PGWR*, 1: 71–75.

52 *"It is ordered that he be discharged"*: Ibid.

53 *"Where it has been observed and complained of"*: GW, General Orders, 22 August 1775, ibid., 346.

53 *"the troops being continuously debauched"*: GW, General Orders, 6 September 1775, ibid., 418.

53 *"Any officer, non-commissioned officer,"*: GW, General Orders, 3 October 1775, ibid., 2: 81.

53 *"every private soldier will detest"*: GW, General Orders, 5 July 1775, ibid., 1: 62–64.

54 *"the great and common cause, in which we are all engaged"*: GW, General Orders, 4 July 1775, ibid., 54–58.

55 *when the Virginians arrive*: The incident to follow is as originally related by Israel Trask, quoted here from *The Revolution Remembered: Eyewitness Accounts of the War for Independence*, ed. John C. Dann (Chicago: Univ. of Chicago Press, 1980), 408–409.

55 *"white linen frocks, ruffled and fringed"*: Ibid., 408.

55 *"and a fierce struggle commenced"*: Ibid., 409.

55 *"With the spring of a deer"*: Ibid.

55 *"less than fifteen minutes' time had elapsed"*: Ibid.

56 *"There [have] been so many great, and capital errors"*: GW to Richard Henry Lee, August 29 1775, *PGWR*, 1: 372–376.

56 *"I pity our good general"*: James Warren to John Adams, 3 December 1775. *The Adams Papers*, Papers of John Adams, ed. Robert J. Taylor (Cambridge: Harvard Univ. Press, 1979) 3: 345–349.

56 *"Could I have forseen, . . ."*: GW to Joseph Reed, 28 November 1775, *PGWR*, 2: 448–451.

57 *"You have no doubt heard of a most horrid conspiracy"*: Extract of a Letter From a Gentleman in New York to his Friend in Hartford, 27 June 1776, *AA*, 6: 1101.

57 *"stop at nothing"*: Ibid.

57–58 *"All our important men were to be seized"*: Ibid.

58 *"From the weight of the persons"*: Ibid.

60 *Wenwood*: Some sources for the story, including GW himself, spell the last name "Wainwood." For example GW to John Hancock, 5 October 1775, *PGWR*, 2: 98–103.

60 *"Wenwood's butter biscuits"*: As advertised by Wenwood himself in the local newspaper, the *Newport Mercury*. Quoted from John Bakeless, *Turncoats, Traitors, and Heroes: Espionage in the American Revolution* (New York: Da Capo Press, 1998), 12.

60 *three British officials*: According to GW, the three officials are "Capt. Wallace," "Mr. Dudley," and "George Rome." GW to John Hancock, 5 October 1775, *PGWR*, 2: 98–103.

61 *"I much wonder you never sent what you promised"*: Quoted from Bakeless, 14.

61 *sitting on the horse just behind the large general*: Ibid., 9–10.

62 *"For a long time, she was proof"*: GW to John Hancock, 5 October 1775, *PGWR*, 2: 98–103.

62 *"at length she was brought to a Confession"*: Ibid.

64 *"Upon his first examination"*: Ibid.

64 *report on the status*: The deciphered letter is Benjamin Church to John Fleming, 23 July 1775, ibid., 103–106. It contains some inaccuracies regarding troop numbers and supplies, which Church later claims represent his attempt to fool the British about the strength of the Continental army.

66 *"wicked and detestable . . . breach of trust"*: Session of the Massachusetts House of Representatives, 3 November 1775, *AA*, 3: 1497.

66 *"I can honestly appeal to Heaven . . . infamy"*: Benjamin Church to GW, 3 October 1775, *PGWR*, 2: 85–87.

67 *the council unanimously agree*: Council of War, 3–4 October 1775, ibid., 82–85.

68 *To this day*: See for example *Encyclopedia of Women in American History*, eds. Joyce Appleby, Eileen K. Cheng, Joanne L. Goodwin (New York: Routledge, 2015), 106.

68 *Benjamin Franklin's own son*: For a biography of William Franklin, see Sheila L. Skemp, *William Franklin: Son of a Patriot, Servant of a King* (New York: Oxford University Press, 1990).

69 *avoid capture by either side*: Some of Robert Rodgers's exploits in both wars are related in his own collected letters and journals. *Journals of Major Robert Rodgers*, Franklin B. Hough, ed. (Albany: Joel Munsell's Sons, 1883).

69 *some experience with intelligence gathering*: GW's early introduction to intelligence gathering during the French and Indian War is documented in

Kenneth A. Daigler, *Spies, Patriots, and Traitors: American Intelligence in the Revolutionary War* (Washington, DC: Georgetown Univ. Press, 2014), Chapter 1.

69 *one of Washington's first big expenditures:* See Bakeless, *Turncoats, Traitors, and Heroes,* 89.

69 *there are more spies around him:* Ibid., 84.

72 *"Resolved: That it be recommended":* AA, 3: 1891.

73 *"The Continental Congress have recommended it":* William Tryon to White-head Hicks, 13 October 1775, ibid., 1052.

73 *"The Members of the Corporation":* Whitehead Hicks to William Tryon, 14 October 1775, ibid., 1052–1053.

74 *"As they have not authorized you":* William Tryon to Whitehead Hicks, 14 October 1775, ibid., 1053.

74 *"be assured that Mr. Tryon is most assiduously":* "The Intelligencer" to John Adams, 16 October 1775, *The Adams Papers,* The Papers of John Adams, 3: 205–208.

74 *much more focused on kidnapping:* From John Adam's notes on the Continental Congress, 6 October 1775. *The Adams Papers,* Diary and Autobiography of John Adams, 192–210.

74 *"the friendly and respectful terms":* Whitehead Hicks to William Tryon, 18 October 1775, *AA,* 3: 1053.

75 *at the home of William Axtell:* Burrows and Wallace, *Gotham,* 226.

75 *"Finding your letter of yesterday insufficient":* William Tryon to Whitehead Hicks, 19 October 1775, Ibid., 1054.

76 Duchess of Gordon: In colonial documents from the period, the spelling "Dutchess" is often used for this ship. We've opted to use the proper British spelling "Duchess" throughout, and in some cases have changed the spelling in quoted original sources to remain consistent.

77 *"We have suffered prodigiously":* Nathanael Greene to Samuel Ward, 31 Dec 1775. *The Papers of General Nathanael Greene,* ed. Richard K. Showman (Chapel Hill: Univ. of North Carolina Press, 1976), 173.

78 *"The Small Pox is an enemy more terrible":* John Adams to Samuel Cooper, 2 July 1776. *The Adams Papers,* Papers of John Adams, 4: 357.

79 *"If we escape the Small Pox in this camp":* GW to Joseph Reed, 15 December 1775, *PGWR,* 2: 551–554.

79 *"Several persons are to be sent out":* Robert H. Harrison to James Otis, 3 December 1775, *AA,* 4: 168.

79 *"By recent information from Boston":* GW to John Hancock, 4 December 1775, *PGWR,* 2: 483–487.

80 *from a family friend . . . Bridgetown:* Chernow, *Washington,* 24.

81 *Having already suffered smallpox:* Ibid, 24–25.

83 *eighty-five slaves:* Ibid. 98.

83 *several dozen more slaves:* Ellis, *His Excellency,* 41.

83 *"Neither negroes, boys unable to bear arms":* GW, General Orders, 12 November 1775, *PGWR,* 2: 353–355.

84 *"I look upon them in general":* John Thomas to John Adams, 24 October 1775, *The Adams Papers,* Papers of John Adams, 3: 230.

84 *"it has been represented to me":* GW to John Hancock, 31 December 1775, *PGWR,* 2: 622–626.

84 *between 6 and 12 percent:* Chernow, *Washington,* 213.

85 *"there is not a man living":* GW to Robert Morris, 12 April 1786. PGWR, 4: 15–17.

85 *he grants freedom to his own slaves:* In his will GW is only able to grant freedom to those slaves under his personal ownership; after his death, some Mount Vernon slaves remain the legal property of his wife's family and are not freed.

87 *"Henry Dawkins, Engraver from London":* Pennsylvania Journal, July 19, 1758.

87 *by the name of Israel Young:* In some documents from the period, Israel Young's last name is spelled "Youngs." In this text we use the spelling "Young" throughout, and occasionally alter the spelling in quoted sources to be consistent. The same applies for Israel's brother Isaac.

88 *That's how Dawkins later remembered it:* Henry Dawkins and Israel Young later provide somewhat differing accounts of how and why they began communicating while Dawkins was in jail. These discrepancies are covered in full in later chapters. Their testimony is contained in *JPC,* 1: 445–447.

88 *On Dawkins's advice:* Dawkins and Young will later concur that Dawkins advised and directed Young regarding the purchase of the press. Ibid.

90 *"pay all his debts this summer":* Charles Friend testimony before New York Provincial Congress, 10 May 1776. Ibid., 1: 437.

90 *"No person was permitted":* Thomas Henderson testimony before New York Provincial Congress, 14 May 1776. Ibid., 445.

91 *"There is one evil I dread":* GW to Josiah Quincy, 24 March 1776, *PGWR,* 3: 528–529.

91 *"The reflection on my situation":* GW to Joseph Reed, 14 January 1776. Ibid., 87–92.

92 *"His Excellency depends upon the Colonels":* GW, General Orders, 11 March 1775. Ibid., 448–449.

92 *"drill'd men":* Ibid.

94 *the Life Guards:* At the time, the grammatical convention was to apply the singular construction "the Life Guard" to refer to the plural group. In this text we apply a more modern usage: the plural "the Life Guards" refers to the full group or to more than one member of the unit, and the singular "Life Guard" refers to only a single member.

95 *ice skates across the bay in the middle of the night:* Joseph Ellis, *His Excellency: George Washington* (New York: Alfred A. Knopf, 2004), 85.

96 *reading military books in his parents' bookstore:* McCullough, *1776,* 58.

97 *roughly 120,000 pounds of artillery:* These numbers and some other details of Knox's trip taken from ibid., 82.

98 *a total of more than three thousand men:* Ibid., 89.

98 *"My God, these fellows":* As reported in a letter from Abigail Adams to John Adams, 16 March 1775, *The Adams Papers,* Adams Family Correspondence, 1: 357–361.

101 *The friend's name is Isaac Ketcham:* In some contemporaneous documents, Ketcham's last name is spelled "Ketchum." We use the spelling "Ketcham" throughout, and sometimes change the spelling in quoted sources to be consistent.

101   *The three-person team is now a four-person team*: The account of Ketcham's initial involvement with Dawkins and the Young brothers, as well as details about the counterfeiters' difficulty finding the proper paper, is provided in later testimony from Dawkins, Young, and Ketcham. *JPC*, 1: 443–448.

103   *"To the inhabitants of New York"*: *The Sentinel,* January 27, 1776.

103   *"Intelligence Office"*: Ibid.

104   *"What in the name of Heaven"*: Ibid.

104   *David Mathews*: In some contemporaneous documents and papers, "Mathews" is spelled "Matthews." In this text we always use the correct spelling "Mathews," and occasionally alter the spelling in quoted sources to be consistent.

104   *"low in estimation as a lawyer"*: Thomas Jones, *History of New York During the Revolutionary War*, ed. Edward Floyd De Lancey (New York: N-YHS, 1879), 2: 121.

104   *"villain"*: This term and the embezzlement accusation are attributed to Mathews's contemporary Peter Dubois. Quoted from Ruma Chopra, *Unnatural Rebellion: Loyalists in New York during the Revolution* (Charlottesville: Univ. of Virginia Press, 2011), 153–154.

105   *three out of the four major gunsmiths*: Tryon bragged about his coercion of New York gunsmiths for the British in a letter to the Earl of Dartmouth on 8 December 1775. The letter is compiled in John Romeyn Brodhead, ed., *Documents Relative to the Colonial History of the State of New-York; Procured in Holland, England and France* (Albany: Weed, Parsons and Co., 1857), 8: 647.

105   *"have it inserted in the several Gazettes"*: William Tryon to David Mathews, 16 March 1775, *AA*, 5: 248.

105   *"prejudice, delusion, and faction"*: William Tryon address to the inhabitants of New York, 16 March 1775. Ibid., 248–249

105   *"It is in the clemency"* . . . *"timely and dutiful submission"*: Ibid.

106   *Around nightfall, the mob*: Details of this incident, including the placard, are from Paul David Nelson, *William Tryon and the Course of Empire: A Life in British Imperial Service* (Chapel Hill: Univ. of North Carolina Press, 1990), 141.

106   *Loyalists . . . cower in their homes*: Ibid.

106   *"My feeling on this occasion"*: Ibid.

108   *"carry'd death in their faces"*: Quoted from Burke Davis, *George Washington and the American Revolution* (New York: Random House, 1975), 74.

PART 3: A Bloody Summer

113   *"The Hudson naturally presented itself"*: Henry Clinton, *The American Rebellion: Sir Henry Clinton's Narrative of his Campaigns, 1775–1782*, ed. William B. Wilcox (New Haven: Yale Univ. Press, 1954), xiv–xvi.

113   *"a kind of key to the whole continent"*: John Adams to George Washington, 6 January 1776, *PGWR*, 3: 36–38.

114   *"The consequences of the enemy's possessing"*: Charles Lee to GW, 5 January 1776, *The Lee Papers* (New York: New-York Historical Society, 1871), 1: 234.

114 *"entirely under the Government of Tryon"*: GW to Joseph Reed, 31 January 1776, *PGWR*, 3: 225–229.

114 *"apples, mutton, and Loyalists"*: Quoted from Henry Belcher, *The First American Civil War* (London: Macmillan and Co., 1911), 2: 110.

115 *"Knowing it to be of the last importance . . . posture of defence"*: GW to Lord Stirling 10 January 1776, *PGWR*, 3: 63–64.

115 *"There is good reason to believe that Tryon"*: GW to Charles Lee, 30 January 1776. Ibid., 221–222.

116 *"Boiling Water"*: Quoted from Barnet Schecter, *Battle of New York: The City at the Heart of the American Revolution* (New York: Walker, 2002), 67.

116 "in flagrante delicto": Quoted from John Richard Alden, *General Charles Lee: Traitor or Patriot?* (Baton Rouge: Louisiana State Univ. Press, 1951), 94.

116 *"Lee says he will send word"*: *Pennsylvania Evening Post*, 6 February 1776. Quoted from Frank Moore, *Diary of the Revolution: A Centennial Volume Embracing The Current Events in Our Country's History From 1775 to 1781* (Hartford, CT: J.B. Burr, 1876), 202.

117 *"What to do with the city"*: Charles Lee to GW, 19 February 1776, *PGWR*, 3: 339–441.

117 *some three hundred cannons . . . were "spiked"*: Thomas Fleming, *1776: Year of Illusions* (Edison, NJ: Castle Books, 1996), 135.

117 *A body called the City Watch*: Ibid.

117 *In response . . . alleged ringleaders*: Alexander Clarence Flick, *Loyalism in New York During the American Revolution* (New York: Columbia Univ. Press, 1901), 90.

118 *"tendered the oath . . . place of security"*: Isaac Sears to Charles Lee, 7 March 1776. Quoted from Thomas Field, *The Battle of Long Island, with Connected Preceding Events, and the Subsequent American Retreat* (Brooklyn: Long Island Historical Society, 1869), 49n2.

119 *"to stop all provisions from the city"*: Charles Lee to GW, 29 February 1776, *PGWR*, 3: 389–393.

119 *"The propensity or rather rage"*: Ibid.

120 *"I have received intelligence that Mr. Tryon"*: Charles Lee to President of the New York Provincial Congress, 16 February 1776, *The Lee Papers*, 1: 301.

120 *"he will not intrigue, cabal"*: Ibid.

121 *known more commonly as Lord Stirling*: Although Gen. William Alexander's claim to royal Scottish ancestry was dubious, he insisted on the title "Lord Stirling" throughout his life in the colonies. The title stuck during his military career, and most army documents and correspondence refer to him as "Gen. Stirling" or "Lord Stirling." Therefore in this text, we almost always use the name "Stirling" or "Lord Stirling" to refer to Alexander.

121 *"all male inhabitants"*: Quoted from Judith L. Van Buskirk, *Generous Enemies: Patriots and Loyalists in Revolutionary New York* (Philadelphia: Univ. of Pennsylvania Press, 2002), 16.

122 *two thousand to the* Duchess of Gordon: *AA*, 4: 1103.

122 *had a meeting with the Governor*: Examination of John Craig, 12 March 1776. Ibid., 4: 978.

122 *"to rig out a sloop"*: Ibid.

123 *"went on board . . . the* Duchess of Gordon": Ibid.

124 *"Attorneys General Kempe and Skinner"*: Ibid.

124 *"By some prisoners taken into custody"*: Lord Stirling to John Hancock, 16 March 1776, *AA*, 5: 248.

126 *"extreme hurry"* . . . *"great speed"*: Quoted from McCullough, *1776*, 116.

126 *His party makes stops*: These and more of GW's stops along route are documented in William Baker, *The Itinerary of George Washington* (Philadelphia: J. B. Lippincott & Co., 1892), 36.

127 *from his newly formed Life Guards*: Referred to as his "personal guard" for this trip in Chernow, *Washington*, 229.

128 *"a third or more"*: See for example Chopra, *Unnatural Rebellion*, 46.

130 *On the morning of April 19, 1776*: The date and subsequent details of Ketcham's trip are from Ketcham's own testimony before the New York Provincial Congress, 14–15 May 1776, *JPC*, 1: 444–445.

131 *Brunswick Landing . . . Levi Lott*: Ibid., 444.

131 *Lott did give Ketcham a very small sample*: Ibid., 445.

131 *describes only as a "Dutchman"*: Ibid., 444.

132 *"Though he at first intended to obtain paper"*: Ibid., 445.

134 *"a continuance of the intercourse"*: GW to the New York Committee of Safety, 17 April 1776, *PGWR*, 3: 77–79.

134 *"relying upon your zeal and attachment"*: Ibid.

134 *"the ship in which Governor Tryon resides"*: Session of the New York Committee of Safety, 18 April 1776, *JPC*, 1: 412.

135 *"Resolved and Ordered, that no inhabitant of this colony"*: Ibid.

136 Constitutional Gazette . . . New-York Journal: See source notes for "Proclamation on Intercourse with British Warships, 29 April 1776," *Founders Online*, http://founders.archives.gov/documents/Washington/03-04-02-0132

136 *"for the purposes of giving intelligence"*: GW, Proclamation on Intercourse with British Warships, 29 April 1776, *PGWR*, 4: 164–165.

136 *"To the end that such evil"*: Ibid.

136 *"I do hereby will and require"*: Ibid.

138 *estate called Mortier's . . . Charlton and Varick Streets*: Property location is as described in Abraham Mortier's will, found in *Abstract of Wills on File in the Surrogate's Office, City of New York* (New York: New-York Historical Society, 1900), 8: 285.

139 *official housekeeper, Mary Smith*: Mary Smith's term as housekeeper began in early April 1776, at roughly the time GW relocated to Mortier's. Nancy K. Loane, "General Washington's Housekeeper," *Tredyffrin Easttown History Quarterly* 43, (Summer 2006) no. 3, 84.

139 *manage . . . expenses*: Ibid., 85.

139 *Two stand at the back*: Harry M. Ward, *George Washington's Enforcers: Policing the Continental Army* (Carbondale: Southern Illinois Univ. Press, 2006), 61.

139 *barricade the door, and take positions*: Ibid.

139 *"any orders delivered by Caleb Gibbs"*: GW, General Orders, 16 May 1776, *PGWR*, 4: 310–311

140 *rechristened the boat*: Seth Harding to Jonathan Trumbull, 20 May 1776. Quoted from Carlos E. Godfrey, *The Commander-in-Chief's Guard* (Washington, DC: Stevenson Smith Co., 1904), 20.

141 *"We have all the reason . . ."*: John Hancock to GW, 25 March 1776. *PGWR*, 3: 532–533.

141 *somewhere close to seventeen thousand:* McCullough, *1776,* 131.

142 *"I fear for you"*: Quoted from Edwin G. Burrows and Mike Wallace, *Gotham: A History of New York City to 1898* (New York: Oxford Univ. Press, 1999), 228.

142 *"complete garrison town"*: Quoted from Van Buskirk, *Generous Enemies,* 14.

142 *"terror and confusion"*: Ibid.

143 *"Troops are daily coming in"*: Quoted from George F. Scheer and Hugh F. Rankin, *Rebels & Redcoats: The American Revolution Through the Eyes of Those Who Fought and Lived It* (New York: World Pub. Co., 1957), 143.

143 *"Oh the houses in New York"*: Quoted from Van Buskirk, *Generous Enemies,* 15.

143 *"many houses taken up"*: GW, General Orders, 17 April 1776, *PGWR*, 4: 75.

144 *"To expect . . . the same service"*: GW to John Hancock, 9 February 1776. Ibid., 3: 274–277.

144 *"We expect a very bloody summer"*: GW to John Augustine Washington, 4 May 1776. Ibid., 4: 411–414.

145 *"I lament much that this movement"*: Henry Clinton to William Tryon, 11 February 1776, Henry Clinton Papers, William Clements Library, University of Michigan, 13:40.

146 *"At length a doubt arose"*: Extract of a Letter to a Gentleman in London, 2 March 1776, *AA*, 5: 44.

146 *transport to England*: Ibid.

147 *farmers and townsfolk will agree*: There are many examples of Tryon's recruiting in the region, some to be highlighted later in the story. One example not otherwise discussed in these pages involves reports from White Plains, NY, of residents making visits to Tryon's ship, and shortly afterward joining an underground network of some seven hundred local Loyalists prepared to raise arms for the British when their fleet arrives. See deposition of John Thomas to White Plains Committee of Safety, 12 July 1776, *CHM*, 1: 421.

149 *"short, thick man" . . . white coat*: For example, examination of James Mason, 20 June 1776, *CHM*, 1: 344.

149 *"Gilbert Forbes, of the City of New York"*: Session of the New York Committee of Safety, 22 March 1776, *JPC*, 1: 381.

150 *soldiers are sent door-to-door*: From Schecter, *Battle of New York,* 91.

151 *"burr-millstone maker"*: A burr-millstone maker was a specialized stonemason who forged the millstones for a gristmill, using a type of rock called burrstone.

151 *In this conversation, Mr. Webb tells Forbes*: Examination of Gilbert Forbes, 29 June 1776, *CHM*, 1: 372.

151 *stash of nine rifles:* Ibid.

151 *"young man who lived with James Rivington"*: Ibid.

152 *eleven "smooth narrow-bored guns"*: Ibid.

152 *"Governor Tryon will give him"*: Ibid.

153 *three guineas in 1776*: Conversion calculated according to Eric W. Nye, *Pounds Sterling to Dollars: Historical Conversion of Currency,* http://www.uwyo.edu/numimage/currency.htm.

153 *mysterious woman named "Mrs. Beck": CHM, 1: 372.*

154 *He will ensure*: Ibid.

154 *he himself will soon be visiting the* Duchess of Gordon: This timeline of Mathews's meeting with Forbes is based on Forbes's later description. Mathews himself will recount a different order of events, in which he met Forbes only after he had already acquired the latter's payment from the *Duchess of Gordon*. For reasons to be explored in later chapters, we favor Forbes's account over Mathews's.

156 *"Every brutal gratification"*: Quoted from McCullough, *1776*, 125.

156 *one drink seller ... twice as many*: Statistics regarding alcohol consumption taken from Benjamin L. Carp, *Rebels Rising: Cities and the American Revolution* (New York: Oxford Univ. Press, 2007), 63-64.

156 *6.7 gallons per year per person:* Ibid., 63. Our calculations for "shots per day" assume that children under sixteen were not rum drinkers, and that men drank more than women.

156 *demanded higher-proof alcohol:* Ibid., 64.

156 *"disgust the sensible"*: Pseudonym "Alcanor," writing in the *New-York Chronicle*, 3 July 1769.

157 *"the suppression of these houses"*: Quoted from Carp, *Rebels Rising*, 68.

157 *"quarreling, fighting, gaming"*: Ibid., 69.

157 *attempted rape, assault, rioting*: Ibid., 68.

157 *"a bowl or two of grog"*: Isaac Bangs, *Journal of Lieutenant Isaac Bangs, April 1, 1776, to July 29, 1776* (Cambridge, MA: John Wilson and Son, 1890), 54.

158 *"the gin shops and other houses"*: Quoted from Marvin Kitman, *George Washington's Expense Account* (New York: Grove Press, 1970), 194.

158 *"General Washington is very solicitous"*: Thomas Mifflin to New York Committee of Safety, 15 April 1776, *JPC*, 1: 408.

158 *"If any soldier shall be found disguised with liquor"*: Quoted from Kitman, *George Washington's Expense Account*, 194.

160 *has uncovered a scheme by which*: Fairfield Committee of Inspection to GW, 14 May 1776, *PGWR*, 4: 298–300.

161 *"The circumstances attending this affair"*: Ibid.

161 *"root out or secure ... truly commendable"*: GW to Jonathan Sturges. Ibid., 321.

161 *an attempt to locate and arrest ... is not successful*: Seth Harding to Jonathan Trumbull, 15 May 1776, *Naval Documents of the American Revolution*, William James Morgan, ed. (Washington, DC: U.S. Navy Department, 1970), 5: 104–105.

161 *"By the enclosed you will discover"*: King's District Committee of Correspondence to GW, 13 May 1776, *PGWR*, 4: 290–291.

162 *"Believe it the plan is as deep as Hell"*: Ibid.

162 *One of the masterminds of this Loyalist plot*: See footnote #1 under "To George Washington from the King's District Committee of Correspondence, 13 May 1776," *Founders Online*, National Archives, http://founders.archives.gov/documents/Washington/03-04-02-0229.

163 *"From these you will readily discover"*: GW to Philip Schuyler, 21 May 1776, *PGWR* 4: 360–361.

163 *"Having the utmost confidence in your integrity"*: Ibid.

163 *"our internal enemies have many projects"*: Ibid.

163 *"a duty I owe myself and my country"*: Philip Schuyler to GW, 28 May 1776. Ibid., 4: 401–403.

163 *"I cannot sit easy under such an infamous imputation"*: Ibid.

164 *"plot being formed for the destruction"*: Mark Hopkins to GW, 26 May 1776, ibid., 387–388.

164 *"The said Convention . . . took all those methods"*: Ibid.

164 *"That there has been a plan forming"*: Ibid.

164 *"some wicked designing men"*: Ibid.

166 *This is where James Mason*: James Mason's arrival in Goshen and the other details in this chapter are taken from his June 20, 1776, testimony before the Committee on Conspiracies within the New York Provincial Congress. *CHM*, 1: 344–345.

166 *a man named William Farley*: William Farley's real name is William Forbes. We've changed Forbes's last name to "Farley" throughout the text to avoid possible confusion with the gunsmith Gilbert Forbes, who is also closely connected to Tryon's plot but bears no relation to William Forbes.

167 *"Governor Tryon would give five guineas"*: Examination of James Mason, 20 June 1776, *CHM*, 1: 344–345.

167 *Farley gets something out of it too*: William Farley, aka William Forbes, denies the accusation that he is a paid recruiter for Governor Tryon. However, his denial contradicts other sources, and the weight of evidence supports Mason's story. For Farley's (aka Forbes's) testimony, see Ibid., 356.

167 *"was to have a bounty from the Governor"*: Examination of James Mason, 20 June 1776, *CHM*, 1: 344–345.

168 *"there are riflemen staged there"*: Ibid.

170 *"Look at New York, where even the church"*: Quoted from Karen Q., "The Indecent Side of Revolutionary Era New York," *Behind the History* (blog). https://patriottoursnyc.com/stories-dont-tell/

170 *By one tally . . . there are about five hundred*: From Edwin G. Burrows and Mike Wallace, *Gotham: A History of New York City to 1898* (New York: Oxford Univ. Press, 1999), 214.

170 *equivalent of some 33,000*: According to the latest U.S. Census Bureau projections from 2017, the population of Manhattan is approximately 1.66 million. Two percent of this number is 33,200.

170 *"at first I thought nothing could exceed"*: Isaac Bangs, 25 April 1776, *Journal of Lieutenant Isaac Bangs* (Cambridge, Mass: John Wiley & Son, 1890), 29.

170 *"bitchfoxy jades, jills, hags, strums, prostitutes"*: Loammi Baldwin to his wife, 12 June 1776. Quoted from John J. Gallagher, *Battle of Brooklyn 1776* (New York: Da Capo Press, 1995), 69.

170 *"continue their employ"*: Ibid.

171 *"castrated in a barbarous manner"*: *Journal of Lieutenant Isaac Bangs* (Cambridge, Mass: John Wiley & Son, 1890), 30.

171 *body of a prostitute*: McCullough, *1776*, 125.

171 *"broke up the knots of men and women"*: Loammi Baldwin quoted from Gallagher, *Battle of Brooklyn*, 69.

172 *"Our Company are now about one half"*: Bangs, *Journal of Lieutenant Isaac Bangs* (Cambridge, Mass: John Wiley & Son, 1890), 64.

172 *afflicted soldiers . . . are ferried to Montresor's Island*: Schecter, *Battle of New York*, 90.

173 *unfit for duty*: McCullough, 131.

175 *"he thought the paper he wanted"*: Examination of Israel Young before the New York Provincial Congress, 15 May 1776, *JPC*, 1: 447.

175 *the only people home at the Youngs' house*: This detail and others taken from Jeremiah Wool testimony before the New York Provincial Congress, 14 May 1776. *JPC*, 1: 443.

175 *"immediately enters"*: Ibid.

176 *going to nearby Huntington*: Ibid.

177 *Mathews would often join them*: On February 15, 1776, the same day Mathews was appointed Mayor, the New York Provincial Congress had granted him open-ended permission to visit Tryon's ship. *JPC*, 1: 302.

178 *"obtain permission from the Governor"*: Examination of David Mathews before the Committee on Conspiracies, 23 June 1776, *CHM*, 1: 354.

178 *"private room"*: Ibid.

178 *"put a bundle of paper money in my hands"*: Ibid.

179 *"Take out five pounds"*: Ibid.

180 *The price of the guns*: The price Gilbert Forbes was originally quoted was "three guineas apiece" for his nine rifles and eleven smoothbore guns; in other words, sixty guineas. One guinea was the equivalent of one pound and one shilling, or slightly less than 1.1 pounds. The total price of his gun shipment would therefore be roughly sixty-five pounds.

182 *On May 17, 1776: JPC*, 1: 450

182 *"dangerous machinations . . . intestine enemies"*: Session of the New York Provincial Congress, 18 May 1776, *JPC*, 1: 450.

182 *"be a Secret Committee" . . . the resolution is passed*: Ibid.

182 *five members . . . any three of them*: Ibid.

183 *"Committee for the Hearing"*: *CHM*, 1: 340.

183 *immediate target of investigation*: Willliam Tryon will soon be the first name on the committee's "List of Suspected Persons" who will become targets of investigation. Ibid.

184 *The Patriots may have started the worst of it*: See for example Gabriel Schoenfeld, *Necessary Secrets: National Security, the Media, and the Rule of Law* (New York: W. W. Norton & Co., 2010), 59.

185 *Skinner's letter, written . . . in December 1775:*, *AA*, 4: 363–364.

185 *"many sentiments and expressions"*: Proceedings of the Provincial Congress of New Jersey, 2 March 1776, *Minutes of the Provincial Congress and the Council of Safety of the State of New Jersey* (Trenton: Naar, Day & Naar, 1879), 403.

187 *Now, he is a familiar presence*: As we'll see, Gilbert Forbes's name will come up repeatedly when authorities examine suspected Loyalists, the gunsmith is frequently described as a regular presence at Loyalist-friendly taverns and inns. Many examples are found in the proceedings of the Committee on Conspiracies of the New York Provincial Congress, *CHM*, 1: 342–372.

188 *Graham is a former British officer*: Examination of Gilbert Forbes before the Committee on Conspiracies, 29 June 1776, *CHM*, 1: 372.

188 *finding and organizing men*: Ibid.

188 *Accounts vary as to exactly how and when*: Forbes and Mathews give different stories of how and when the transaction occurs, but after initial denials both men eventually confess to the money changing hands (*CHM*, 1:

354–355, and *AA*, 6: 1085). Other witnesses will also testify to having knowledge of the transaction.

189 *"exerted himself . . . and raised enough men"*: CHM, 1: 372.

191 *"Paper money was in those times"*: Benjamin Franklin, *The Life of Benjamin Franklin, Written by Himself*, ed. John Bigelow (Philadelphia: J.B. Lippincott & Co., 1902), 3: 354.

191 *half the money in circulation is fake*: See for example Stuart Hatfield, "Faking It: British Counterfeiting During the American Revolution," *Journal of the American Revolution*, 7 Oct 2015. https://allthingsliberty.com/2015 /10/faking-it-british-counterfeiting-during-the-american-revolution.

191 *The first report comes from a Cold Spring Harbor resident*: The resident's name is Charles Friend, who says he learned of the matter largely through another resident named John Anderson. *JPC*, 1: 437.

191 *unusual tools and supplies*: Ibid. See also Examination of Thomas Henderson, ibid., 445.

192 *"Whereas . . . without delay"*: Ibid., 437.

192 *Jeremiah Wool makes the trip:* These and other details of Captain Wool's mission to Cold Spring Harbor are from his testimony before the New York Provincial Congress on May 14, 1776. Ibid.: 443–444.

192 *"Isaac Young came to the door"*: Ibid., 443.

193 *"they proceeded to a room"*: Ibid.

193 *"At the head of one of the beds in that room"*: Ibid.

193 *"proceeded up the said stairs"*: Ibid.

194 *"the press, . . . two dollar bill of Continental money"*: Ibid., 443–444.

194 *"employed in this business to get paper"*: Ibid., 444.

194 *initial statement from Dawkins*: Ibid.

196 *Following directions they were given back in Elizabethtown*: These and other details of the group's journey are primarily from James Mason's examination before the Committee on Conspiracies on June 20, 1776, *CHM*, 1: 344–345. See also William Forbes's (aka William Farley's) examination on June 23, ibid., 356. William Forbes's testimony is less reliable as it contains self-serving and unpersuasive denials of his own role as a recruiter.

197 *"McLean and Farley whispered together"*: Ibid., 344–345. We have changed the original text such that "Forbes" is written as "Farley" in this quote.

197 *"McLean had sent and recommended them"*: Ibid.

198 *"qualified"*: Ibid., 345.

198 *"swear not to divulge anything"*: Ibid.

198 *"to be sent to the Governor"*: Ibid.

198 *"Gilbert Forbes promised"*: Ibid.

198 *"Forbes said that he could not help it"*: Ibid.

199 *"he had enlisted about sixty men"*: Ibid.

200 *"Internal secret enemies"*: James Thacher, *Military Journal During the American Revolution, 1775–1783* (Boston: Richardson & Lord, 1823), 55.

200 *must swear an oath of secrecy*: Details about this oath, including the wording, are found in the proceedings of the New York Provincial Congress of May 19, 1776. *JPC*, 1: 453.

201 *"WHEREAS his Excellency"*: Language is from the secret committee's "Report on Disaffection," 21 May 1776. *CHM*, 1: 338–340.

201 *"WHEREFORE, as well out of regard"*: Ibid.

203 *In what will be a long and expansive career*: One recent biography of John Jay is Walter Stahr's *John Jay: Founding Father* (New York: Diversion Books, 2012).

207 *"The encouragements given by Governor Tryon"*: GW to John Hancock, 10 Jun 1776, PGWR, 4: 487–489.

208 *two men at Corbie's begin a conversation*: The description of this scene is a composite based on the testimony of William Green on June 26, 1776, before the general court-martial (*AA*, 6: 1085) and the examination of Gilbert Forbes before the Committee on Conspiracies on June 29, 1776 (*CHM*, 1: 372).

208 *Mr. Corbie himself*: We don't know definitively that this meeting took place at Corbie's; however, both the close proximity of Corbie's to Mortier's estate and the common use of Corbie's by Loyalists to hold clandestine meetings make it the likeliest location. Also, we know that Gilbert Forbes has utilized Corbie's in the past for activities related to Tryon's plot; for example his swearing in of James Mason and William Benjamin as described in *CHM*, 1: 344–345.

PART IV: A Most Infernal Plot

211 *arrested and taken to New York City*: As documented at the end of Jeremiah Wool's testimony before the New York Provincial Congress. *JPC*, 1: 444.

212 *He also presents the physical evidence*: The transcripts of Wool's testimony include mention of the physical evidence he presents to the Congress. Ibid., 443–444.

212 *None of the suspects' accounts matches another*: The bulk of the counterfeiters' combined testimony before the Provincial Congress, given on May 14 and May 15, 1776, is found in ibid., 443–448.

212 *"Israel Young frequently came to visit"*: Henry Dawkins's examination before the New York Provincial Congress, 14 May 1776. Ibid., 1: 445–446 and 447–448.

212 *"after he . . . had been a day or two at Cold Spring"*: Ibid.

213 *"requested him to do it immediately"*: Ibid.

213 *"showed him how to press the bills"*: Ibid.

213 *"he never had any hand in counterfeiting money"*: Israel Young's examination before the New York Provincial Congress, 15 May 1776. Ibid., 447.

213 *"that he does not know that Dawkins"*: Ibid.

214 *"he did not know that Henry Dawkins was engraving"*: Isaac Young's examination before the New York Provincial Congress, 14 May 1776. Ibid., 446.

214 *"it was a sin"*: Ibid.

214 *"had not been concerned"*: Isaac Ketcham's examination before the New York Provincial Congress, 14 May 1776. Ibid., 444.

217 *this little group of a half dozen*: The general characterization of the guards in this chapter is derived from the combined testimony of several witnesses and suspects eventually examined by the Committee on Conspiracies or before the general court-martial, including William Green, Gilbert Forbes, James Mason, William Welch, William Forbes, and John Craig.

217 *"five feet six inches high"*: Quoted from Washington Irving, *The Life of George Washington* (New York: William L. Allison Co., 1856–1859), 2: 81.

217 *"a favorite"*: Benson J. Lossing, "Washington's Life Guard," *Historical Magazine* 2, no. 5 (May 1858): 131.

217 *They complain about the Continental army*: As above, this depiction of Green, Hickey, Lynch, et al. is derived from the combined testimony of multiple witnesses and suspects.

218 *the Continental army under Washington's personal command*: This characterization does not include the failed Battle of Quebec on December 31, 1775, fought by northern detachments of the Continental army under the command of Maj. Gen. Philip Schuyler.

219 *One night in the first week of June*: This and the coming depiction of Green's interactions are drawn from his June 26 testimony before the general court-martial (*AA*, 6: 1085). Gilbert Forbes gives a different version of the meeting (ibid. and also *CHM*, 1: 372), and also suggests a much earlier date. Forbes's date is not plausible given the full timeline of events.

219 *"conversation on politicks"*: *AA*, 6: 1085.

219 *"I had repeated conversations with Forbes"*: Ibid.

219 *"He invited me to dine with him"*: Ibid.

220 *He's been sent by his boss*: The details of William Leary's story in this chapter are taken from Leary's examination before the Committee on Conspiracies on June 20, 1776. *CHM*, 1: 342–343.

221 *"Forbes ran . . . prevent[s] him from using the said pistol"*: Ibid.

221 *James Mason, a part-time miller*: James Mason is never questioned regarding this meeting with Leary, so we don't know his account of it. All details are based on William Leary's account.

222 *"might see them if he would take an oath"*: Ibid.

222 *"go and be qualified"*: Ibid.

222 *"intending to decoy them thither"*: Ibid.

223 *"they discovered [my] pistols"*: Ibid.

225 *"I had no doubt when I left this city"*: GW to John Hancock, 10 June 1776, *PGWR*, 4: 487–489.

228 *On Thursday, June 13*: *JPC* 1: 492.

228 *"diligently, impartially, without fear"*: Ibid., 495.

228 *Divided by region, the list includes every person*: The "List of Disaffected Persons" is found in *CHM*, 1: 340–41.

228 *"William Tryon, on board the Ship of War"*: Ibid., 340.

230–31 *"the persons under guard"*: *JPC*, 1: 464.

231 *"WHEREAS it has been represented"*: Ibid.

231 *On May 30, two days after*: Ibid., 467.

231 *on June 1, authorities apprehend . . . Philip Young*: Ibid., 470.

231 *one from Dawkins and one from . . . grief-stricken father*: The petitions can be found, respectively, in *CHM*, 1: 296 and 321.

232 *"is injured by the leg irons"*: *JPC*, 1: 481.

232 *a sister of Israel and Isaac Young*: *JPC*, 1: 485.

232 *"deeply impressed with shame and confusion"*: Petition of Isaac Ketcham, 9 June 1776, *AA*, 6: 1410.

232 *"dangerously ill by sore sickness"*: Ibid.

233 *With the guards out of earshot*: This depiction of events in the cell is based

on the combined testimonies of Isaac Ketcham before the New York Provincial Congress on June 17, 1776 (*JPC*, 1: 497) and his testimony before a general court-martial on June 26, 1776 (*AA*, 6: 1085–1086).

235 *twenty-six members*: This tally and other minor details of the morning's session are taken from *JPC*, 1: 496–497.

236 *The first . . . written more than a week ago*: This is Ketcham's June 9 petition letter described in the previous chapter. *AA*, 6: 1410.

236 *"I . . . have something to observe to the honorable House"*: Petition of Isaac Ketcham, 16 June 1776, *CHM*, 1: 325.

236 *On June 9*: Some records suggest the congressmen also received an earlier letter from Ketcham, supposedly written on June 8 (*AA*, 6: 1410). This letter states that Ketcham's coconspirator Israel Young also has a story to share about a plot he learned about in the jail, and that Young specifically requests an audience with John Jay to share it. However, the wording and content of the letter suggest that it has been filed under the wrong date, and was probably written June 18, after Ketcham's current testimony.

237 *Ketcham's cryptic request:* The congressional records indicate that Ketcham may have also included an additional "memorandum" attached to the June 16 note. If so, the memorandum is now missing. For more on this, see the related endnote below referring to p. 239 of the text.

237 *"Ordered, that the officer commanding the guard"*: *AA*, 6: 1410.

238 *Ketcham answers: It has to do*: This depiction of Ketcham's testimony is based on the congressional transcripts from June 17, 1776, found in *JPC*, 1: 497. Some emphasis and clarity are also borrowed from Ketcham's later June 26 testimony on the same subject before the general court-martial, found in *AA*, 1085–1086.

238 *Ketcham overheard them speaking*: The transcript of Ketcham's testimony is confusing in that they begin with him speaking as if the subject has already been introduced (for example "he had further conversations with the two soldiers"). Our suspicion is that the transcripts missed the opening part of his actual testimony, in which he first reveals what he learned in the jail.

239 *Gilbert . . . "Horbush"*: Ketcham probably misheard "Forbes" to be "Horbush." As we'll see, the committee figures out the mistake. In some historical manuscripts (for example *AA*) the correct spelling is actually printed within Ketcham's original testimony, ignoring his apparent misstatement.

239 *"piece of paper"*: Ibid.

239 *This piece of paper . . . no longer exists*: Elsewhere in the congressional records, there is also a mention of a "memorandum" that Ketcham attached to the letters he originally sent to Congress asking for an audience (*CHM*, 1:325). This memorandum, like the "piece of paper" alluded to during his testimony, has since gone missing. Our suspicion is that these two documents are one and the same. In other words, Ketcham attached the memorandum to his petition to speak to congress, and then alluded to it during his testimony before them a few days later. The content is likely some sort of list of conspirators that was intended to be sent to the British ships, but that Hickey or Lynch gave to Ketcham instead.

As other authors have also covered, we know of the memorandum because Ketcham's original petition to the Congress has a handwritten note on it, added by someone later, with the words "The application of Isaac Ketcham and the memorandum which finally ended in the execution of Thomas Hickey for high treason" (Ibid.). This suggests that the missing memorandum may contain some key piece of unknown evidence that could shed new light on the plot. However, if the memo was, as we suspect, simply a written list of conspirators that contained Thomas Hickey's name, that would justify the handwritten note without substantially altering the scope of what we know about the conspiracy.

239 *"showed and gave to"*: Ibid. The full sentence in the congressional record refers to "a piece of paper (as they showed and gave the examinant, and is by him delivered to the committee)"

239 *two Continental soldiers had indeed been arrested*: Nathanael Woodbull to GW, *JPC*, 394.

240 *resolved to send the two soldiers back to the army*: Ibid.

242 *"The charge of secrecy was given"*: *JPC*, 1: 497.

242 *"Ordered, that Mr. Ph. Livingston"*: Ibid.

243 *separate confidential records*: The standard records for the New York Provincial Congress, archived in the volumes called *Journal of the New York Provincial Congress, Provincial Convention, Committee of Safety and Council of Safety of New York State, 1775–1777* do not include the transcripts or other records from the Committee on Conspiracies. The latter records were later archived by the New York Secretary of State's office in a volume called *Calendar of Historical Manuscripts, Relating to the War of the Revolution, in the Office of the Secretary of State*. Both publications are listed in this book's bibliography, and referenced frequently in these notes.

243 *Some of the most critical and sensitive information*: As we'll soon discuss, no records were kept of what must have been dramatic first interrogations of the suspected Life Guards themselves: Hickey, Green, Lynch, Johnson, and Barnes. In fact, there is no record of anything said by Lynch, Johnson, and Barnes at all. Similarly, there are no records of the top investigators and officers discussing or debating the evidence of the case.

244 *"Rifle-men . . . Cape Cod men"*: *JPC*, 1: 497.

245 *The chairman of the Dutchess County Committee of Safety*: *JPC*, 1: 499.

245 *"The militia in the county"*: Ibid.

247 *"to confer with General Washington"*: *AA*, 6: 1412.

248 *"I have been up to view the grounds about King's Bridge"*: GW to John Hancock, 20 June 1776, *PGWR*, 5: 55–58.

249 *"Our affairs are hastening to a crisis"*: John Hancock to New York Provincial Congress, 4 June 1776, *AA*, 6: 1377–1378.

249 *"It is to be hoped that, if our cause is just"*: GW to John Augustine Washington, 4 June 1776, *PGWR*, 4: 411–414.

249 *"We have nothing, my dear sir, to depend upon"*: The anecdote portrayed in this chapter is difficult to verify, although it was often repeated in texts from the time. GW to John Adams, 15 April 1776. Ibid., 67.

252 *He had been sent by his boss*: The details of Leary's story are taken directly from his testimony before Jay and Morris, *CHM*, 1: 342–343.

252 *"took hold of Benjamin"*: Ibid.

253 *"go on board the Man-o-War"*: Ibid.

253 *"employed by the Mayor or Governor"*: Ibid.

253 *"expected a large body of men to join them from Goshen"*: Ibid.

253 *"employed by the Mayor or Governor"*: *JPC*, 1: 499.

255 *Mason's story, like Leary's*: The details of Mason's story are taken directly from his testimony before Jay and Morris. Ibid., 344–345.

256 *"Governor Tryon would give five Guineas bounty"*: Ibid.

256 *"employed by the Governor"*: Ibid.

256 *"qualified"*: Ibid.

256 *"short, thick man"*: Ibid.

257 *"Gilbert Forbes is at the head [with] the Mayor & the Governor"*: Ibid.

257 *"Green of the General's Guards"*: Ibid.

257 *"one Hickey of the General's Guards"*: Ibid.

258 *"one Barnes of the General's Guards"*: Ibid.

258 *"is to have one dollar per man"*: Ibid.

260 *"Sir: Whereas David Mathews"*: Jay, Morris, and Livingston to GW, 21 June 1776. Ibid., 347.

261 *"General Greene is desired to have"*: GW to Nathanael Greene, 21 June 1776. Ibid.

262 *"surround his house"*: Nathanael Greene, 22 June 1776. Ibid.

263 *"seized his person precisely"*: Ibid.

263 *"Vigilant search was made"*: Ibid.

263 *When the Committee on Conspiracies convenes*: The nine-member committee convenes that Saturday morning for a session, and meanwhile Jay and Morris convene separately to conduct a series of examinations related to the plot. Ibid., 347–350.

264 *another Continental soldier*: Examination of Thomas Fletcher, 22 June 1776. Ibid., 350.

264 *"List of Tories in New York and Orange County"*: The list can be seen in ibid., 351.

265 *"Some days past, the General"*: Webb's journal entry is written as June 21, 1776, but the actual date must be June 22. He writes of David Mathews having already been arrested, which did not occur until the early morning of June 22. The entry is found in Samuel Webb, *Correspondence and Journals of Samuel Blachley Webb*, ed. Worthington Chauncey Ford (New York: Wickersham Press, 1893.), 1: 148–149.

265 *"To our great astonishment"*: Ibid.

267 *"This day a most horrid plot was discovered"*: William Heath, 22 June 1776. William Heath Papers, Massachusetts Historical Society, Boston.

270 *"on Broadway, across from Hull's Tavern"*: Examination of James Mason, 20 June 1776, *CHM*, 1: 344–345.

271 *From the start of the examination*: Details are taken directly from Mathews's examination before the Committee on Conspiracies, 23 June 1776. Ibid., 354–355.

272 *"the Governor took him into a private room"*: Ibid.

272 *"Governor Tryon had put a matter on his shoulders"*: Ibid.

272 *a rather convoluted account*: In addition to Mathew's examination, some interesting details about the transaction can be found in the later examination of the acquaintance—a man named George Brewerton—who helped Mathews locate Forbes. Brewerton's examination is found in ibid., 363–364.

272 "*he would be hanged if he was found out*": Examination of Mathews, ibid., 354–355.

273 "*begged of him to desist*": Ibid.

273 "*has no further knowledge*": Ibid.

274 *including the recruiter William Farley*: The examination of Farley (aka William Forbes) is in ibid., 356.

275 *obtained by the* Pennsylvania Journal: Taken from Frank Moore, *Diary of the Revolution: A Centennial Volume Embracing the Current Events in Our Country's History from 1775 to 1781* (Hartford, CT: J. B. Burr, 1876), 256n2.

276 "*Yesterday the General's housekeeper*": Ibid. The letter is also found in *AA*, 6: 1054, with the title "Extract of a Letter Dated New York, June 24, 1776."

276 "*occasion to part . . . inconvenience*": GW to James Clinton, 28 June 1776, *PGWR*, 5: 132.

276 *various infamous theories*: We'll address some of these theories in chapter 80 of this book.

278 *According to one version of events*: The anecdote portrayed in this chapter has not been fully verified, although it was often repeated in texts from the time. The story comes primarily from the extract of an anonymous letter, 24 June 1776, *AA*, 6: 1054.

278 "*his time was very short*,": Ibid.

279 "*This had the desired effect*": Ibid.

279 *save his formal examination for later*: Forbes's official examination before the Committee on Conspiracies will occur several days later, on June 29, 1776 (CHM, 1: 372). As we're about to see, before this formal examination Forbes will be asked to provide more limited testimony.

PART V: Sacricide

285 *He was originally from Ireland . . . Wethersfield*: Details taken from Benson J. Lossing, "Washington's Life Guard," *Historical Magazine* 2, no. 5 (May 1858): 131. Lossing's account of the plot is unreliable, but the depiction of Hickey's background is generally accepted.

285 "*dark hair*": Ibid.

287 "*enemies of the Colonies*": The resolution was drafted by the Continental Congress on June 24, 1776, and brought in session before the New York Provincial Congress on June 26. *JPC*, 1: 506.

288 *These are the thirteen officers who are called to serve*: The list of officers and other details of the court-martial are from *AA*, 1: 1084–1086.

289 "*Thomas Hickey, a private sentinel*": Ibid., 1085.

289 "*[A]bout three weeks ago*": Deposition of William Green. Ibid.

290 "*I asked him where the money*": Ibid.

290 "*Forbes left it with me to inlist and swear the men*": ibid.

290 "*Hickey agreed to the scheme*": Ibid.

290 "*I was pleased with the notion*": Ibid.

290 "*I mentioned the matter . . . to Hickey*": Ibid.

291 "*A night or two after General Washington arrived*": Deposition of Gilbert Forbes. Ibid.

291 "*But in repeated applications from him*": Ibid.

292 *"In a day or two Green gave me"*: Ibid.

292 *"I received upwards of a hundred pounds"*: Ibid.

295 *"In different conversations he informed me"*: Deposition of Isaac Ketcham, ibid., 1086.

295 *"asked me to be one of them"*: Ibid.

295 *"eight of the General's Guard"*: Ibid.

295 *"[T]he enemy would soon arrive"*: Deposition of William Welch, ibid., 1085.

296 *"I did not relish the project"*: Ibid.

297 *"The prisoner being here called"*: Ibid., 1086.

299 *"The Court being cleared"*: Ibid.

300 *"The General communicated to the Council"*: Council of War, 27 June 1776, *PGWR*, 5: 114–116.

301 *"Thomas Hickey belonging to the General's Guard"*: GW, General Orders, 27 June 1776. Ibid., 112–113.

301 *"all the officers and men off duty"*: Ibid.

303 *This particular morning Washington updates Hancock*: GW to John Hancock, 28 June 1776. Ibid., 132–136.

304 *"Congress I doubt not will have heard"*: Ibid.

305 *"The plot had been communicated"*: Ibid.

305 *"I am hopeful this example"*: Ibid.

305 *present-day Grand and Chrystie Streets*: Lossing, "Washington's Life Guard," 131.

306 *close to twenty thousand people*: Crowd size as reported at the time by the *Constitutional Gazette*, New York City, 29 June 1776.

306 *"twenty men, from each Brigade"*: GW, General Orders, 27 June 1776, *PGWR*, 5: 112–113.

307 *"He appeared unaffected and obstinate"*: Letter of William Eustis, 28 June 1776, *New England Historical and Genealogical Register* 23, no. 1 (1869): 208.

307 *"With his last breath"*: Ibid.

310 *"By virtue of, and in obedience to"*: Warrant signed by Provost Marshal William Morony, 28 June 1776, *AA*, 6: 1120.

311 *"The unhappy fate of Thomas Hickey"*: GW, General Orders, 28 June 1776, *PGWR*, 5: 129–130.

311 *"And in order to avoid those crimes"*: Ibid.

313 *"This forenoon, was executed in a field . . . "*: Quoted from Moore, *The Diary of a Revolution*, 256–257.

313 *"ministerial myrmidons"*: The word "myrmidon" refers to an ancient Greek legend about a race of ant-people created by the Gods. "Ministerial" refers to the British monarchy, so the writer is essentially comparing the coming British soldiers to ants who work in service to the King.

314 *"A hellish plot has been lately discovered"*: Joseph Hewes to Samuel Johnston, 8 July 1776. *AA*, 5th Series, 1: 117.

314 *"Their design was upon the first engagement"*: Letter of William Eustis, *New England Historical Register*, 208.

314 *"any set of men could be so lost"*: Ibid.

315 *"It is hoped the remainder"*: Quoted from Chernow, *Hamilton*, 76.

318 *100,000 copies in three months*: Beeman, *Our Lives, Our Fortunes*, 320.

318 *"not only of her Parliament but of her Crown"*: John Adams to Abigail Adams, 17 May 1776, *Adams Papers*, Adams Family Correspondence, 1: 410–412.

320 *"Objects of the most stupendous magnitude"*: John Adams to William Cushing, 9 June 1776, *Adams Papers*, Papers of John Adams, 4: 244–246.

321 *After circling back and communicating*: Joseph Davison to GW, 27 June 1776, *PGWR*, 5: 119–120.

322 *The* Greyhound *was last spotted*: Ibid.

322 *he quickly sends messages*: For example, GW to William Livingston of New Jersey; GW to Massachussetts General Court, both 28 June 1776 (*PGWR*, 5: 136–139). The next day Washington will write similar letters to officials in Connecticut and Pennsylvania.

323 *"upstairs in an out-house"*: Daniel McCurtain, 29 June 1776. Quoted from Schecter, *The Battle for New York*, 99.

323 *"in about ten minutes the whole bay"*: Ibid.

323 *between forty and fifty ships*: McCullough, *1776*, 134.

324 *now it's over one hundred ships*: Ibid., 135.

324 *vacates New York city . . . away from battle*: *JPC*, 1: 512.

324 *Washington sends messages*: See GW to John Hancock, 30 June 1776, *PGWR*, 5:159–60; GW to John Hancock, 14 August 1776, *PGWR* 6:22–25; for more on the volume of ships arriving see McCullough, 146–148.

324 *"The time is now near at hand"*: GW General Orders, 2 July 1776, *PGWR*, 5: 179–182.

326 *"lie on the table"*: Department of State, *The Declaration of Independence 1776* (Washington, DC: Literal Print, 1911), 10.

326 *On July 2, after furious debates*: Ibid.

327 *for another few weeks*: Ellis, *Revolutionary Summer*, 61.

328 *"dainty food of reconciliation"*: GW to John Augustine Washington, 31 May 1776, *PGWR*, 4: 411–414.

329 *he orders each brigade of soldiers*: GW, General Orders, 9 July 1776, ibid., 5: 245–247.

329 *Tuesday, July 9, 1776*: Ellis, *Revolutionary Summer;* 71. A few sources differ on the exact date, and suggest Washington receiving his copy of the Declaration one day earlier, on July 8 (Chernow, *Washington*, 237).

329 *the troops converge on the Commons*: McCullough, 137.

330 *the entire crowd . . . lets out a massive cheer*: See for example Schecter, *Battle of New York*, 102.

330 *Tear down the massive lead statue*: See for example Joseph Ellis, *Revolutionary Summer: The Birth of American Independence* (New York: Alfred A. Knopf, 2013.), 72. One of many contemporary accounts of this night is found in Moore, *Diary of the American Revolution,* p. 270–271.

330 *head in a wheelbarrow*: Detail is from Solomon Drowne to William Drowne, 13 July 1776, in *New York City During the American Revolution*, Mercantile Library Association, ed. (New York: Mercantile Library Association, 1861), 80.

PART VI: Aftermath

336 *over four hundred British ships*: Schecter, *Battle of New York*, 4.

336 *a total of roughly 34,000*: Ibid.

336 *too few troops stationed on Long Island*. See for example McCullough, *1776*, 152.

336   *In the so-called Battle of Brooklyn:* Several details of the Battle of Brooklyn taken from Schecter, *Battle for New York*, 146–153.

337   *kept far too many troops in Manhattan:* For more on Washington's decision to divide his troops, and of his other mistakes, see Ellis, *His Excellency*, 95–96. Also Schecter, *Battle for New York*, 147-153.

344   *One noteworthy example:* Irving, *Life of Washington*, 2: 215.

344   *with the plate of lethal peas in front of him:* A classic version of the poisoned peas story, and the one that arguably started the rest, is reported in Benson J. Lossing, "Washington's Life Guard," *Historical Magazine* 2, no. 5 (May 1858): 131.

344   *daughter of Samuel Fraunces:* Ibid.

345   Minutes of a Conspiracy Against the Liberties of America: There are a few versions of this unusual text, sometimes containing different titles. A relatively accessible edition from the 19th century is *Minutes of a Conspiracy Against the Liberties of America* (Philadelphia: John Campbell, 1856). The originally-published British version is called *Minutes of the Trial and Examination of Certain Persons in the Province of New York, Charged with Being Engaged in a Conspiracy Against the Authority of Congress, and the Liberty of America.* (London: J. Bew, 1786).

345   *Two fictional women:* For the fictionalized testimony concerning Mary Gibbons and "Judith," see *Minutes of a Conspiracy*, 20–25.

347   *"most hellish report that has been propagated":* David Mathews to John McKessen, 20 August 1776, Force, *AA,* 5th Series, 1: 1085.

347   *"You well know the cause of that treatment":* Letter to David Mathews, 28 August 1776. Ibid., 1: 1551.

348   *"formed a plan for the taking of Mr. Washington.":* Quoted from McBurney, *Abductions in the American Revolution*, 16.

349   *a plan to kidnap him . . . more likely:* Writers who take the general position that the goal of the plot was most likely to kidnap Washington include Christian McBurney in *Abductions in the American Revolution: Attempts to Kidnap George Washington, Benedict Arnold and other Military and Civilian Leaders* (2016) and John Bakeless in *Turncoats, Traitors, and Heroes: Espionage in the American Revolution* (1998).

349   *they would be hanged as traitors:* Early in the war, while Washington's army was still in Boston, the British Commander Thomas Gage used colorful language to inform Washington and other colonial leaders of the potential fate of prisoners of war: "your prisoners, whose lives by the laws of the land are destined to the cord" (Thomas Gage to GW, 13 August 1775, *PGWR,* 301–302). In other words, captured rebels can expect to be hanged as traitors. Washington himself also voiced this assumption; see Chernow, *Washington*, 237.

350   *captured officers like Charles Lee:* Maj. Gen. Charles Lee was captured by the British in New Jersey, in December 1776. After over a year of negotiations between the two armies, the British exchanged Lee back to the Americans in exchange for a British general named Richard Prescott. See for example Jared Sparks, *Lives of Charles Lee and Joseph Reed* (Boston: Little, Brown and Company, 1864), 143–153.

350   *"Mathews was installed":* New York City Parks Department. https://www .nycgovparks.org/parks/matthews-muliner-playground/history.

352   *crafted by a playwright:* The Joseph Addison play *Cato, a Tragedy*, written

in 1712 but popular during the Revolution, contains the line "what a pity it is/that we can die but once to serve our country."

352 *spies and double agents known as the "Culper Ring"* : Two recent books that explore the Culper Ring are Brian Kilmeade and Don Yaeger, *George Washington's Secret Six: The Spy Ring That Saved the American Revolution* (New York: Penguin Group, 2013) and Kenneth A. Daigler, *Spies, Patriots, and Traitors: American Intelligence in the Revolutionary War* (Washington, DC: Georgetown University Press, 2014).

352 *didn't even know there* was *a Culper Ring until the 1930s*: See Rhodri Jeffreys-Jones, *Cloak and Dollar: A History of American Secret Intelligence* (New Haven: Yale University Press, 2002) 17–18; also, Brian Kilmeade and Don Yaeger, *George Washington's Secret Six: The Spy Ring That Saved the American Revolution* (New York: Penguin Group, 2013), xvi–xvii.

353 "*inquiring into, detecting and defeating*": From *Minutes of the Committee and of the First Commission for Detecting and Defeating Conspiracies in the State of New York* (New York: New-York Historical Society Collections), 2.

354 "*America's first counterintelligence chief*": The title is applied to Jay on the CIA's own website. P.K. Rose, "The Founding Fathers of American Intelligence," https://www.cia.gov/library/center-for-the-study-of-intelligence/csi-publications/books-and-monographs/the-founding-fathers-of-american-intelligence/art-1.html#john-jay-america-s.

354 *conference room named after Jay*: From Matthew H. Williamson, "The Networks of John Jay, 1745–1801: A Historical Network Analysis Experiment" (PhD diss: Northeastern University, 2017), 105.

354 *he gives Jay first choice of any position*: John Brown Scott, "John Jay, First Chief Justice of the United States," *Columbia Law Review,* Vol. 6, No. 5 (May 1906), 311.

355 *Washington wrote a letter to his wife*: GW to Martha Washington, 18 June 1775, *PGWR,* 1: 3–6.

Selected Bibliography

PRIMARY SOURCES

Abbot, W. W., Philander D. Chase, Edward G. Lengel et al., eds. *The Papers of George Washington*. Revolutionary War Series. Vols. 1–8. Charlottesville: Univ. of Virginia Press, 1985–1998.

Adams, John. *The Adams Papers*. Diary and Autobiography of John Adams. 4 Vols. Edited by L. H. Butterfield. Cambridge: Harvard Univ. Press, 1961.

———. *The Adams Papers*. Papers of John Adams. Vols. 1–6. Edited By Robert J. Taylor. Cambridge: Harvard University Press, 1977–1983.

Bangs, Isaac. *Journal of Lieutenant Isaac Bangs: April 1, 1776–July 29, 1776*. Cambridge, MA: John Wiley & Son, 1890.

Brodhead, John Romeyn, ed. *Documents Relative to the Colonial History of the State of New-York; Procured in Holland, England and France*. Vol 8. Albany: Weed, Parsons, and Co., 1857.

Calendar of Historical Manuscripts, Relating to the War of the Revolution, in the Office of the Secretary of State. 2 Vols. Albany: Weed, Parsons, and Co., 1868.

Clark, William B., William J. Morgan, eds. *Naval Documents of the American Revolution*. Washington, DC: U.S. Dept. of the Navy Naval History Division, 1964–1972.

Clinton, Henry. *The American Rebellion: Sir Henry Clinton's Narrative of His Campaigns, 1775–1782*. Edited by William B. Willcox. New Haven: Yale Univ. Press, 1954.

———. Henry Clinton Papers. William Clements Library, University of Michigan, Ann Arbor.

The Colonial Records of North Carolina. Vols. 8–9. Edited by William Saunders. Raleigh: Edwards & Broughton, 1886.

Davies, K. G., ed. *Documents of the American Revolution*. Vols. 7–12. Dublin: Irish University Press, 1772–1776.

Force, Peter, ed. *American Archives: Consisting of a Collection of Authentick Records, State Papers, Debates, and Letters and Other Notices of Publick Affairs*. 4th Series. 6 Vols. Washington, DC: M. St. Clair Clarke & Peter Force, 1837–1853.

———. *American Archives: Consisting of a Collection of Authentick Records, State Papers, Debates, and Letters and Other Notices of Publick Affairs*. 5th Series. 3 Vols. Washington, DC: M. St. Clair Clarke & Peter Force, 1837–1853.

Franklin, Benjamin. *The Life of Benjamin Franklin, Written by Himself*. Ed. John Bigelow. Philadelphia: J.B. Lippincott Co., 1902.

Greene, Nathanael. *The Papers of General Nathanael Greene*. Vol. 2. Edited by Richard K. Showman. Chapel Hill: Univ. of North Carolina Press, 1976.

Hamilton, Alexander. *The Papers of Alexander Hamilton*. Vols. 1–5. Edited by Harold C. Syrett. New York: Columbia Univ. Press, 1961–1962.

Heath, William. *Memoirs of Major-General William Heath*. Edited by William Abbott. New York: William Abbott, 1901.

———. William Heath Papers, Massachusetts Historical Society, Boston.

Jay, John. Papers of John Jay. Columbia University Libraries, Columbia University, New York.

Journals of the American Congress: From 1774 to 1788. 4 Vols. Washington, DC: Way and Gideon, 1823.

Journals of the Continental Congress, 1774–1789. Vols. 1–5. Edited by Worthington C. Ford. Washington, DC: U.S. Government Printing Office, 1904–1906.

Journals of the Provincial Congress, Provincial Convention, Committee of Safety and Council of Safety of the State of New-York, 1775–1777. Vol 1. Albany: Thurlow Weed, 1842.

Lee, Charles. *The Lee Papers*. Vol 1. New York: New-York Historical Society, 1871.

Martin, Joseph Plumb. *A Narrative of a Revolutionary Soldier: Some of the Adventures, Dangers, and Sufferings of Joseph Plumb Martin*. New York: Penguin Putnam, 2001.

Mercantile Library Association of New York City. *New York City During the American Revolution, Being a Collection of Original Papers From the Manuscripts in the Possession of the Mercantile Library Association of New York City*. New York: Mercantile Library Association, 1861.

Minutes of the Committee and of the First Commission for Detecting and Defeating Conspiracies in the State of New York. Vol 1. New York: New-York Historical Society Collections, 1924.

Nash, Solomon. *Journals of Solomon Nash, a Soldier of the Revolution, 1776–1777*. Edited by Charles I. Bushnell. New York: Privately printed, 1861.

Nuxall, Elizabeth M., ed. *The Selected Papers of John Jay*. Vol 1. Charlottesville: University of Virginia Press, Rotunda, 2010.

Paine, Thomas. *The Writings of Thomas Paine*. Edited by Moncure Daniel Conway. 2 vols. New York: G. P. Putnam's Sons, 1894.

Rush, Benjamin. *The Letters of Benjamin Rush*. Vol 1. Edited by Lyman H. Butterfield. Princeton: Princeton Univ. Press, 1951.

Smith, William. *Historical Memoirs of William Smith from 16 March 1763 to 25 July 1778*. Edited by W. H. W. Sabine. New York: New York Times and Arno Press, 1969.

Thacher, James, M.D. *Military Journal During the American Revolution, 1775–1783*. 2nd ed. Boston: Cottons & Barnard, 1827.

Tryon, William. *The Correspondence of William Tryon and Other Selected Papers*. Vol 2. Edited by William S. Powell. Raleigh, NC: Division of Archives and History, 1981.

Washington, George. *This Glorious Struggle: George Washington's Revolutionary War Letters*. Edited by Edward G. Lengel. Charlottesville: Univ. of Virginia Press, 2007.

———. *The Writings of George Washington*. 39 Vols. Edited by John C. Fitzpatrick. Washington, DC: U.S. Government Printing Office, 1931–1944.

Webb, Samuel Blachley. *Correspondence and Journals of Samuel Blachley Webb.* Vol 1. Edited by Worthington Chauncey Ford. New York: Wickersham Press, 1893.

SECONDARY SOURCES

Alden, John Richard. *General Charles Lee: Traitor or Patriot?* Baton Rouge: Louisiana State Univ. Press, 1951.

Bakeless, John. *Turncoats, Traitors, and Heroes: Espionage in the American Revolution.* New York: Da Capo Press, 1998.

Baker, William. *The Itinerary of George Washington.* Philadelphia: J. B. Lippincott Co., 1892.

Beeman, Richard R. *Our Lives, Our Fortunes & Our Sacred Honor: The Forging of American Independence, 1774–1776.* New York: Basic Books, 2013.

Belcher, Henry. *The First American Civil War.* 2 Vols. London: Macmillan and Co., 1911.

Blakely, Phyllis R., and John N. Grant, eds. *Eleven Exiles: Accounts of Loyalists of the American Revolution.* Toronto: Dundurn Press, Ltd., 1982.

Borden, Morton, and Penn Borden, eds. *The American Tory: Great Lives Observed.* Englewood Cliffs, NJ: Prentice-Hall, Inc., 1972.

Burrows, Edwin G., and Mike Wallace. *Gotham: A History of New York City to 1898.* New York: Oxford Univ. Press, 1999.

Calhoun, Robert McCluer. *The Loyalists in Revolutionary America, 1760–1781.* New York: Harcourt Brace Jovanovich, 1965.

Carp, Benjamin L. *Rebels Rising: Cities and the American Revolution.* New York: Oxford Univ. Press, 2007.

Chernow, Ron. *Washington: A Life.* New York: Penguin Press, 2010.

———. *Alexander Hamilton.* New York: Penguin Press, 2004.

Chopra, Ruma. *Unnatural Rebellion: Loyalists in New York during the Revolution.* Charlottesville: Univ. of Virginia Press, 2011.

Daigler, Kenneth A. *Spies, Patriots, and Traitors: American Intelligence in the Revolutionary War.* Washington, DC: Georgetown University Press, 2014.

Dann, John C. *The Revolution Remembered: Eyewitness Accounts of the War for Independence.* Chicago: Univ. of Chicago Press, 1980.

Daughn, George C. *Revolution on the Hudson: New York City and the Hudson River Valley in the American War of Independence.* New York: W. W. Norton & Company, 2016.

Ellis, Joseph. *His Excellency: George Washington.* New York: Alfred A. Knopf, 2004.

———. *Revolutionary Summer: The Birth of American Independence.* New York: Alfred A. Knopf, 2013.

Field, Thomas W. *The Battle of Long Island, With Connected Preceding Events, and the Subsequent Retreat.* Brooklyn: Long Island Historical Society, 1869.

Fitch, William Edward. *Some Neglected History of North Carolina, Being an Account of the Revolution of the Regulators and of the Battle of Alamance.* New York: Fitch, 1914.

Fleming, Thomas. *1776: Year of Illusions.* Edison, NJ: Castle Books, 1996.

Flexner, James Thomas. *George Washington: The Indispensable Man.* New York: Little, Brown, and Co., 1974.

Flick, Alexander Clarence. *Loyalism in New York During the American Revolution.* New York: Columbia Univ. Press, 1901.

Freeman, Douglas Southall. *George Washington: A Biography*. 7 Vols. New York: Charles Scribner's Sons, 1948–1957.

Godfrey, Carlos E. *The Commander-in-Chief's Guard*. Washington, DC: Stevenson Smith Co., 1904.

Hoock, Holger. *Scars of Independence: America's Violent Birth*. New York: Crown, 2017.

Hughes, Rupert. *George Washington*. 3 Vols. New York: William Morrow and Co., 1926–1930.

Irving, Washington. *The Life of George Washington*. 5 Vols. New York: William L. Allison Co., 1856–1859.

Jones, Thomas. *History of New York During the Revolutionary War*. 2 Vols. Edited by Edward Floyd DeLancey. New York: New-York Historical Society, 1879.

Kitman, Marvin. *George Washington's Expense Account*. New York: Grove Press, 1970.

Long Island Historical Society. *The Campaign of 1776 Around New York and Brooklyn*. Brooklyn: Long Island Historical Society, 1878.

Lossing, Benson J. "Washington's Life Guard." *Historical Magazine* 2, no. 5 (May 1858): 129–134.

McBurney, Christian. *Abductions in the American Revolution: Attempts to Kidnap George Washington, Benedict Arnold and Other Military and Civilian Leaders*. Jefferson, NC: McFarland & Co., Inc., 2016.

McCullough, David. *1776*. New York: Simon & Schuster, 2001.

Minutes of the Trial and Examination of Certain Persons in the Province of New York, Charged with Being Engaged in a Conspiracy Against the Authority of Congress, and the Liberty of America. London: J. Bew, 1786.

Moore, Frank. *Diary of the Revolution: A Centennial Volume Embracing The Current Events in Our Country's History From 1775 to 1781*. Hartford, CT: J.B. Burr, 1876.

Nagy, John A. *George Washington's Secret Spy War: The Making of America's First Spymaster*. New York: St. Martin's Press, 2016.

Nelson, Paul David. *William Tryon and the Course of Empire: A Life in British Imperial Service*. Chapel Hill: Univ. of North Carolina Press, 1990.

O'Callaghan, E. B. *The Documentary History of the State of New York*. Vol 3. Albany: Weed, Parsons & Co., 1850.

Rose, P. K. "The Founding Fathers of American Intelligence." Washington, DC: Center for the Study of Intelligence, Central Intelligence Agency, 1999. https://www.cia.gov/library/center-for-the-study-of-intelligence/csi-publications/books-and-monographs/the-founding-fathers-of-american-intelligence/art-1.html.

Sabine, Lorenzo. *Biographical Sketches of Loyalists of the American Revolution*. 2 Vols. Port Washington, NY: Kennikat Press, 1864.

Sabine, William H. W. *Murder, 1776 and Washington's Policy of Silence*. New York: Theo Gaus' Sons, 1973.

Schecter, Barnet. *The Battle for New York: The City at the Heart of the American Revolution*. New York: Walker, 2002.

———. *George Washington's America: A Biography Through His Maps*. New York: Walker, 2010.

Scheer, George F., and Hugh F. Rankin. *Rebels & Redcoats: The American Revolution Through the Eyes of Those Who Fought and Lived It*. New York: Da Capo Press, 1957.

Shattuck, Gary. "Plotting the 'Sacricide' of George Washington." *Journal of the American Revolution*. July 25, 2014. https://allthingsliberty.com/2014/07 /plotting-the-sacricide-of-george-washington.

Toner, J. M., ed. *Washington's Rules of Civility & Decent Behavior in Company and Conversation*. Washington, DC: W. H. Morrison, 1888.

Van Buskirk, Judith L. *Generous Enemies: Patriots and Loyalists in Revolutionary New York*. Philadelphia: Univ. of Pennsylvania Press, 2002.

Ward, Harry M. *George Washington's Enforcers: Policing the Continental Army*. Carbondale: Southern Illinois Univ. Press, 2006.

Williamson, Matthew H. "The Networks of John Jay, 1745–1801: A Historical Network Analysis Experiment." PhD diss., Northeastern University, 2017.

Wood, Gordon S. *Revolutionary Characters: What Made the Founders Different*. New York: Penguin Press, 2006.

Index

Read on for
Exclusive
Bonus Content

The Mystery of
George Washington's Teeth

We asked authors Brad Meltzer and Josh Mensch if there were any secrets about George Washington that they stumbled onto. They told us there was one unusual detail that they originally intended to write about, but that never found a place in their book. So here's an exclusive look at one final George Washington secret just for Barnes & Noble readers: Washington's missing teeth.

This is a story about George Washington—but it's not about the battles he fought as a general, or the momentous decisions he made as a statesman or president.

It's about his teeth. George Washington's teeth.

It's a subject we happen to know something about, because a few years ago, we produced a story on this subject for *Brad Meltzer's Lost History* (a documentary series that aired on H2 and the History Channel). It's a story that's hard to forget, and it shines a light on one of the most painful struggles of Washington's life. Then it ends with a truly baffling mystery that is still with us today.

The story begins back in 1756, when George Washington was twenty-four years old. By all accounts, Washington was a strapping young man, tall and strong, with a stamina tested by many trips through the wilderness as a land surveyor and a young military officer. But there was one area where Washington was *not* healthy, and that was in his mouth. He was plagued by dental problems. In his twenty-fourth year he had his first tooth pulled. It was replaced by a fake one made of ivory.

Thus would begin a lifelong odyssey for Washington of having his real teeth removed, then gradually replaced by a changing array of false teeth. By middle age, the state of Washington's dental health is downright terrible. In 1781, towards the end of the Revolutionary War when he was in his late forties, Washington began wearing a set of partial dentures to compensate for several missing teeth. In 1789, George Washington delivered his first inaugural address with only a single natural tooth in his mouth; by this time, he was wearing a full set of fake teeth.

Given the dental technology of the time, what all of this also means is that George Washington was in a state of near-constant physical pain throughout his adult life. In Washington's diaries and journals, where he is reticent about most personal subjects, he makes repeated references to swollen gums, soreness, abscesses, and the need to have yet another tooth pulled.

Most of us know what it's like to have a bad cavity, or a root canal, or have experienced the painful healing that comes after having wisdom teeth removed. Well, in Washington's time, there was no anesthesia, no aspirin, no fancy surgical tools, and only a primitive knowledge of how to perform oral procedures. So for Washington, the repeated process of having his teeth pulled, and then getting crude fake teeth fitted, would be by today's standards almost unthinkably excruciating, with ongoing bleeding, swelling, infection, and periods of sustained soreness.

In other words, George Washington's mouth was very possibly wracked with pain when he crossed the Potomac, when he led the Continental army to victory in the Battle of Yorktown, and while he presided over the Constitutional Convention. And indeed, at that first inaugural address—delivered with that one real tooth and a set of dentures—his mouth was in such bad shape he had to speak very softly, such that his speech could only be heard by those sitting in the front.

In fact, you know that famous picture of George Washington on the dollar bill, where his cheeks appear sort of puffy? That's because the crude dentures he wore while sitting for the portrait forced his cheeks out, as if he had cotton in his mouth.

We know, we know—you'll never look at the dollar bill the same way again.

Also, when we say "dentures" in the context of the late eighteenth century, we're not talking about white enamel or the cutting-edge synthetic materials we have today. At the time, dentures were usually made from ivory—in Washington's case, the ivory from a hippopotamus—mixed in with actual animal teeth, and held together with crude metal fixtures. And that's not all. Dentures also sometimes included *human* teeth, to complement the animal teeth and ivory. How were those human teeth acquired?

Here's where it gets really nasty. Dentists would put out public notices offering to buy healthy teeth, and strangers would come forward—usually the very poor, or in some cases, slaves—and allow a healthy tooth or two to be extracted manually for a guinea or two. This is how dentists served the wealthier clients who could afford to pay for fake teeth.

Aside from highlighting what today seems like a barbaric practice of pulling healthy teeth from the poor to service the wealthy, these facts dispel a myth sometimes passed along about George Washington: that he wore wooden teeth. To be clear, this isn't true—but there's a reason people at the time thought it was. Basically, ivory dentures would get so stained, that they inevitably turned brown, and probably looked like wood. So some of Washington's contemporaries described his teeth as being wooden, and the misconception spread for a few generations before the myth could be properly dispelled.

In any case, by the time of his death in December 1799, Washington had a total of four full sets of dentures. After his death, the dentures were passed on to his descendants' families, who eventually donated them to museums or historical institutions. Three of the four sets are currently housed in such places; for example, a full, intact set of Washington's dentures is now held at the Mount Vernon Museum and Education Center in Virginia.

So if three sets are in museum or research institutions, where is the fourth?

That's where the mystery comes in.

Washington's descendants originally gave his last set of dentures—a set created in 1795, and worn by Washington when he sat for the portrait we now see on the dollar bill—to the University of Maryland School of Dentistry. Then in 1965, the school loaned the dentures to the Smithsonian National Museum of Natural History, in Washington, D.C., where they remained for many years, either on display or kept in their storage facility.

Then, things took an unexpected turn.

On June 19, 1981, the Smithsonian's curator went to retrieve the dentures from storage, and discovered something shocking: the teeth were gone.

Disappeared.

What happened?

There was only one explanation: the dentures were stolen. And why would someone steal such a thing? Quite simply, for money. Historical artifacts are often valuable, and anyone in possession of Washington's original dentures could probably sell them for a good price on the black market, or to a private collector. Or, because there was some gold inlaid in the upper dentures, the teeth could be melted down for the precious metal.

Now, it so happens that stealing something from the Smithsonian is a big deal. The Smithsonian is federal property, so a theft from the museum is a federal crime. The case therefore fell under the jurisdiction of the Federal Bureau of Investigation.

From there, federal agents examined the scene of the crime. At the time, museums didn't have motion sensors or surveillance cameras, so all the agents could do was question the staff and search for forensic evidence. They found no fingerprints or footprints, no strands of hair, nothing. Once they thoroughly investigated the crime, they did however come to a pretty strong theory of the case: the theft was an inside job.

Why? No one but an employee could have gained access to the storage facility, or would have even known where to look. Also, for an outsider to break into the building and access the storage unit without tripping any alarms would've been impossible.

Still, neither the museum directors nor the authorities had any idea who among the staff may have committed the theft. For about a year, the case went cold. Then, a shocking piece of evidence showed up in the Smithsonian itself. The lower part of the dentures—just the bottom half of the teeth—mysteriously reappeared in a storage room, near where the full set was originally kept. Once again, no fingerprints, no footprints, and no further clues.

This bizarre occurrence served to reinforce a key supposition of the case: the original theft must have been an inside job. No one else but an employee could have or would have returned the stolen property to the high-security storage facility. But the question remains: Why would someone take the risk of carefully returning just the bottom part of Washington's false teeth, and keep the rest?

The only theory anyone could come up with was that the thief must have kept or sold the top half for the value of the gold, and returned the now-worthless bottom half out of guilt. Or maybe, the thief just wanted to confuse everyone. Either way, it's a very strange development in the centuries-long saga of a set of teeth that were once in the mouth of our first President.

When we covered this story for *Lost History,* we interviewed experts and asked viewers to send in any tips for where Washington's last set of dentures may be. We still don't have the answer, and to this day no one knows who stole those teeth or where they may be now.

Just like *The First Conspiracy,* some aspects of George Washington's missing teeth are still shrouded in mystery.

So if you have any clues, or have an idea where they might be, please let us know.

References.

1. Fort George in
   Lat. 40. 11. 58.
2. Trinity Church
3. St. Pauls Church
4. St. Georges Chapel
5. Old Dutch Church
6. New English Dutch Ch.
7. New Dutch Cal. Church
8. Presbyterians Meeting
9. New Do
10. French Church
11. Lutheran Church
12. New Lutheran Do
13. Calvinist Church
14. Morravians Meeting
15. Anabaptist Do

16. New Scots Meeting
17. Quakers Meeting
18. Jews Synagogue
19. The College
20. Free Eng. School
21. Sanctuary Office
22. City Hall
23. The Prison
24. Poor House
25. Exchange
26. Barracks
27. Fish
28. Oldslip
29. Fly Market
30. Docks
31. Sewage

NORTH OR HUDSON'S RIVER

to Greenwich

Fresh
Water

Scale of 2000 Feet